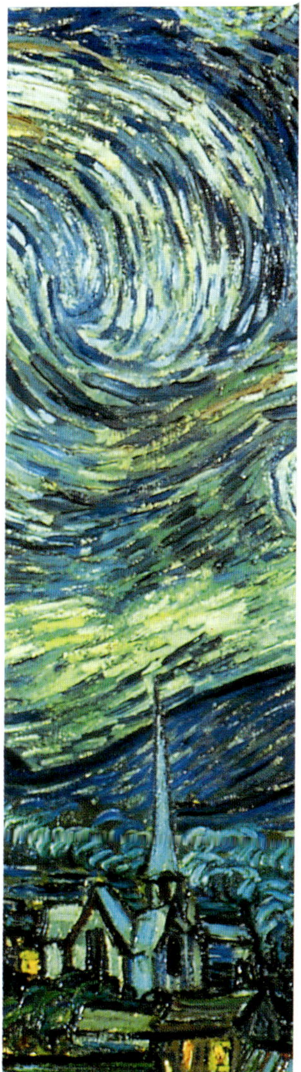

PocheCouleur

Artistic Director
Ahmed-Chaouki Rafif
Assistant
Marie-Pierre Kerbrat
Translation
Jonathan Steele Kundra
Revision
Joan Collett

ISBN 2-86770-111-2
ISSN 1248-6981
N° d'éditeur 1112/1
Dépôt légal 1er trimestre 1998

Printed in France

VINCENT VAN GOGH

The Path of Light

Jean-Jacques Lévêque

ACR Edition

PocheCouleur

Contents

The Luminous Quest

Prologue

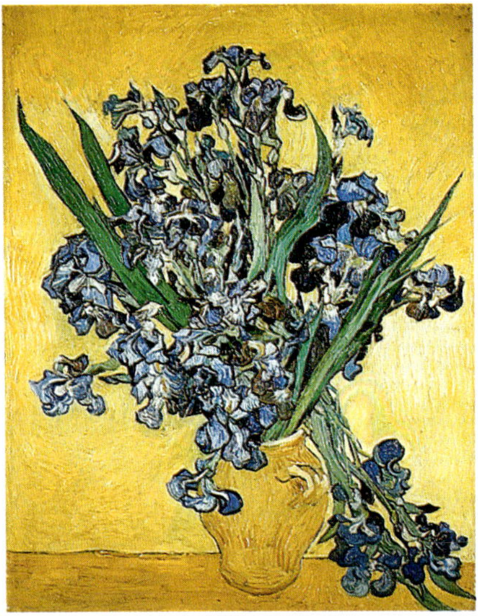

Irises. *Rijksmuseum Vincent Van Gogh, Amsterdam.*
The sumptuous bouquet of irises is overpowering in its intensity and presence. A superbly personal vision, revealing the artist's intimate feeling for nature.

Vincent Van Gogh's unique paintings cannot disassociated from their creator. His life and art are a hymn to human experience, the product of immense suffering and an incandescent faith in existence itself, shared and communicated through his art despite the many trials of his tragic life.

The intimate of sorrow, the companion of distress, Van Gogh created works which went beyond the limits of the ordinary, beyond the boundaries of reality itself, as he transformed the pain of his life into pure painted passion with all the determination of an artist intent on forging both a sublime new aesthetic and an uncommon destiny.

For Vincent, the act of painting was neither pleasurable nor a simple question of mastery or technique; rather, it was the logical outcome of a quest rooted in his intimate knowledge of the misery of mankind - of the men and women he knew - whose existence he attempted to portray and sanctify through the religion that was his art.

Vincent was an attentive and passionate reader of the Bible. For him, beyond their narrative beauty, the Gospels expressed essential truths. As moral and ethical models, he would ceaselessly attempt to integrate their idealism into his life and art.

From conflict to painful conflict, Vincent progressively abandoned any trace of self-pity or complacency toward himself. He early confronted the darkest abysses and most hopeless situations of his fellow-men. Thwarted in his desire to became an evangelist and pastor, he was rejected for his uncompromising practice of charity and compassion. Ultimately, there remained only art,

Self-Portrait. *The Art Institute of Chicago (Illinois).*
Vincent would paint many portraits of himself and each time in a different manner, according to his state of mind and the period of his life. His self-portraits were always extreme but lucid representations: beyond his features, they also revealed his soul.

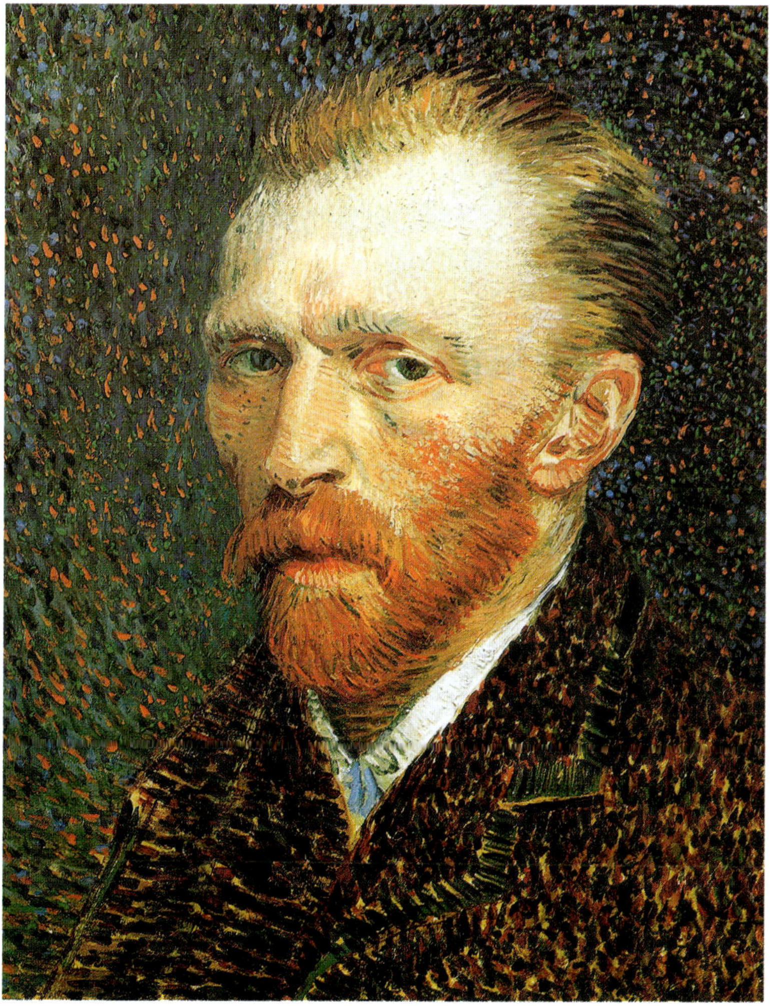

for which he had always felt an instinctive attraction. In his hands, it became an instrument for transcending the limitations of the human condition and the failure of his earlier ambitions.

Given his sincerity and idealism, he ignored considerations such as success, social prestige and even physical comfort. Although all of this would be refused to him, none of it seemed to matter. His goal was to plunge as far as possible into his own inner depths - and beyond those limits where madness lies - to reach the ultimate point in which the path of personal existence merges with that of the stars, and the horizon opens with the grace of a paradise regained.

Vincent's art testifies to search, discovery and final loss. It is a voyage traversed by extremes of darkness and light, and moments when the spirit becomes one with the mind, filling it with its force and sacred joyousness. It was the solitary, impossible quest of a saint or a madman - a path forgotten or deemed too perilous by common mortals.

Alone and unguided in this adventure of the soul, confronted by his own demons and misunderstood by those about him, he shattered. As the bonds linking him to his origins, to society and to his very being progressively disintegrated, the issue could only be fatal.

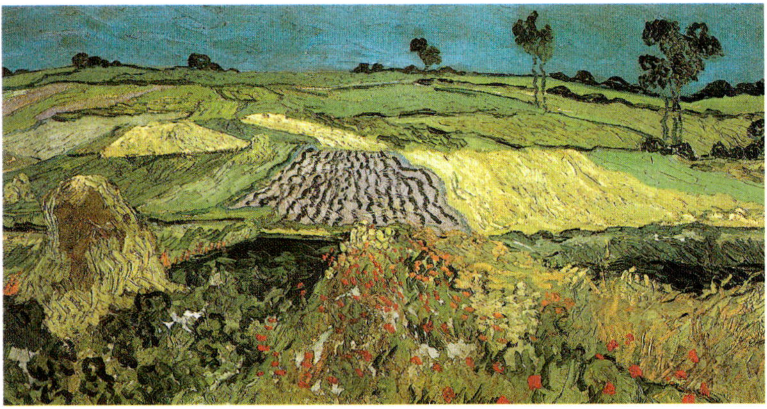

Auvers Plain. *Österreichische Galerie in der Stallburg, Vienna.*
If the landscapes of the Ile-de-France offered a visual complexity that the countryside of Holland lacked, Vincent alone saw their tragic aspects: a reflection of his own life.

No other painter had travelled this road before him. Beyond all normality, normal criteria for judging him are useless; superbly incomparable, no point of comparison exists. By the implicit grandeur of his quest and his efforts to attain it, Van Gogh placed

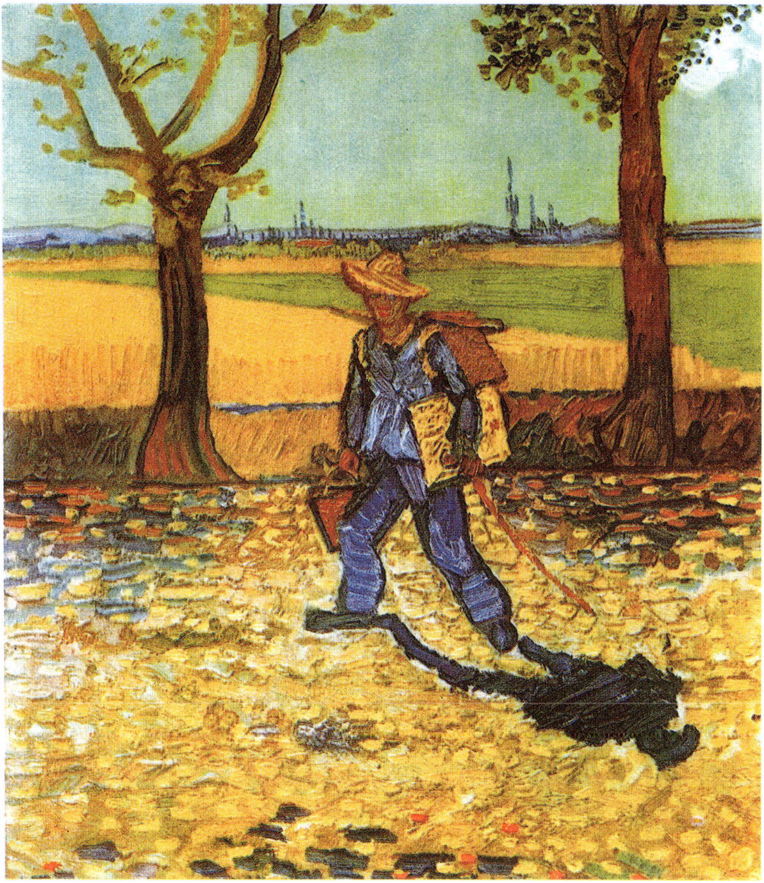

himself in a dimension inhabited by saints, heroes and martyrs.

If neither his life nor his art can be judged by usual standards, they fascinate by their very difference, and by our difficulty in separating the legend of the man from the beauty of his art: works whose vision of humanity and innate nobility remain fascinatingly contemporary even a century after the death of their creator.

The Painter on the Road to Tarascon. *(Non-Extant).*
Van Gogh as he saw himself: crushed by the sun, loaded down like a beast of burden with his paints and easel. And always alone.

A Road of Shadows:

l'Œuvre au Noir

The Well of Solitude

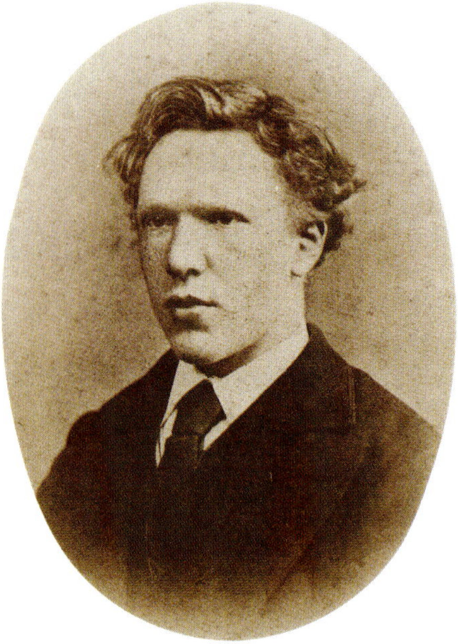

Van Gogh in 1871. *Photographic portrait. The body is pinched, the suit dignified and conventional. Vincent's features are sharp and severe: the face of a young man desperately in search of himself.*

Like Breughel or Bosch, the origins of the Van Gogh family name can be traced back to a territory and a village. His ancestors, already well-established in the seventeenth century, were comfortable burghers, holding positions of authority in their community and the church. His father, Theodorus, was a Calvinist pastor, and if there was no fundamental contradiction between the austere path of his life and that of the other members of his family who had chosen more materially rewarding or active careers, Vincent himself would be deeply affected by the implicit duality separating spirituality from worldly occupations.

His father's straight-laced respectability was counterbalanced by the gentler, more romantic personality of his mother Anna, who practised the art of watercolours and light prose with equal talent. A well-bred product of her class and social station, she remained faithful to the upbringing of her girlhood years, strongly marked by an appreciation of art and literature.

Far-removed from the populist spirit which was to influence his life so powerfully, Vincent's family was of the type that creates solid personalities, capable of confronting the hard realities of existence, individuals whose inner strength was firmly anchored in religious faith and an appreciation of life, but always in the most conventional sense. It was a cultivated, even cultured environment, but severely limited by established tradition and acceptable behaviour, and any departure from accepted norms was both unthinkable and scandalous. Vincent would early chafe against the limitations of these representatives of a well-meaning but complacent social class, certain of their legitimacy, confident of their power and secure within their network of protective relationships. Destined to share their privileges, his growing awareness of his own differences gradually forced him to the edges of both a family and a society whose moral codes and restrictive values he neither shared nor respected.

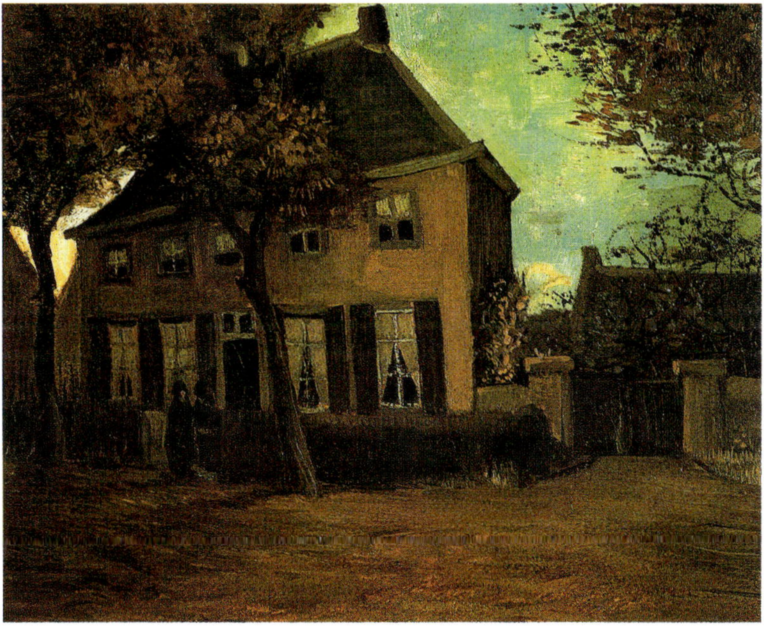

The Presbytery in Nuenen. *Rijksmuseum Vincent Van Gogh, Amsterdam.*
The Pastor Theodorus Van Gogh's residence. Vincent found his family intolerable but nevertheless remained both emotionally and materially dependant upon them during all of his adult life.

A particularly significant element in Vincent's life, and the subject of psychoanalytical studies concerning the artist, was the fact that he had been preceded by a brother - also named Vincent - who was stillborn a year before his own birth in March 1852.

For Vincent's parents, comfortably installed in their otherwise placid existence, the tragedy was a continual source of remorse, and could not have failed to haunt Vincent's impressionable mind as well.

Among his first experiences were the family visits to the cemetery. There, surrounded by the tombs of those whose lives had been cut short by the capricious forces of destiny, Vincent would contemplate his own name carved into the headstone that marked his brother's resting-place.

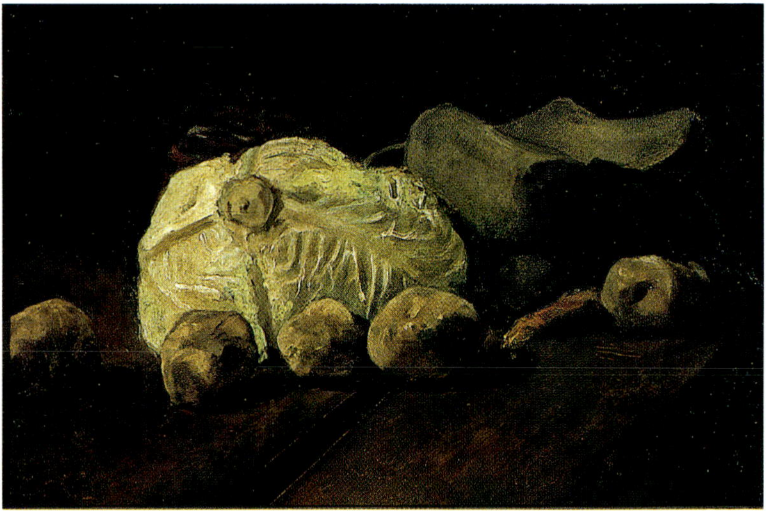

Still Life: Cabbage, Clogs and Potatoes.
Rijksmuseum Vincent Van Gogh, Amsterdam.
A celebration of austerity. Although Vincent's initial desire for recognition resulted in conventional subjects treated in conformity with established Dutch traditions, the severity of his manner betrays the uncompromising honesty of his approach.

The long, silent minutes spent before the grave of the brother whose name he carried - and with whom he strongly identified - had a profound effect upon Vincent, who progressively became introverted and moody.

Haunted by his brother's shadow, unconsciously believing himself to be his usurper and in some mysterious way responsible for his death, Vincent was predestined for the suicide which would finally release him both from his burden of guilt and the abnormally intense bond of love which united him to his younger brother Theo.

Theo the protector, Vincent's shelter from the storm, who in time would become his confessor, the privileged witness of Vincent's hopes, failures and ultimate tragedy. And all the while, woven into their relationship like a golden thread, was their correspondence: the impression of contact and comprehension provided by the endless exchange of letters with Theo was Vincent's only light in the tunnel.

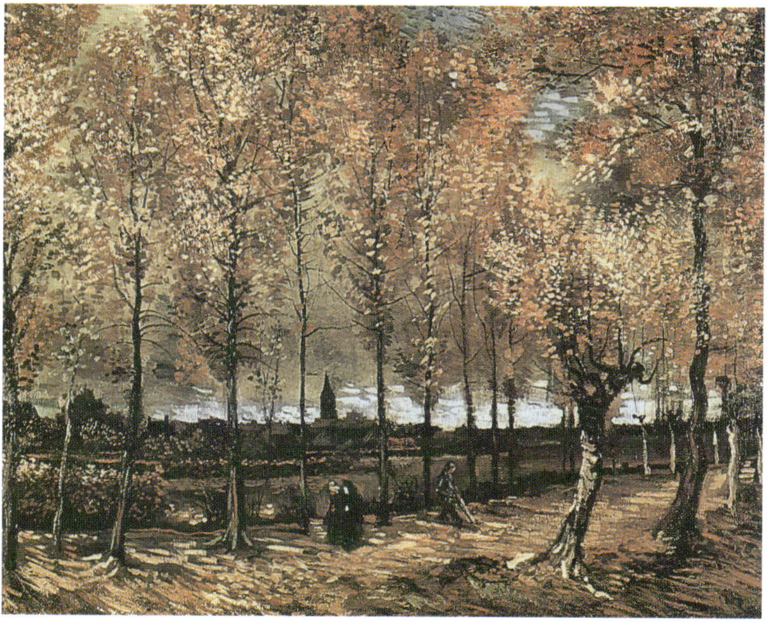

Path with Poplars Near Nuenen. *Boymans-Van Beuningen Museum, Rotterdam. Vincent projected his eternal melancholy upon this scene, painted in the countryside surrounding his father's presbytery. The sense of loneliness and distance in the composition speaks of repressed desire and echoes Vincent's perception of life in his parent's home.*

A Portrait of the Artist as a Young Dog

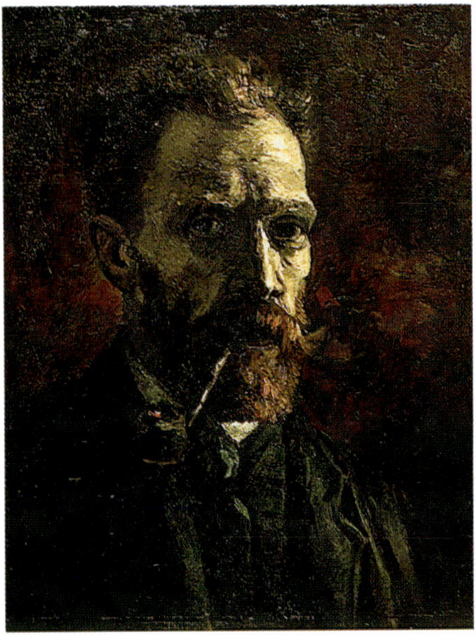

Self-Portrait with Pipe. *Rijksmuseum Vincent Van Gogh, Amsterdam. Vincent's eyes fix the viewer, all complacency absent from his regard. A prisoner of his own solitude, he appears to be searching for the answer to an unvoiced question.*

The destinies of exceptional individuals are often inscribed upon their very features: future greatness can be read in their faces.

Vincent Van Gogh was no exception: indeed, he was an exemplary case.

Many contemporary accounts testify to his appearance. They describe a young man who although afflicted by an uncommon lack of good looks, nevertheless radiated a presence which impressed all who came in contact with him.

"More stocky than tall, his back slightly bent from the unfortunate habit of never raising his eyes from the ground, his reddish-blond hair was cropped short under the straw hat that obscured the strangeness of his face. Despite his youth, there was something old about him. His forehead was already marked by premature lines; the eyebrows, accentuating the heavy brow, were drawn together in perpetual contemplation of the unseen, while his deep-sunken eyes would change from green to blue, depending upon the nature and depth of his thoughts." Thus wrote Elizabeth Hubert, Vincent's sister, who added: "Although lacking any grace and despite his extreme youth, he was already remarkably striking: his features reflected the depth of his spirit. His brothers and sisters were as strangers to him; moreover, he was a stranger to himself and to his own youthfulness. He was already possessed by genius before reaching adulthood - and was never aware of it."

His regard unflinchingly turned toward the world and its realities,

Skull with Cigarette. *Rijksmuseum Vincent Van Gogh, Amsterdam.*
A rare moment of levity for Vincent, even if the humour is distinctly black. The volumes and articulations of the skeleton are skilfully rendered, while the grinning smile of the skull is like an insolent commentary on the absurdity of life.

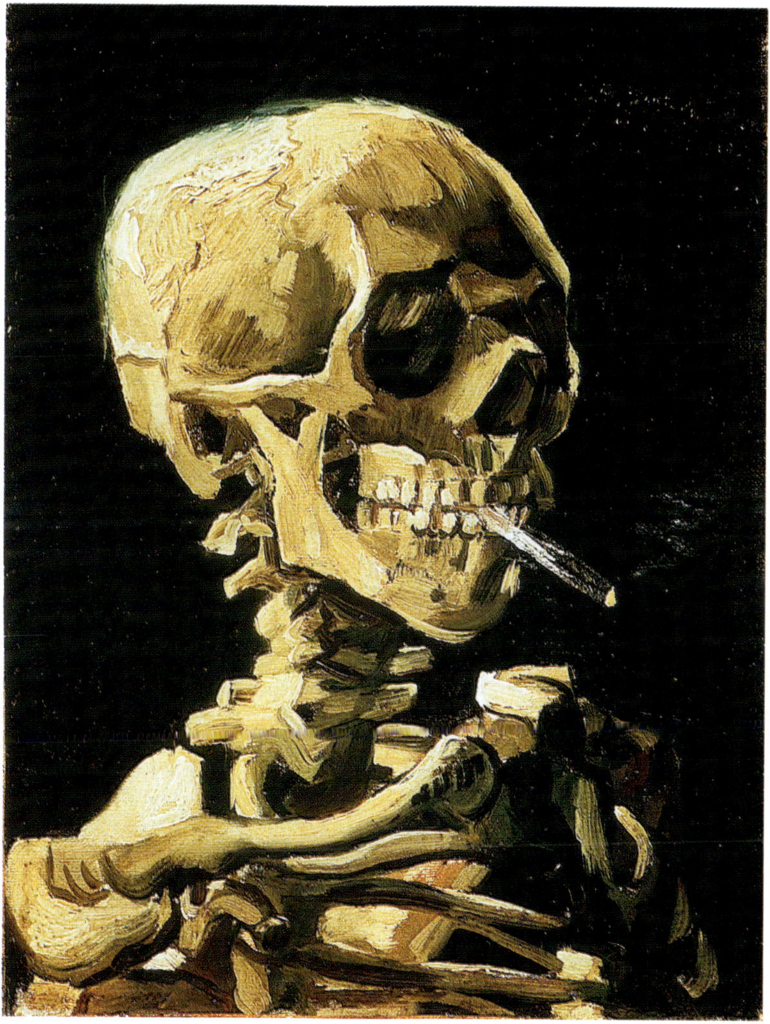

Vincent was a witness to many of life's darkest aspects; invariably, his path would lead him to those who suffered: the victims and outcasts of a society whose principles and prejudices he would refuse. A pure product of his own inner fire, the white heat of his quest for absolutes would literally destroy his body, even as it purified and forged the resolution of his heart. As his sister soberly observed: "Nature itself spoke to him with a thousand voices, and to all of them, his soul listened attentively."

A photographic portrait of Vincent, discovered in the 1950s by the historian Marc Edo Tralbaut, offers a striking resemblance to the young Arthur Rimbaud. When it was shown to Picasso, the latter remarked: "What a similarity - especially in those fiery and piercing eyes!".

If Vincent would often scrutinise his face in a mirror, it was less out

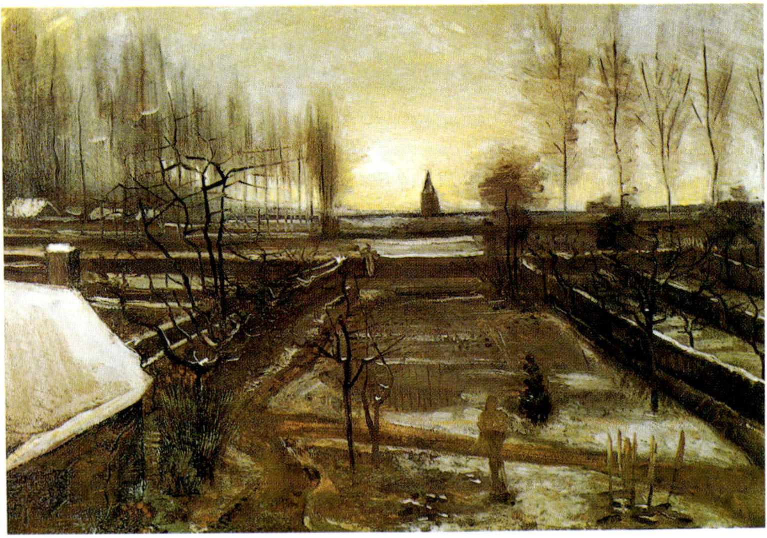

The Presbytery Garden at Nuenen in Winter. *Armand Hammer Museum, Los Angeles.*
Illuminated by the wan light of winter, the low horizon is broken only by the strong vertical thrust of the bell-tower positioned in the centre of the composition. It provides both a human and religious note in the otherwise desolate scene.

of pure vanity than in an obsessive questioning of his very identity. Haunted by Rimbaud's famous maxim: "I am the other," Vincent saw in his reflection the manifestation of a presence other than his own: something unquiet, untamed, and toward the end of his life, Christ-like in its saintliness.

The moment he became aware of his physical degradation - during his stay in Antwerp - Van

Gogh began the first of his many self-portraits.

He had just completed what was to be one of his strangest works: *Skull with Cigarette.* Despite its macabre black humour, the sheer force of expression of the grinning skull is more telling than the provocative mockery of the subject itself. By its sinister verve and morbidity, it foreshadows the series of self-portraits which were to follow, all of them representing a man old before his time, riveting the spectator with a questioning and unquiet gaze. Van Gogh's regard expresses an implicit challenge that precludes any possible response; soon enough, his works reflected this same unique and devastating quality.

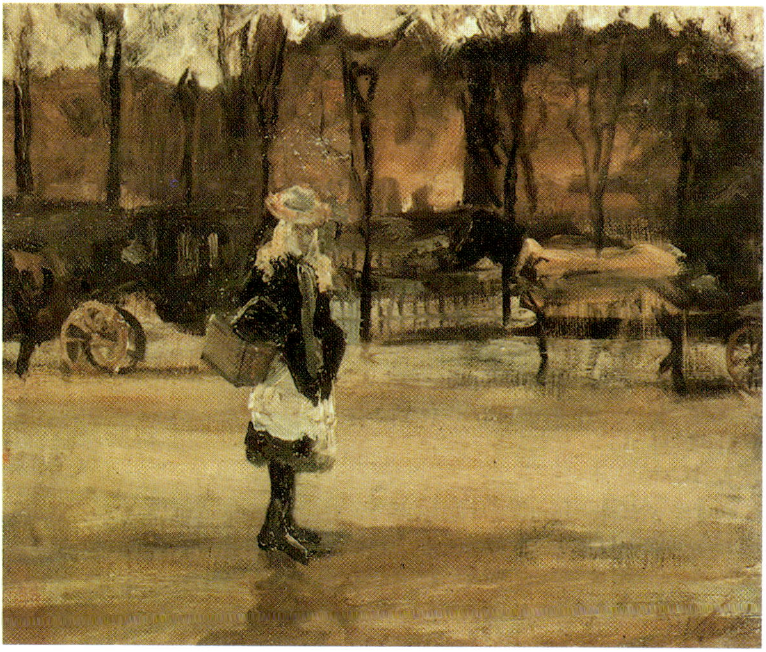

The Carriage Station. *Jäggli-Hahnloser Collection, Winterthur.*
A street-scene treated in the manner of a rapid sketch. Vincent communicates the atmosphere of the scene in a style close to that of the Impressionists.

To the Manner Born

Many members of the Van Gogh family either were or had been involved in the art business, including two uncles - one also named Vincent (1820-1888), and Cornelis Marinus (1824-1908). In time, Vincent's brother Theo also entered the profession and would become his sole and ever-faithful source of moral and financial support.

Encouraged by his family, the young Vincent accepted an apprentice position at the Goupil gallery in The Hague in July 1869. Successful and well-established, Goupil possessed branches in Brussels, London and Paris, where Vincent would be sent for additional training.

Whether obliged by his family to persevere in his new career or simply hesitant to chose a different path more in keeping with his character, Vincent soon found himself in a situation that was totally unsuited to his temperament and ambition - as well as his appearance and behaviour. The only real advantage for him - and he made the most of it - was the possibility that the job offered him of learning about art through his daily contact with the works exhibited in the gallery. In his letters to Theo (who would occupy a managerial position at Goupil in 1873), Vincent devoted long passages to the description of this heady and enriching experience.

His aesthetic sense was enriched by his visits to galleries where many paintings of his contemporaries were shown, and frequent visits to local museums.

At work, Vincent carried paintings from the storeroom to the display easels where they were offered for the appreciation of Goupil's stolid bourgeois clients - often narrow-minded and motivated by a desire for social status far-removed from the sublime idealism of the quest taking form in Vincent's spirit and already alluded to in his correspondence with Theo.

Art at this time was as reassuring as it was conventional, the product of fashionable painters who rarely adventured beyond the accepted canons of academic realism. Vincent nevertheless absorbed what he needed, reshaping to his own ends what he had learned from studying the

The Girl in the Forest. *Rijksmuseum Kröller-Müller, Otterlo.*
The distant image of the young girl under the trees expresses all of Vincent's reserve toward women.

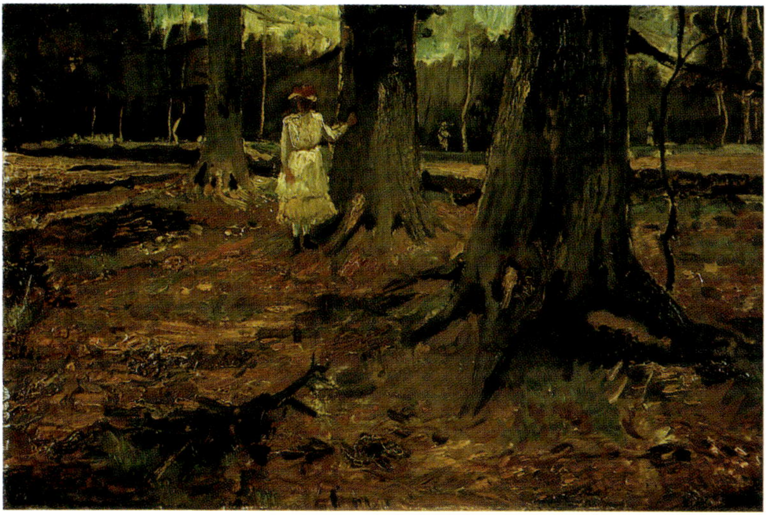

works of Troyon, his fellow-countrymen Jacob and William Maris and his uncle Anton Mauve, who for several years would serve as his mentor.

In addition to the artists of the Hague School, whose works exercised a certain fascination on the sensibility of the young Vincent, the Goupil began to promote a group of French painters whose works, in the purest tradition of the Barbizon School, encompassed the vivid brushwork of Jongkind, the eye for detail of Diaz, as well as such seasoned artists as Corot and Daubigny.

They were exhibited in the discreetly luxurious atmosphere of the gallery, whose panelled doors opened onto a succession of richly-appointed rooms furnished with heavy period furniture and exquisite art objects. Here, commerce was less a question of pure salesmanship than of possessing a gift for light banter and the proper social graces, leisurely exercised on plush sofas and comfortable wing-chairs. In many respects, the atmosphere of the gallery was not very different from that of a high-class bordello; many of its clients frequented both, passing indifferently from one to the other with all the assurance and cynicism of the rich. Confident of their own opinions, certain of their rights, secure in their newly-acquired wealth but terribly limited in their tastes and choices, they were the same type of individuals that would appear in the short stories of Guy de Maupassant and the novels of Zola. Theirs was a world dominated by wealth and power, where love was often venal and personal ambition usually unlimited. Women served as the ornaments of the successful, who covered them in jewels and furs to emphasise their own importance, even as they gave vent to their most secret desires in bordellos whose ostentatious luxury mirrored the same over-blown and doubtful tastes of their clients.

The walls of the gallery, lined with velvet and precious hangings, offered row upon row of gilt-framed paintings - works which would ultimately adorn the mansions and apartments of the wealthy across the capitals of Europe.

From one city to the next, the style was the same, the image of a society in full expansion in which the reputation of an artist was increasingly dependant upon international exposure. Such was the case of the Impressionists, who although promoted by the more audacious galleries such as Durant-Ruel in Paris, were largely ignored until the latter opened a branch in New York.

Although Goupil was well-established, it too would progressively modernise its operations. In Paris, Theo Van Gogh was put in charge of Goupil's new gallery on Boulevard Montmartre, created to expose the works of a new generation of painters such as Pissarro, Monet and Degas. The main gallery, located on Rue Chaptal and in the same neighbourhood in which many of these painters had their studios, was still hesitant to give them any consequent exposure.

It was in this atmosphere, strongly codified and respectful of established hierarchies, that Vincent would begin learning about the workings of the art market and the techniques of the painters who were fuelling it.

But by his volatility and directness of expression, as well as his uncompromising and often disturbing candour, Vincent's career at Goupil - like so many other of his undertakings - was doomed to failure from the very beginning. Neither the quality of the gallery's works nor the mission of convincing clients to purchase them corresponded to his youthful ideals and ambitions.

In the meantime, he found himself transferred from The Hague to Brussels in January 1873 and to London in June of the same year; to Paris in October 1874; back to London again, and thence to Paris in May 1875. Lacking any sense of tactful diplomacy and openly critical of the gallery's choice of artists, Vincent rapidly fell from favour with his employers. Rather than waiting to be fired, he offered his resignation on April 1, 1876.

It was the end of the career that his parents had hoped for him, a natural continuation of family ties and traditions. Vincent's experience at Goupil nevertheless gave

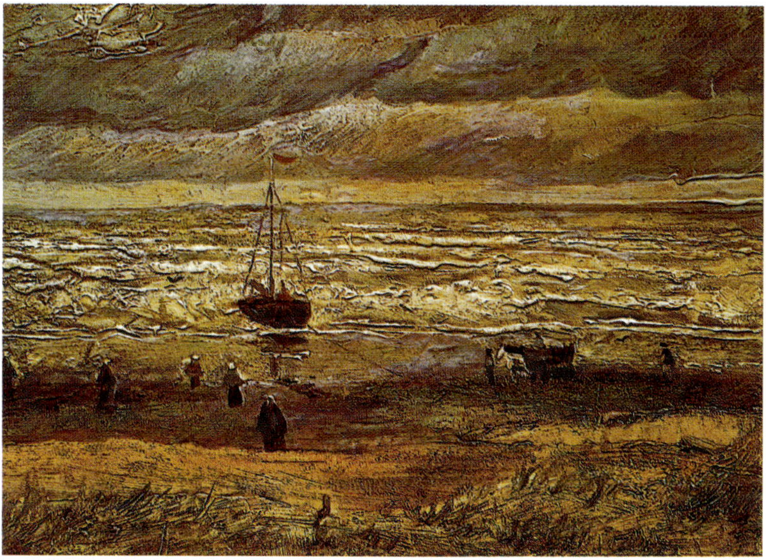

him the opportunity to discover the nature of the gallery-going public, as well as the connoisseurs and critics whose support he would need to succeed as an artist. But at this point in his life, he was still unaware of his destiny. All he knew, as he returned home to his parents, was that he had failed miserably. It was the first of the many failures which would follow, the first step on the long and inevitable descent into his own private Inferno.

Beach Scene. *Rijksmuseum Vincent Van Gogh, Amsterdam.*
In a work whose spirit is closer to Courbet than Boudin, Vincent employed sweeping brushwork to suggest the force of the elements and the melding of the sea and sky.

The Descent to Hell

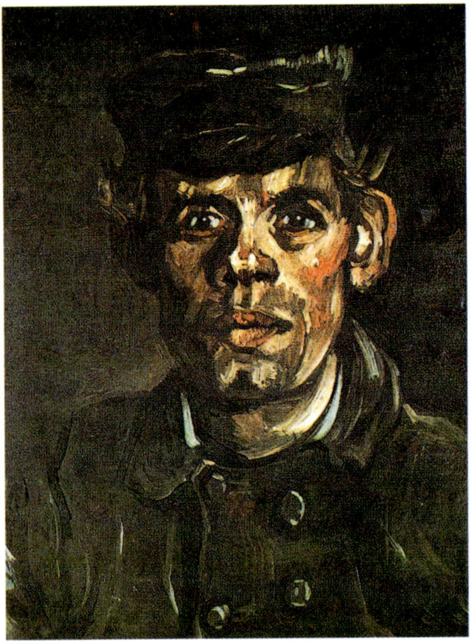

Peasant with Cap. *Royal Museum of Fine-Arts, Brussels.*
Vincent often chose common people for his subjects, representing them with a radically new vision of authenticity and humanism.

The concept of eternal damnation occupied a special place in the popular imagination of the nineteenth century. It was a place associated with suffering, proffered as a menace to those who strayed from the straight and narrow path of virtue traced by religion and enforced by society.

Deviations from this path resulted in finding oneself thrown into the bottomless, fiery pit so well-described by generations of writers and artists who often seemed to take a particular pleasure in revealing its horrors in exquisite and terrifying detail.

Those who were thus punished were generally there for eternity. Nevertheless, mythology and legend offer examples of individuals for whom a descent into the inferno signifies a rite of initiation or a sublime act of heroism motivated by a higher ideal: such was the love of Orpheus, who entered Hades to find Euridice and lead her back to the world of the living.

For others, hell exists on earth; this was Vincent's case, and his heroic quest was that of a compassionate soul intent on saving others - perhaps more than himself - from an existence of misery and injustice.

Vincent's experience in the Borinage coal fields of Belgium reveals a striking similarity between objective reality and poetic imagination. Penetrating the dark world of the coal pits, he described the shadowy, Dantesque universe of the mine:

"We descended 700 meters and explored the farthest reaches of this underground world. The mine has five levels; the topmost three have already been worked and abandoned, for there is no more coal. If one were to sketch these galleries, the images would be astonishing, unimaginable, totally new. Imagine a series of small cells dug into the walls of a low and narrow corridor supported by heavy wooden beams. Each of the cells is inhabited by a miner. Dressed in rough work clothes as filthy as those of a chimney-sweep, the miner picks at the coal face with his tools by the weak flame of a small lamp. In some of the cells, the miners can work standing up; in others, the seam of coal is so low that they must lie flat on their stomachs. The multitude of cells are like those of a beehive, an underground prison or perhaps the interior of a tomb.... Everywhere, water sweats from the walls and trickles down, while the play of the lamp-light produces strange reflections, as if upon the

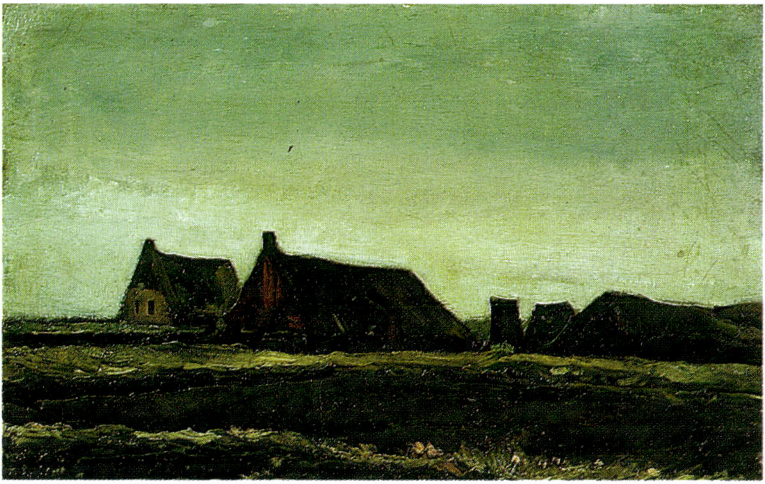

The Small Holdings. *Rijksmuseum Vincent Van Gogh, Amsterdam.*
The low horizon is nearly indistinguishable from the somber fields, while the massive volumes of the houses appear to be rooted in the earth. All here speaks of the dark misery of peasant life.

stalactites of a cavern. Some of the miners work at breaking the coal free from the seams; others load it into wagons that they push on rails like those of a tramway. Many of these workers are children: young girls as well as boys. Seven-hundred meters down, I saw a stable and the seven old horses used for pulling several wagons at a time to the mine-shaft from where they are hoisted to the surface. Still other workers were reinforcing old galleries to prevent them from collapsing, or excavating new ones."

Vincent's exploration of existence was always a painful experience, even as his growing asceticism led him to seek out extremes which played havoc with his mind and body:

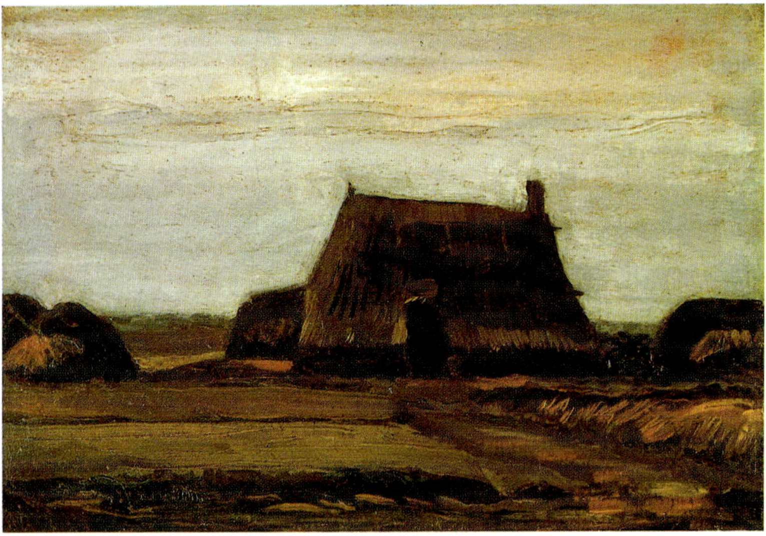

The Cottage. *Rijksmuseum Vincent Van Gogh, Amsterdam.*
Nothing has been idealised in this rural landscape, for Vincent was seeking to portray all the hopeless misery of the scene. His objective as an artist was to proclaim the truth; in this quasi-religious quest, the easel had become his pulpit.

"Even though this journey was so difficult that I returned exhausted, my feet torn, and in a more or less melancholic state of mind, I have no regrets, for what I saw was fascinating. I am learning to see clearly, and with new eyes, even despite all this misery....
I once had to spend the night in an abandoned carriage in the middle of the fields. In the morning, it was

white with frost and most uncomfortable. Another time, I slept on a heap of firewood and thereafter in a pile of hay, which would have been a fairly comfortable nest, were it not for the fine rain which contributed little to my sense of well-being."

Strangely enough, the mental and physical tribulations that Vincent traversed, and which would have soon discouraged most men, both revitalised his being and clarified his vision. Unlike Orpheus, he did not return from these descents into raw experience with a beloved Eurydice, but with a new purity of spirit, and in his memory, the material for sketches of all that he had witnessed.

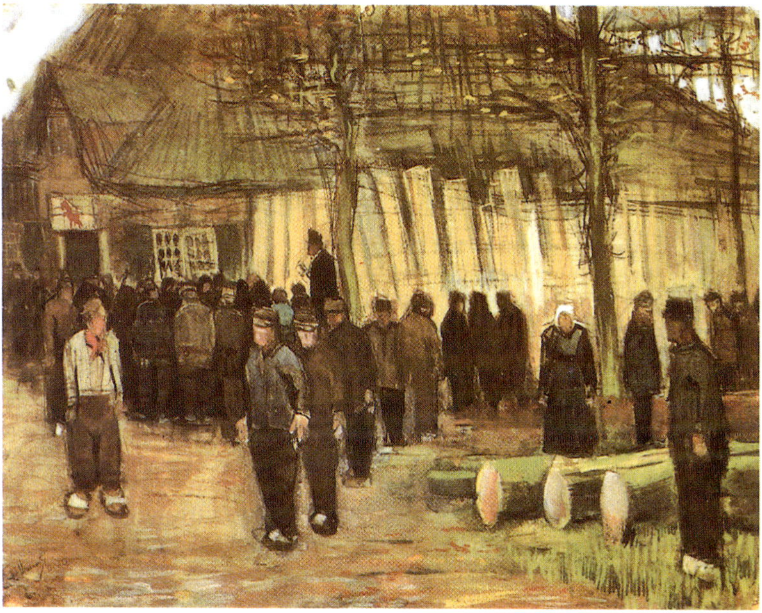

The Wood Auction. *Rijksmuseum Vincent Van Gogh, Amsterdam.*
For Vincent, the anecdotal quality of a scene was far less important than its implicit moral message. The individuals portrayed here are the product of their condition, of which the artist is both participant and witness.

The Ugly Duckling

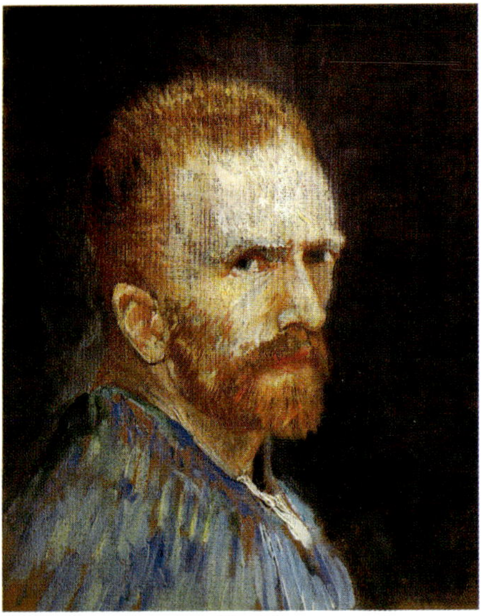

Self-Portrait. *Wadsworth Atheneum, Hartford (Connecticut).*
More than in any other of his self-portraits, Vincent appears to have withdrawn into a private world of anguished soul-searching and doubt, as if dimly aware of his tragic destiny.

The bland normality of Vincent's family rendered his own behaviour and appearance all the more shocking. Seemingly indifferent to the opinion of others, he was seen as an individual who refused to obey rules that everyone else accepted and respected.

As he confessed to Theo: "Like many others, you feel that there are problems concerning my behaviour, my way of dressing and my language, problems which are serious enough (and apparently without solution) to result in the progressive destruction (as has been the case over the years), of our relationship as brothers. The fact is, you are an important man at Goupil, while I am only a black and errant sheep."

Even those who admired his moral strength and the qualities of his immense heart could not help remarking Vincent's indifference to his physical appearance and the degree to which he discouraged those who attempted to approach him. Judged only by his superficial aspects by those unable to comprehend his uncommon integrity, Vincent was seen as a misfit, an individual in rebellion against society. Rare were those who could perceive his essential goodness and rare compassion for his fellow-men.

Although it is tempting to compare Vincent's temperament to that of Arthur Rimbaud, there is at least one essential difference: the latter attempted to transcend his personal identity by his famous

Self-Portrait. *Rijksmuseum Vincent Van Gogh, Amsterdam.*
Vincent emerges from a dimension which is no longer of this world, the image of the visions filling his mind.

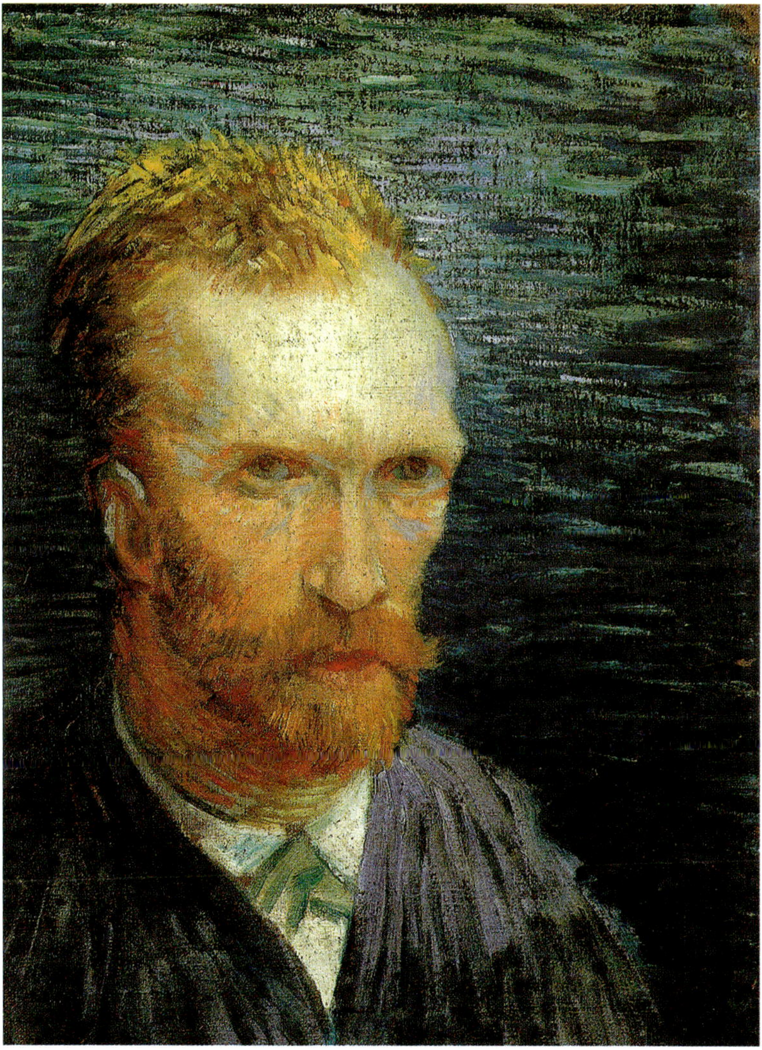

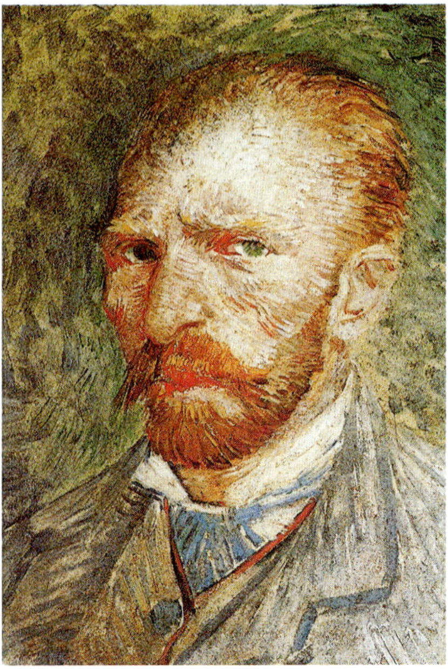

Self-Portrait. *Rijksmuseum Kröller-Müller, Otterlo.*
For Vincent, the rapidity of his brushwork was the natural corollary of his passion as an artist.

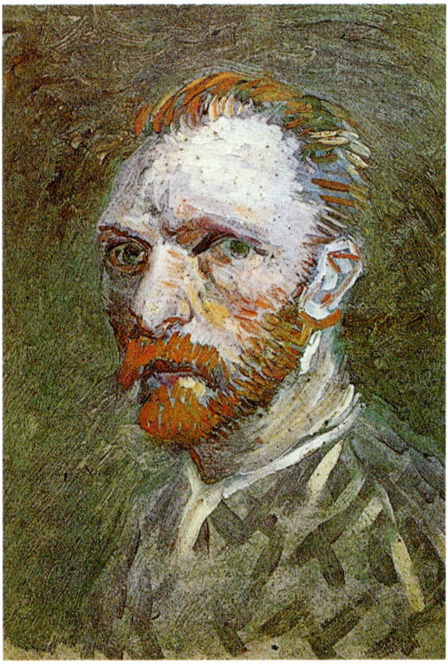

motto, "I am the other," whereas Vincent attempted to rescue others by identifying with their misery. His consciousness of humanity's distress was expressed in lines that fairly cried his own: "Man is often powerless, a prisoner of some unknown cage; it is horrible, horrible, simply horrible".

All those who knew Vincent in his youth, remarked how solitary and unapproachable he was: "He was a homely, red-haired boy who loved taking frequent and long walks across the fields - alone".

If Vincent was aware of the effect of his appearance on others, as well as the degree to which it intensified his solitude, he also saw certain of its advantages: "You are well aware that I neglect my appearance. I know this too, and admit that it is shocking. But if my poverty is in part the reason for this, as is the deep discouragement I feel, it is nonetheless a way of assuring myself the solitude necessary for going deeper into whatever question happens to be occupying my mind".

Vincent's relational problems were often due to the fear he provoked in others by his brusqueness, his uncompromising character and the intensity of his moods. As if this were not enough, he almost never made an effort to please, and when he did, he tried too hard. His opinions

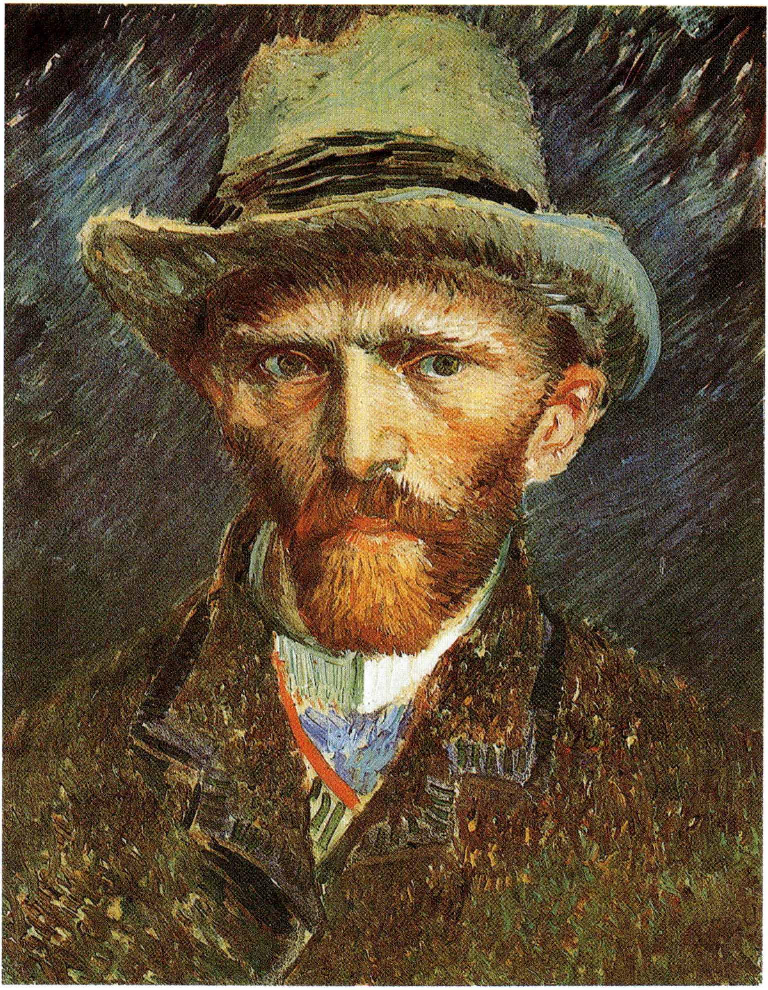

Self-Portrait. *Rijksmuseum Vincent Van Gogh, Amsterdam.*
His eyes are riveted to the mirror, as if willing himself to confront reality; in reality, night was his only friend and refuge.

Self-Portrait. *Stedelijk Museum, Amsterdam.*
The hat is a sign of social distinction. Here, Vincent portrays himself in an uncustomary bourgeois mode, as if dressed for a polite visit to middle-class neighbours of his own invention. An impossible dream for this inveterate outsider.

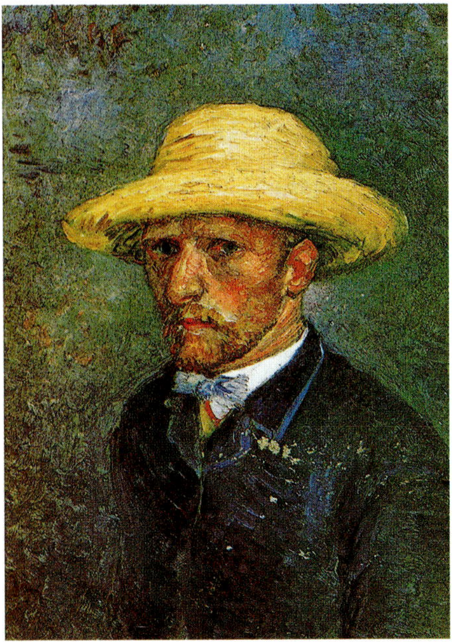

Self-Portrait. *Rijksmuseum Vincent Van Gogh, Amsterdam.*
Lacking models to pose for him in Paris, he posed for his own portrait, representing himself as the artist he was: alone, with only the sun for company.

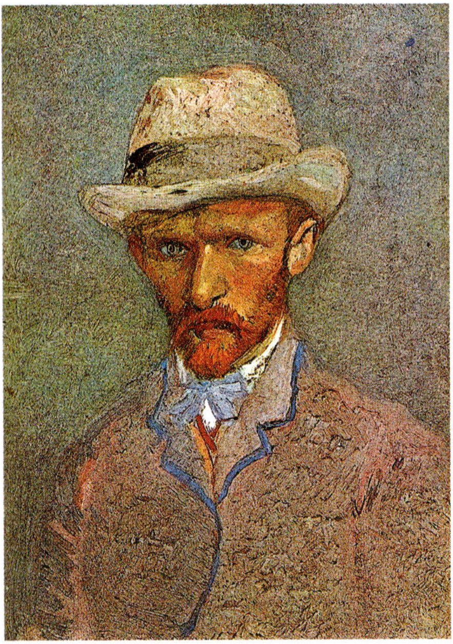

were as categorical as he was tactless in their expression. All of this suggested a certain self-destructiveness, which manifested itself in his systematic choice of experiences which were invariably damaging to his physical health and psychological stability.

Penniless, miserable and badly-dressed, his appearance generally frightened off those who were not already acquainted with him. His inflexibility could be read in the severity of his features, framed by a thin red beard like that of a vagabond: for a vagabond he was, both in his life and in his restless soul.

His obsession for serving others rendered him indifferent to superficial appearances. He was often considered as being either mildly insane or at best, a naively innocent and idealistic dreamer. And yet despite this, he was loved, but always from a safe distance, for his love of others was so consuming that it inspired a sense of unease verging on terror. Instinctive terror of the unknown, for Vincent's passionate altruism was too extreme, and corresponded to no known model of conventional charity. He was like a man inhabiting the shadows of some metaphysical night, an intimate of the forest's mysteries, the emissary of an unknown and timeless place from which sprang seers and prophets, tyrants and saints, madmen and poets.

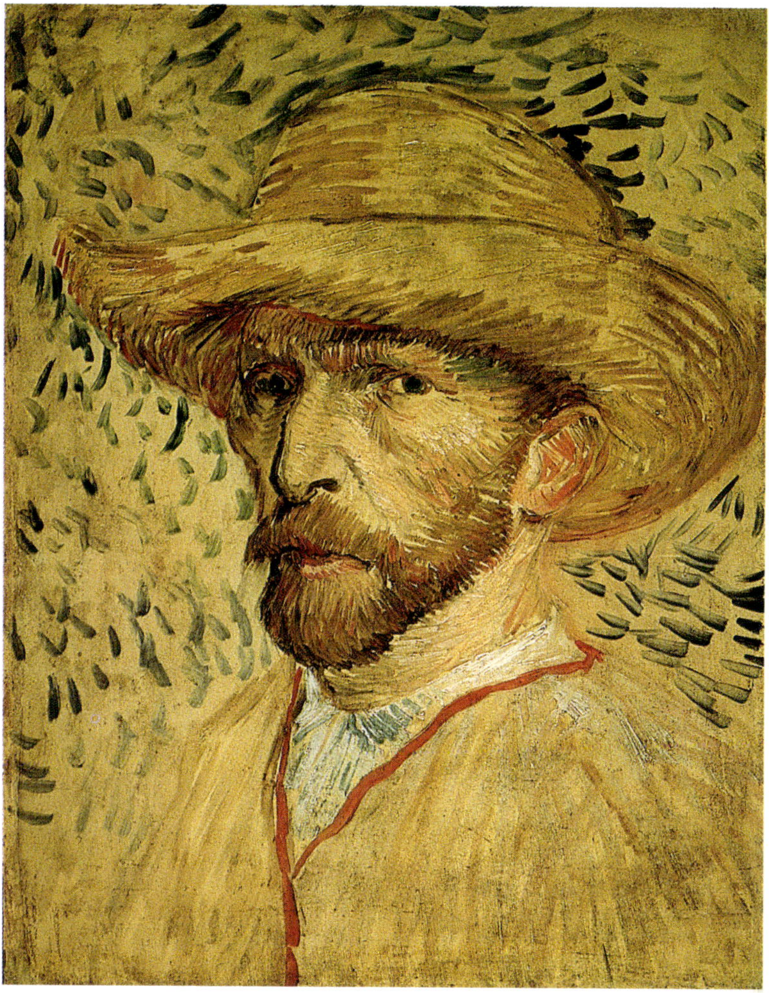

Self-Portrait. *Rijksmuseum Vincent Van Gogh, Amsterdam.*
Among Theo's relations, Vincent encountered artists like himself: talented but as yet unrecognised. If their company helped alleviate his solitude, even his dress-clothes fail to mask the sense of isolation that he carried with him like his own shadow.

Self-Portrait. *Rijksmuseum Vincent Van Gogh, Amsterdam.*
More than the reflection of his own features, Vincent's portrait represents a self-sufficient artistic statement.

A Man of *His* Word

"For I shall be the guardian of Your Word...". Absorbed in reading the Bible during his successive sojourns in England or the Dordrecht bookshop where he briefly worked from January to May 1877, Vincent incessantly studied the words of the Gospels, filling his being with their timeless beauty and power.

For Vincent, the Scriptures were nothing less than revealed truth. He took them literally and strove to practice them in his daily life. His quest was as intense as it was tragic, for it only distanced him even further from society and from those near to him. Progressively, he entered the rarefied sphere of the great solitaries - individuals like Rimbaud in Harrar, John the Baptist, or the Desert Anchorites. The lives would serve as the inspiration for many novels of the time, including Gustave Flaubert's *The Temptation of Saint Anthony*.

Solitary Vincent, a man alone. Yet, a man who believed that all men were his brothers.

Pondering the direction of his life, Vincent concluded that his destiny was "the path leading to the ministry." As he would confess to Theo: "The only possible choice for me is to become either a teacher or a pastor - or a combination of both: an evangelist." To this he added, "I shall go amongst the workers and the poor and preach the message of the Bible."

And this was indeed the road which he desired from the bottom of his heart.

He would begin during his stay with the miners in the Borinage coal-fields of Belgium: "I have often spoken before the public in a large hall intended for religious meetings. Certain evenings, I have also spoken in workers' halls."

At the same time, Vincent's boundless admiration for the French historian and humanist Jules Michelet made him envy "his life of ink and paper."

His allusion to the basic materials of the graphic artist was significant: a premonitory, unconscious reference, as if he were already dimly aware that his destiny would ultimately lead him to chose art as a means of expression. And when he did chose it as his vehicle, it would be to better communicate his vision of existence, so profoundly influenced by the teachings of the Bible.

Words given and words received, transformed into images intended to liberate man from his earthly condition of pain and misery.

Still Life with Open Bible. *Rijksmuseum Vincent Van Gogh, Amsterdam.*
Reading the Bible was an integral part of life in the Van Gogh household and an activity that Vincent would practice with avidity as an adult. For him, the Word was sacred; represented here alongside Zola's newly-published La Joie de Vivre, *it takes on the aspect of an indestructible monument. the lessons of the Gospels would guide his actions and shape his art all his life.*

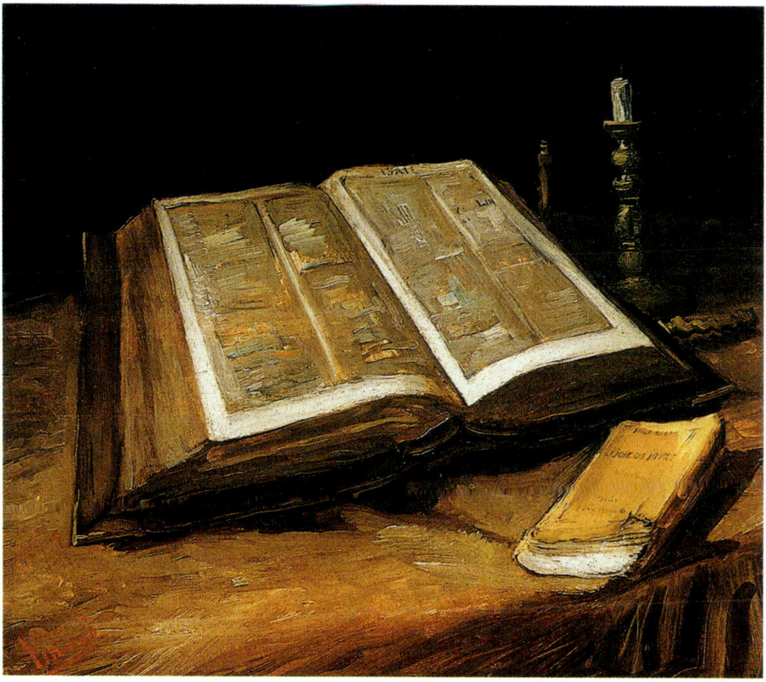

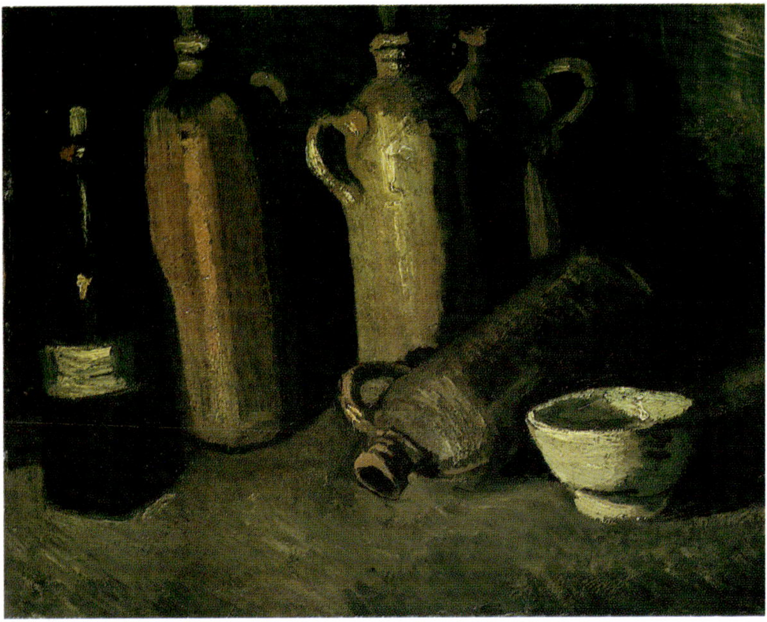

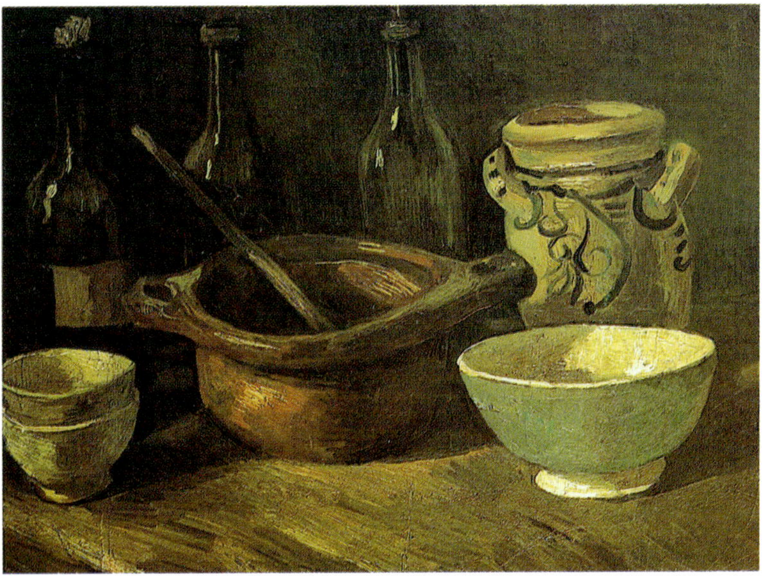

Still Life with Bottles and White Bowl.
Rijksmuseum Kröller-Müller, Otterlo.
Many of Vincent's early still-lifes were a continuation of an ancient Dutch stylistic tradition.

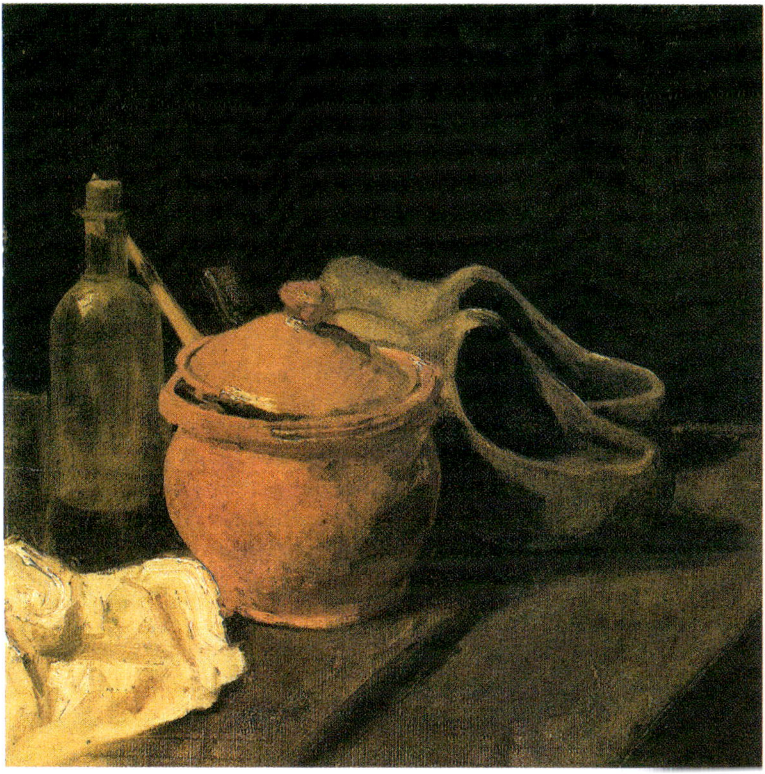

Still Life with Domestic Objects.
Rijksmuseum Vincent Van Gogh, Amsterdam.
A representation of the accumulated memory of the objects, as well as their physical reality. Their patina reveals the passage of time: long years of use have endowed them with an innate beauty born of necessity rather than of superficial style.

Still Life: Earthen Pot and Clogs.
Rijksmuseum Kröller-Müller, Otterlo.
The manner is similar to Chardin's, but a Chardin who would have abandoned the bourgeois comfort of Paris for the hardships of country life and the company of peasants.

The Hague School

Vincent was familiar with the artists of The Hague School even before he began painting, and admired the works of its most representative members such as Anton Mauve, Jozef Israëls, Gérard Bilders and William Roelofs. Although their choice of themes and subjects perpetuated an extremely ancient Dutch pictorial tradition, their approach was more audacious, expressive and marked by a depth of feeling which was no longer that of the anecdote but of painting as a mirror of emotions inspired by nature itself.

Their manner was similar to the artists of the Barbizon School, but with one essential difference: the Dutch painters had maintained the tradition of portraying the social and human context of their scenes, paying particular attention to the details of daily life and work.

The works of the Hague School were contemporary echoes of the golden age of seventeenth-century Dutch landscape painting. Their personalised manner, often emphasised by dramatic effects of sky and clouds had nothing of the sombre artificiality of Romanticism, for their approach was more pragmatic. The scenes were overflowing with life, expressive of the forces of nature and the elements. To this was added - in the appropriate context - human activity, portrayed with a new realism: the hallmark of a style which chronicled the lives of the humble, most often in a pastoral setting.

The tone here was less melancholic than naively idealistic: "Groups of labourers, sweating and breathless - Rise and march onwards - Your brows marked by the dream of a useful victory - Yours bodies broad and hard, your hands violent and strong - Treading, hurrying, stopping, struggling in your efforts - What fluid contours in your marvellous movements - Your procession inscribed profoundly in my memory - I love you, o farmhands and drovers - Amidst your teams of flashing and powerful horses - And you, ruddy woodsmen of the fragrant forests - Or you, aged, rough-hewn peasants of the white-painted villages - With your cherished fields and humble paths - Sowing great handfuls of seed - Straight before you, into the skies, into the light -

So that they may live a little, before falling back to earth...".

These lines by the poet Emile Verhaeren are charged with the vision of man that Van Gogh would express in his approach to the Dutch tradition of landscape painting.

Immersed in its poetry, he would enlarge its scope in a totally new élan of artistic vitality. Vincent, the man of sorrow and artist of the abyss, would begin his race against time by re-inventing a tradition, endowing his native Dutch landscapes with new energy, new realism and ultimately, new meaning.

He would give without limits, receive nothing in return and thus ignored, heartbroken he would perish.

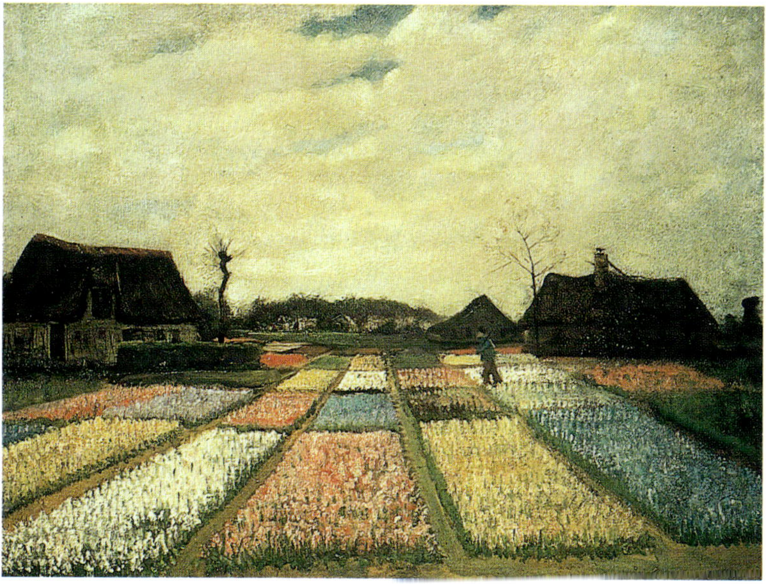

Tulip Fields in Holland. *The Mellon Collection, National Gallery of Art, Washington.*
The treatment is influenced by the painters and artistic traditions that Vincent admired, but the juxtaposition between the dark buildings and the colourful flower-beds reveals his awakening to the possibilities of bright colours. Despite the conventionality of the scene, it foreshadows the luminosity of his later works.

Shadow and Light

Poplars in Autumn. R*ijksmuseum Vincent Van Gogh, Amsterdam.*
The pathway cuts through the heavy shadows toward light, home, and the promise of peaceful repose.

"You know that one of the fundamental truths, not only the Gospels but of the Bible itself, is that from shadow and darkness, we come forth into light."

This passage from Van Gogh's writings prefigures his approach to life and art.

In was during his stay in the Drenthe that like a man inspired by a Divine mission, he would transpose these words directly into painting.

For the landscape of the region fascinated him: it was a majestic yet tragic place, whose stark solitude was punctuated by the heavy, dark outlines of low houses scattered among the moors. Its pervading atmosphere of desolation was attenuated only by man's presence, which infused it with life and movement.

Up to then (1881), and aided by his mentor and uncle, the artist Anton Mauve, Vincent had struggled to develop a personal style. He was determined to transcend the influence of the group of painters that he so admired - principally Millet for his powerful and generous humanism and Jules Breton, whose work was honoured in official exhibitions. Although he still imitated their manner, he was also progressively distancing himself from them.

Along with his landscapes there now appeared the still-lifes. Although initially tentative and still marked by the formalism of the Academy, his manner evolved rapidly but always within the limits of Dutch tradition. It was as if by conforming to it, Vincent was hoping to facilitate his recognition as an artist, for he was already concerned about the acceptance and eventual market for his works.

Despite the banality of works such as *Cabbage, Clogs and Potatoes* and his representations of boots, bottles, bowls and other everyday objects, Vincent's still-lifes possessed an existence of their own.
And even if their underlying

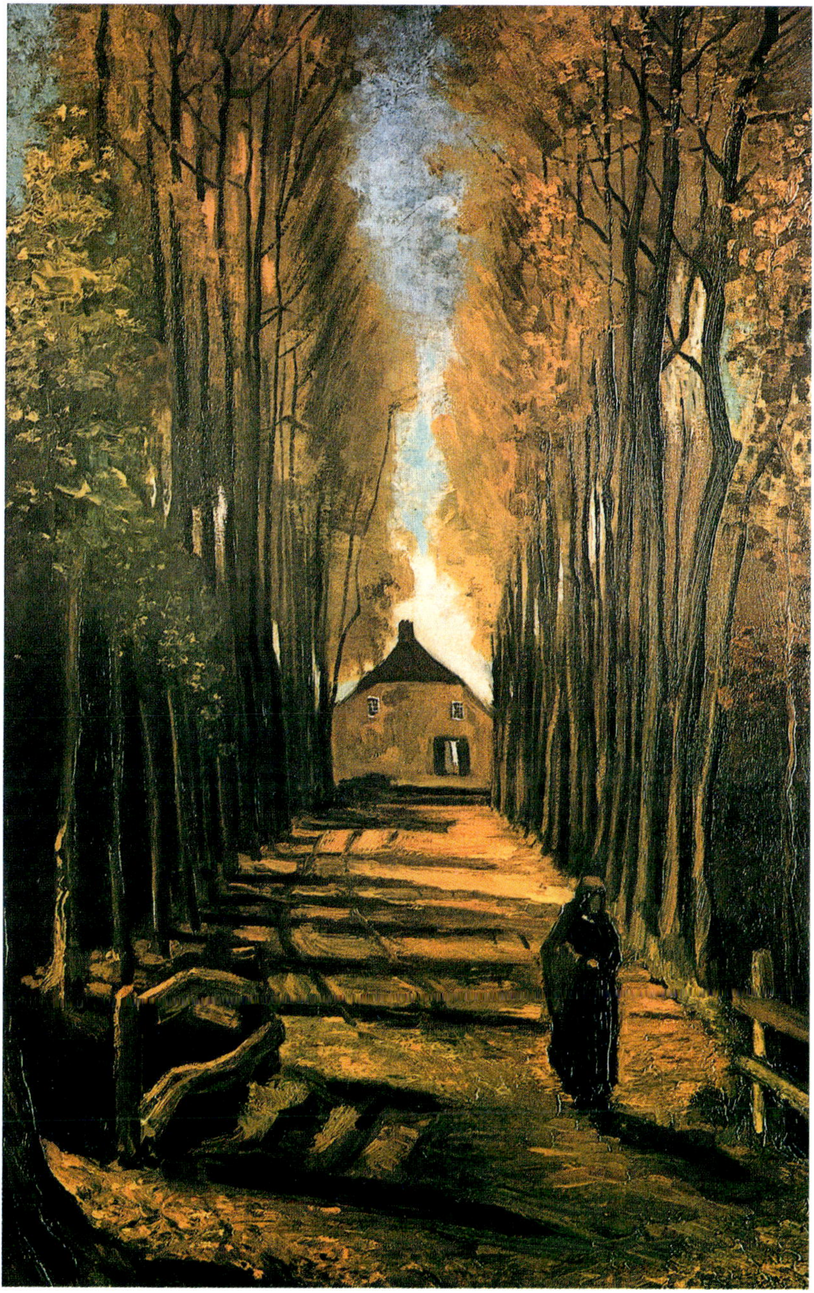

current of melancholy did not in itself constitute an obstacle to their recognition as authentic art according to the criteria of the period, they were of little interest to collectors whose choices were oriented toward more polished and sophisticated works.

Traditionally, one of the artistic conventions of the still-life was in the opulence of the objects themselves and the attention paid to detail. Artists were careful to render the brilliance of metals such as copper or silver, the transparency of glassware, the sheen of precious fabrics and the appetising succulence of fruit, game and fowl.

Vincent ignored all of this; his still-lifes expressed less a sense of renunciation and pathos than the reality of the objects themselves,

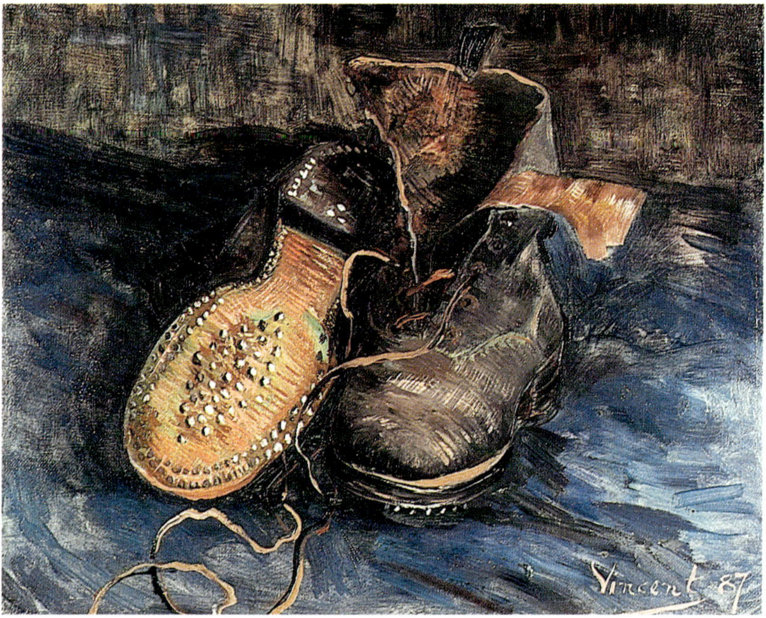

Boots. *Baltimore Museum of Art, Baltimore.*
The heavy, well-worn, metal-cleated shoes eloquently speak of foot-travel, long journeys and the wandering life of an artist that would be Van Gogh's.

intensified by their commonplace familiarity.

His *Boots* - shapeless and worn like those of a tramp's - are more than simple, mute objects, for they convey a sense of poverty and endless wandering. Here, the representation of the object also contains an implicit commentary on its human history and despite its underlying melancholy, the vision is positive and even life-affirming.

In Vincent's still-lifes, the worn yet useful objects convey all the difficulty of his existence and at the same time, his fierce will to exist. In his quest for realism and his desire to express inner truth, these encounters between the object and the canvas were like a combat, marked by the spontaneous expression of pure emotion.

Although he continued to admire the works of the contemporary painters who were treating similar themes, such as Wilhelm Roelofs and Jan Hendrik Weissenbruch, Vincent's own works were already marked by an exceptional force and originality of expression.

His landscapes and dunes (on the Scheveningen beachfront), fishermen, wind-shaken trees, sowers - all communicated the passion and intensity of his vision. And if the works of this period often lacked the stylistic qualities of a seasoned artist, they nevertheless clearly announced the direction his troubled genius would take in the future.

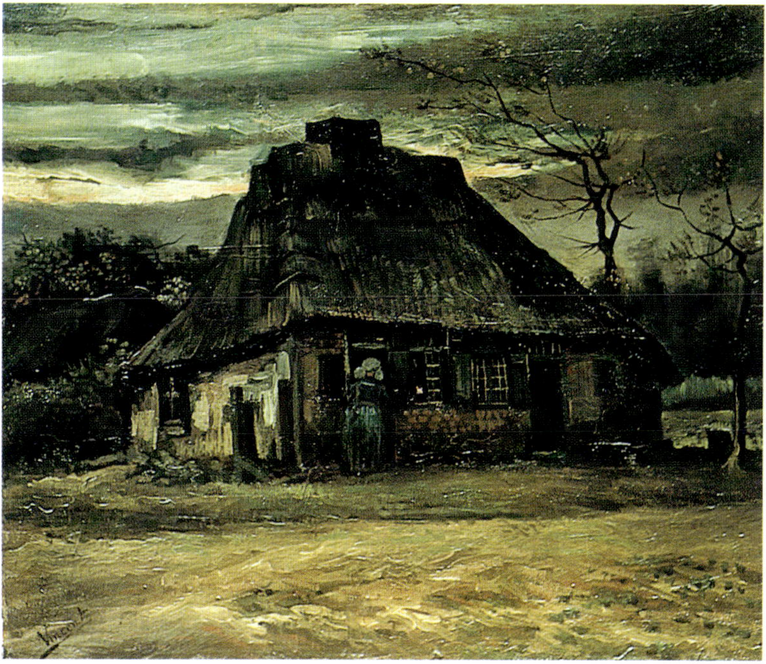

Thatched Cottage at the Close of Day. *Rijksmuseum Vincent Van Gogh, Amsterdam. A masterful rendering of pure atmosphere: with the pale, cloud-streaked sky, wind-blown trees and the peasant-woman before the door of her cottage, Vincent created a vision of solitude and the starkness of nature.*

Tentacular Cities

This was the title given by Emile Verhaeren to the collection of his poetry that was published in 1895, in which he expressed his horror of the modern metropolises that were emerging all across Europe.

Confronted by the triumph of industrialisation and the inhuman transformation of the cities, Verhaeren voiced his indignation.

In doing so, he used poetry to address a reality both new and full of menace for humanity. For all but the wealthy, cities had become grim and inhospitable places. The conviviality of the village had been replaced by the supremacy of the work ethic, while the constant growth of urban centres only increased their atmosphere of imprisonment and suffocation.

Vincent, living in a rural context as yet untouched by rampant industrialisation, viewed the concept of work somewhat more positively, while remaining fully conscious of the misery that often accompanied it.

He believed in the essential nobility of work and felt that man - by striving to overcome his condition - could attain his full measure of dignity. By domesticating the brute forces of nature and transforming its rich potential into a source of productivity, man could cease to be its slave. Vincent's ideal of man and his labour was not passive submission to a callous god of mechanisation, but of a partnership between man and technological progress, of modernity anchored in tradition.

In his art, Vincent celebrated the basic gestures of this creative act, such as that of the sower silhouetted against the immensity of the sky, or the weaver, framed in the horizontality of his loom.

The theme of the weaver took on a particularly symbolic aspect in the way by which Van Gogh rendered the shadowy, nocturnal atmosphere of what was essentially still a cottage industry.

The forceful, geometric lines of the loom made the weaver appear like the conductor of some strange vehicle, while emphasising both the solitude and fragility of his body, surrounded by the powerful machine.

His coal miners were portrayed in the cramped and painful positions of their underground prisons, slave-like and twisted, their flesh sculpted by the immensity of their efforts. But for Vincent, the weavers remained the masters of their machines - in the epicentre of the

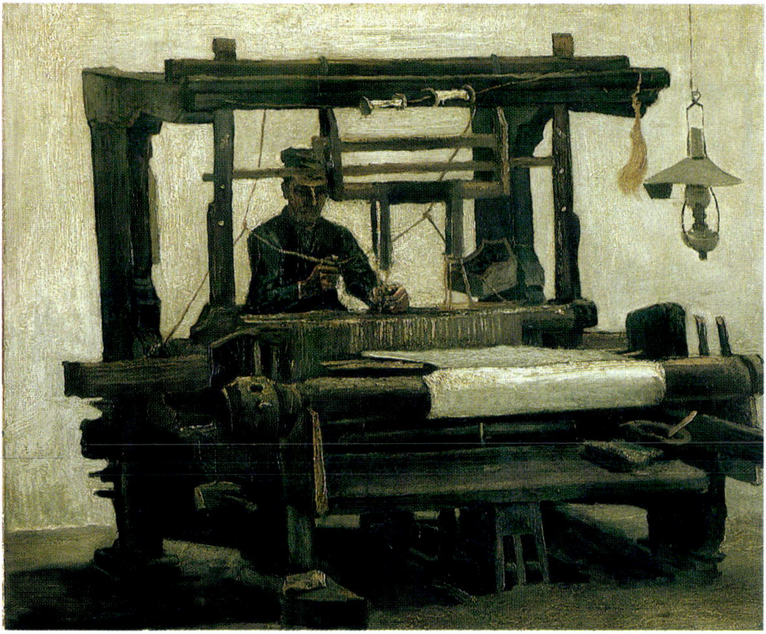

ceaseless motion and incessant noise of their complex mechanisms - even if they were physically dominated by their sheer size. The deep shadows of the weaving-rooms were illuminated by the light of man's labour: honest, skilled, intelligent and useful.

The Loom (*also known as* The Weaver). *Rijksmuseum Kröller-Müller, Otterlo. Solitary and concentrated in the centre of his loom, the weaver has become one with his machine, both master and servant of the industrial age.*

Sorrow's Sister

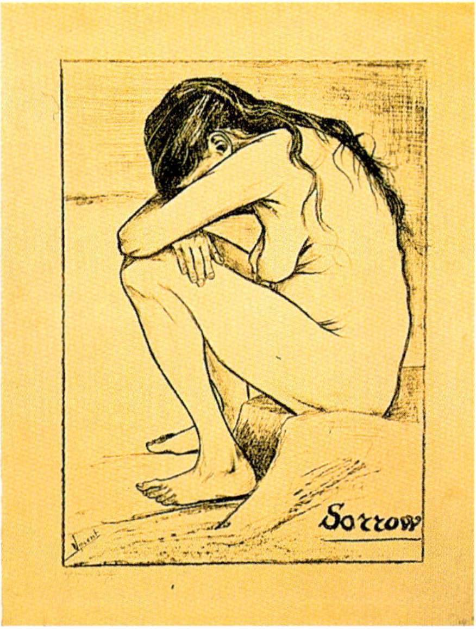

Sorrow. *Rijksmuseum Vincent Van Gogh, Amsterdam.*
The female body was never represented as an object of pleasure by Van Gogh, but as a means of illustrating the condition of women in society. Here, his model - the prostitute Sien with whom he lived - reveals all the misery of her existence in a vision touched with both pathos and compassion.

"What am I for most people? A nobody, an eccentric, a failure who will never amount to anything: in short, less than nothing at all."

For those who knew Vincent, this was indeed their judgement. For them, his choices in life were misguided and tragic, as was his uncompromising determination to express his ideals and ambitions at whatever the personal cost.

During his unsuccessful attempts at becoming a pastor and evangelist, he tried to express his sense of generous altruism by aiding those more miserable than himself. His actions were judged excessive by his superiors, who duly ejected him out of their midst; but this deep-seated need could not be repressed and was re-channelled into art. The choice implied a long and difficult apprenticeship, and even if success might be long in coming, Vincent was ready to accept its constraints. His will was unvarying, since art - like charity - offered the same potential for achieving spiritual progress, even as it offered the possibility of gaining one's livelihood.

The prospect of immediate success was more than hypothetical however, and it was only thanks to Theo's modest but essential financial support that Vincent was able to launch himself and persevere upon his chosen path.

He was perceptive enough not to count on innate artistic genius or spontaneous talent, for it was evident that both these qualities were lacking. But their absence was more than compensated by the efforts he made to master his craft and the passion with which he would express his vision of reality.

His efforts were met with scepticism, while his dependence upon his brother's aid was judged to be unethical and parasitic. As more, his refusal of a 'normal' existence of work and family resulted in his condemnation as an oddly eccentric and potentially dangerous social misfit.

Both his uncle Anton Mauve, who previously had been so supportive, and Tersteeg, the director of the Goupil gallery, disapproved of Theo's financial aid to his brother. Vincent's total dependence constituted a serious affront to their principles, while their succession of acid comments and harsh judgements soon began to strain Theo's professional relationship with the gallery.

The situation became a source of anguish and guilt for Vincent, for he feared that his brother would be subjected to the same process of exclusion as himself. The possibility of his continuing as an artist depended upon Theo's support: if ever his loyalty weakened and he gave up, Vincent would have no other choice but to do the same.

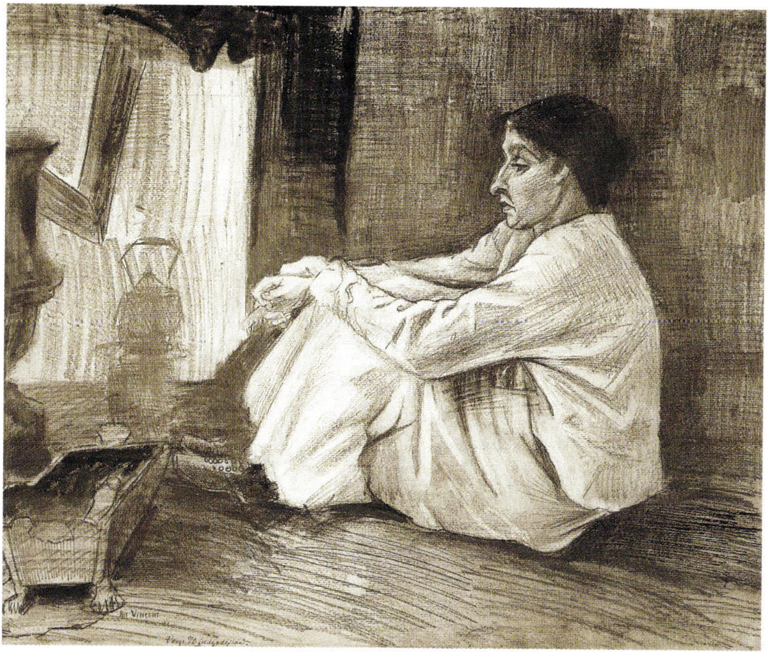

Sien Smoking a Cigar. *Rijksmuseum Kröller-Müller, Otterlo.*
The intimacy of the scene belies its quiet accusation of a society indifferent to the sufferance of its outcasts. Pregnant, alcoholic and in ill-health, Sien was offered a refuge from the streets under Vincent's roof. The scandal that this provoked obliged him to abandon her shortly thereafter.

The scandal provoked by Vincent's non-conformist existence considerably worsened after the arrival of a woman in his life: Clasina Maria Hoornik, otherwise known as Sien.

Sien was a famished, alcoholic prostitute, pregnant with another man's child. For Vincent, she became the living symbol of the misery that can be seen in his portrait of *Sien Smoking a Cigar,* itself the counterpart to *Sorrow,* both executed in April, 1882. The latter work portrays Sien in a moment of silent lassitude. Her unspoken despair mirrors that of Vincent's and most likely, the moral dilemma in which he now found himself, for not content with simply taking this unfortunate woman under his roof, he had also decided to marry her.

His portrayal of her physical and spiritual distress recalls that of the Biblical Job, who suffered in a similar attitude of mute, uncomprehending submission; it also reveals the underlying self-destructiveness of his need to involve himself in hopeless situations as a means of stimulating his creative energies.

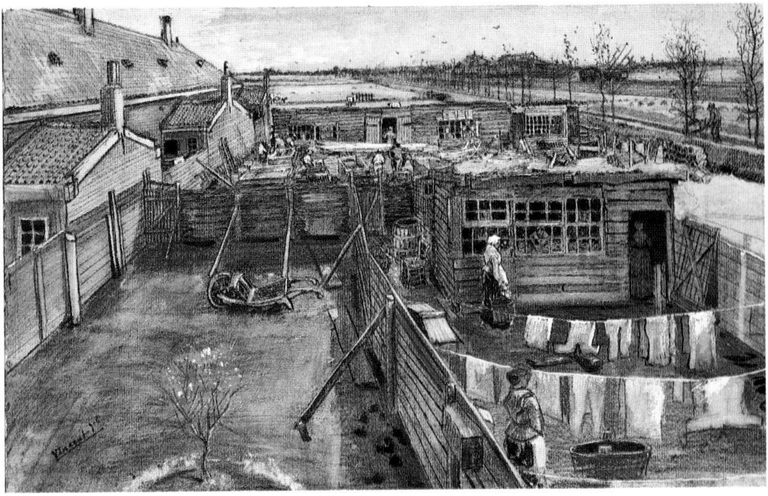

Behind the Schenkweg. *Kröller-Müller Museum, Otterlo.*
A view from the rear window of Vincent's studio in The Hague. The scene takes in a vast panorama filled with diverse structures and activities, the details of which are rendered with great precision.

Working Girl. *Rijksmuseum Vincent Van Gogh, Amsterdam.*
Influenced by Ruben's palette, Vincent began to experiment with a wider range of more vivid colours. Here, his nervous brushwork contrasts with the quiet intensity of the young girl whose portrait is a study in authenticity and strength.

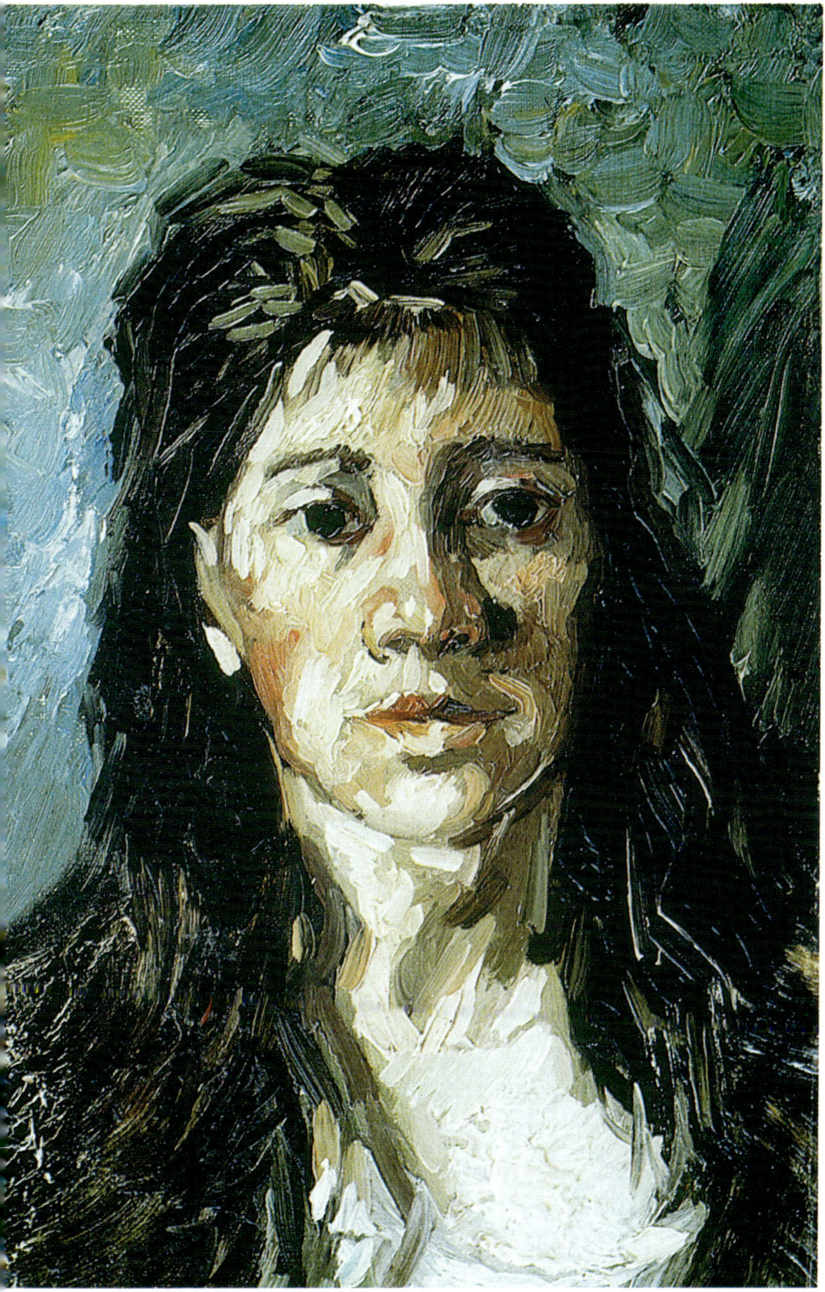

Family Life

The Chapel in Nuenen. *Rijksmusuem Vincent Van Gogh, Amsterdam. Both literally and figuratively, Vincent's family lived in the shadow of the Church.*

Daily life within the family circle of the Pastor Theodorus Van Gogh was anything but joyous. His exemplary existence, high ideals and willingness to extend a helping hand to those in need made him feel that he had the right to expect the same qualities from others. In time however, the admonitions of his ecclesiastical superiors succeeded in dampening his spirit of selfless altruism. He began preaching acts of charity rather than performing them.

It was Vincent who picked up the torch of selflessness - fuelled by his acute sense of compassion - once his father had definitively laid it down. And it was precisely this that his family found so unacceptable, and which would in time accentuate the lack of mutual understanding between them. As he repeatedly transgressed the limits of bourgeois respectability whose hypocrisy he found so intolerable, Vincent was progressively excommunicated from the Van Gogh family circle.

Vincent's mother Anna was somewhat more indulgent with him. A typical product of her middle-class upbringing, she possessed a certain talent for prose and water-colour paintings, but it would be an error to imagine that this light veneer of conventional culture was the hereditary source of Vincent's own creative drives: his passion for art was rooted in an infinitely richer and more turbulent ancestral substrate, particularly on his mother's side of the family.

There was the heritage of a wide circle of uncles and aunts: Johanna Wilhelmina (1812-1883), Hendrick-Vincent (1814-1877); Dorothea Maria (1815-1882), Johannes (1817-1885), Willem Daniel (1818-1872), Vincent (1820-1882), Elizabeth Huberta (1823-1895), Cornelis Marinus (1824-1908), Geertruida Johanna (1826-1891) and Maria Johanna (1831-1911). Vincent's immediate family included his sisters Anna Cornelia (1855-1930), Elizabeth Huberta (1859-1936), and Wilhelmina Jacoba (1862-1941). His brothers were Cornelis Vincent (1867-1900) and the most important of all, Theodorus (1857-1891), familiarly known as Theo. It was he who would constitute Vincent's most loyal and lasting link during his long fall from his family's grace.

If he became all but lost to them, it was because of who and what he was. From the very beginning, he was the wayward child in a brood of siblings governed by reason and good sense, dominated by an authoritarian father and the collective wisdom of a plethora of aunts and uncles. All of this constituted a tightly organised and loyal unit into which the family vainly attempted to integrate Vincent. Their efforts were to no avail, and he became the object of criticism, doubt and ultimately, rejection. Progressively ejected from the moderating effects of the family circle, he would give full rein to the originality and excessiveness of his personality elsewhere: in the tragedy of his life and the splendour of his art.

As a child, Vincent already preferred taking long, solitary walks in the fields to staying at home with

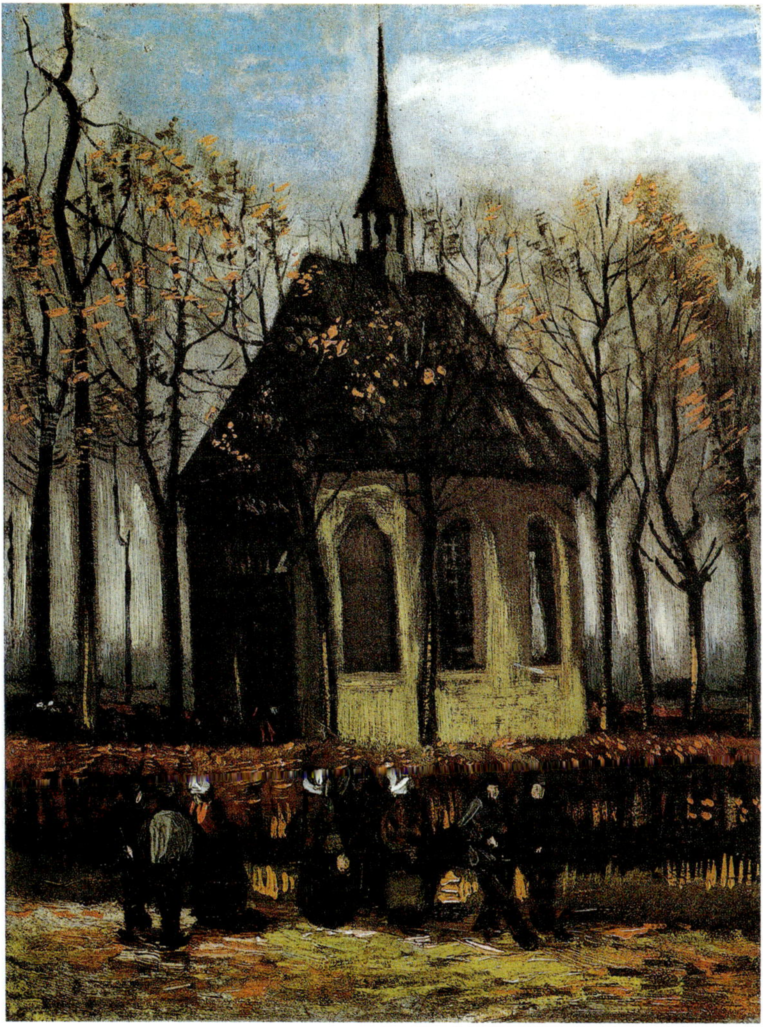

his family. If he was seen as being somewhat untamed and withdrawn, his forays into the countryside were less a means of expending his boundless energy than the result of his profound interest in nature, the details of which he observed with all the passion of the very young. Fascinated by the world of animals, insects and plants, he studied the forces and processes of a nature whose expression is seen in humble, everyday phenomena. The tiny grains which once planted soon become a waving field of wheat represented one of the innumerable mysteries which fuelled his childhood dreams.

Vincent repeatedly disappointed his parents by his successive failures: at Goupil - a career which

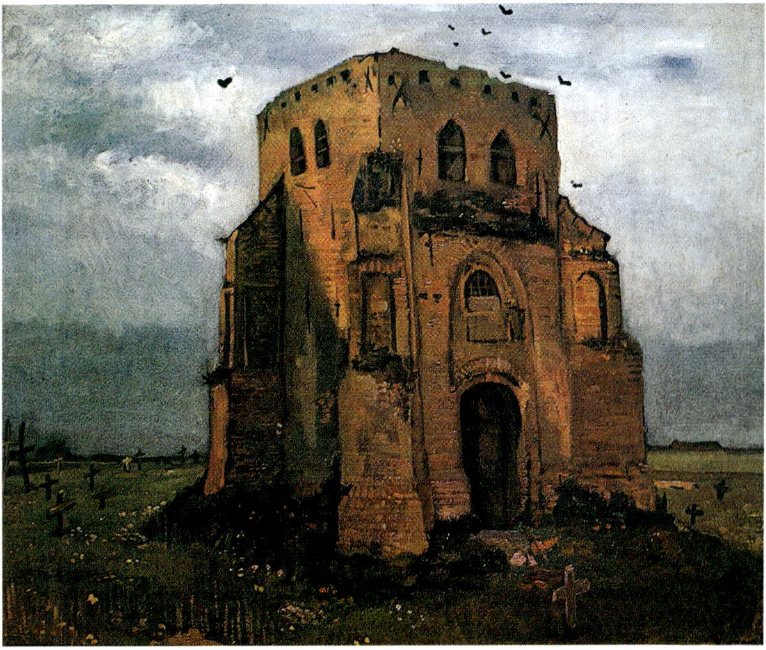

Bell-Tower in Nuenen Cemetery. *Rijksmuseum Vincent Van Gogh, Amsterdam.*

seemed a natural choice in a family of art merchants - in his vain attempts to become an evangelist in England, and by an identical lack of success (after having been recommended for the job by his relatives) as a clerk in the Dordrecht bookstore from which he would be fired.

In 1877, Vincent decided to de-

The Water-Mill at Gennep. *Rijksbureau voor Kunst, The Hague.*

vote himself exclusively to religion, a choice which entailed formal theological training and studious discipline. Over the next two years, he would try to gain admission or be dismissed from various schools and religious institutions in both Holland and Belgium. A thorn in the side of his instructors and unable to accept the limitations that were imposed upon him, santly travelled back and forth between various cities in Holland, England, France and Belgium, while desperately trying to decide on his real calling in life. In the meantime, his father had been successively posted to Zundert and Etten before being transferred to the village of Nuenen in 1882. When Vincent, who had spent the preceding two years drawing and

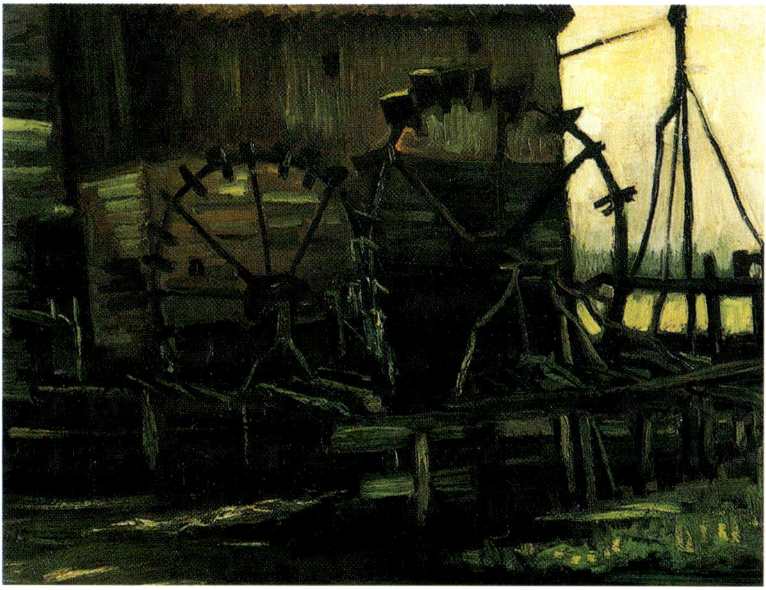

Vincent was finally sent on a six-month mission as a lay-evangelist to the Borinage region of Belgium in January 1879. Once again, his zeal proved to be too much for his superiors, and his position was never renewed.

During the years following his first posting at Goupil's Hague branch in 1869, Vincent inces- painting thanks to Theo's aid, arrived at his father's presbytery in December 1883, he was exhausted, out of money and seriously in need of shelter.

He left again in autumn of the same year. The last family reunion took place in 1884: shortly thereafter in March 1885, the good pastor Theodorus passed away.

The Good Earth

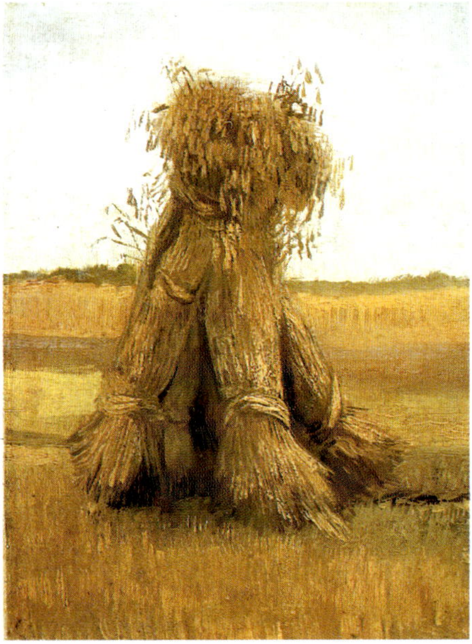

Wheat Sheaves. *Kröller-Müller Museum, Otterlo.*
Beyond the reference to Millet, Vincent affirms his highly personal vision and manner of portraying a typical detail of rural life.

With *The Potato Eaters* (April-May 1885), Vincent finally attained the first of the many summits of his art that were to follow. It was his breakthrough: after the long years patiently learning his craft, after the pain, humiliation and doubt, a single painting of his own creation expressed everything he had absorbed during his long wanderings among the desolate landscapes of the Drenthe.

He had once again returned to Nuenen, discouraged and depressed by a sentiment of failure. And once again, he received only charity instead of the love and understanding he so desperately needed.

Speaking of his family, he observed: "Their well-meaning but half-hearted compromise saddens me - their lack of awareness of this error is even worse than the error itself. Instead of really doing something to make us feel more at ease here, their lack of real acceptance paralyses me, weighing on my spirit and energy like lead...The reality of life here is horrible - and seems endless."

Vincent was still undermined by his experience with Sien: he had negotiated a separation and fled from the sterile misery of their existence without having been able

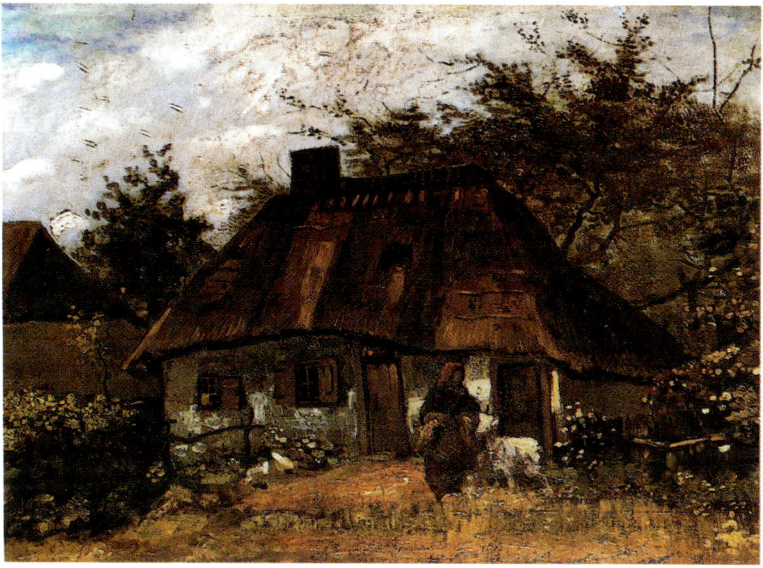

to save her from her own luckless destiny.

In Nuenen, he was received with a mixture of condescension and pity; a small studio was arranged for his use in one of the buildings adjoining the presbytery, but he soon left and moved in with the sexton of the village's Catholic church.

Among his few personal effects were the portraits and scenes of

Cottage with Peasant Woman and Goat.
Städelsches Kunstinstitut, Städtische Galerie, Francfort-sur-Main.
Every element in this composition contributes to its overbearing atmosphere of laboriousness and melancholy.

country life that he had executed during the years of poverty, solitude and estrangement from those he loved.

His work showed visible progress: the brushwork was freer, at once more powerful and confident, while his use of colour - given the sombre tonalities of his palette - was masterful in its range of expression.

All of this testified to painstaking labour: *The Potato Eaters* was not the miraculous result of spontaneous genius, but of lessons patiently learned. The painting itself was preceded by an excellent preliminary sketch, full of energy and emotion.

"I wanted it to suggest a totally different existence from our civilised lives...to show these humble peasants eating their potatoes right off the platter under the lamp light. The difficulty of their existence and its meagre rewards. In

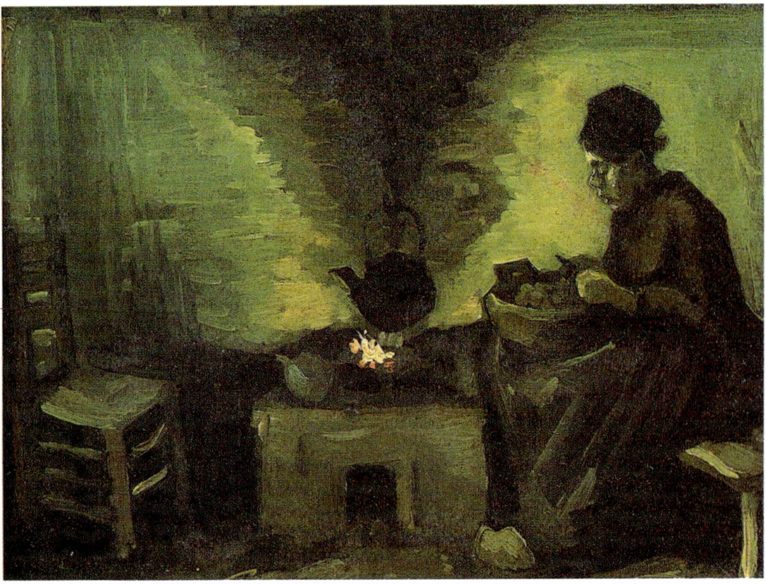

Peasant Woman and Hearth. *Orsay Museum, Paris.*
Vincent's intimate contact with peasant life strongly influenced his work. While sharing - and identifying - with their condition, he nevertheless portrayed their misery without condescension or false sentimentality.

painting it, I thought about what has been so rightly said about Millet: that his peasants appear to have been painted with the very soil they cultivate."

Vincent's comment was significant, for it prefigured all the final brilliance of the period in the south of France, where the landscapes he painted under the brilliant sun of the Midi mirrored his own state of self-consuming incandescence. Paintings filled with absolute light, just as *The Potato Eaters* was a study in absolute shadow. Both his life and his art were marked by the same extremes, which ultimately gave way to breakthroughs so radical that they were like a new life after the finality of death.

There was something Promethian in Van Gogh's attitude.

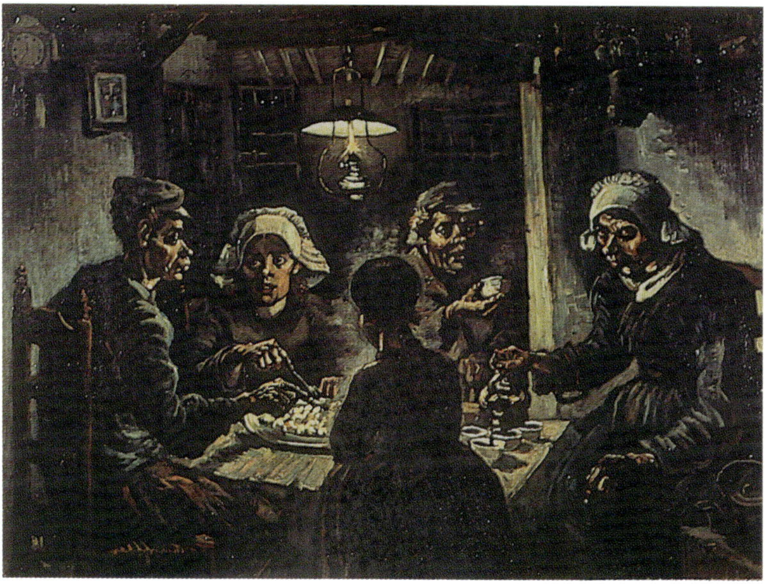

The Potato Eaters. *Rijksmuseum Vincent Van Gogh, Amsterdam.*
The work embodies all of Vincent's experience among the peasants of the Drenthe. This intimate scene of their daily life is touched by solemnity, as if portraying the celebrants of a mysterious ritual.

The Universe of Zola

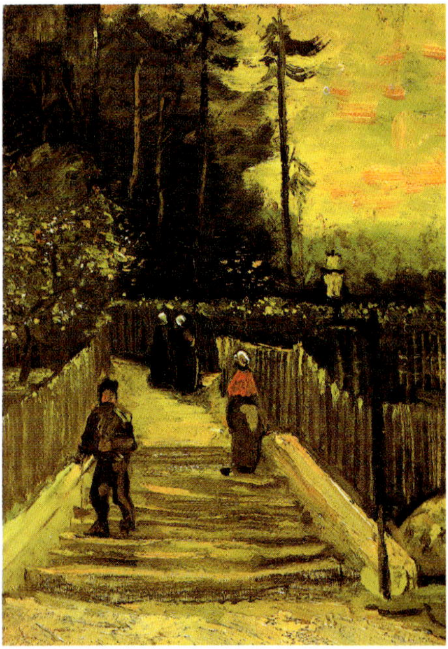

View of Montmartre. *Rijksmuseum Vincent Van Gogh, Amsterdam.*
In Vincent's time, Montmartre was still a peaceful hilltop village surrounded by gardens and tree-lined paths.

"Zola's novels are beautiful; above all, *l'Assommoir.*" Although Vincent often enthusiastically evoked the works of the celebrated French author in his letters to Theo, the full scope of Zola's universe was unknown to him.

Vincent's vision of the world was extremely fragmented; born into a respectable, middle-class family, he would chose to live amongst society's most disinherited members, whose existence he perceived all the more clearly for sharing it on a daily, intimate basis.

Van Gogh the painter of misery and shadow did not yet possess either the experience or the depth of vision that he would progressively acquire toward the end of his life. Only then, navigating at the ultimate edge of his own madness, would he emerge as a prophet of light.

It was Zola the chronicler of the outcasts of society that fascinated Vincent, less out of an appreciation for the writer's consummate talent than his ability to reveal the inner workings of society, representing in broad strokes of his pen the diverse personalities which composed it.

In his art as in his life, Vincent explored society's most insignificant and commonplace aspects.

Self-Portrait. *Gemeente Museum, The Hague.*
A pitiless confrontation with his own image.

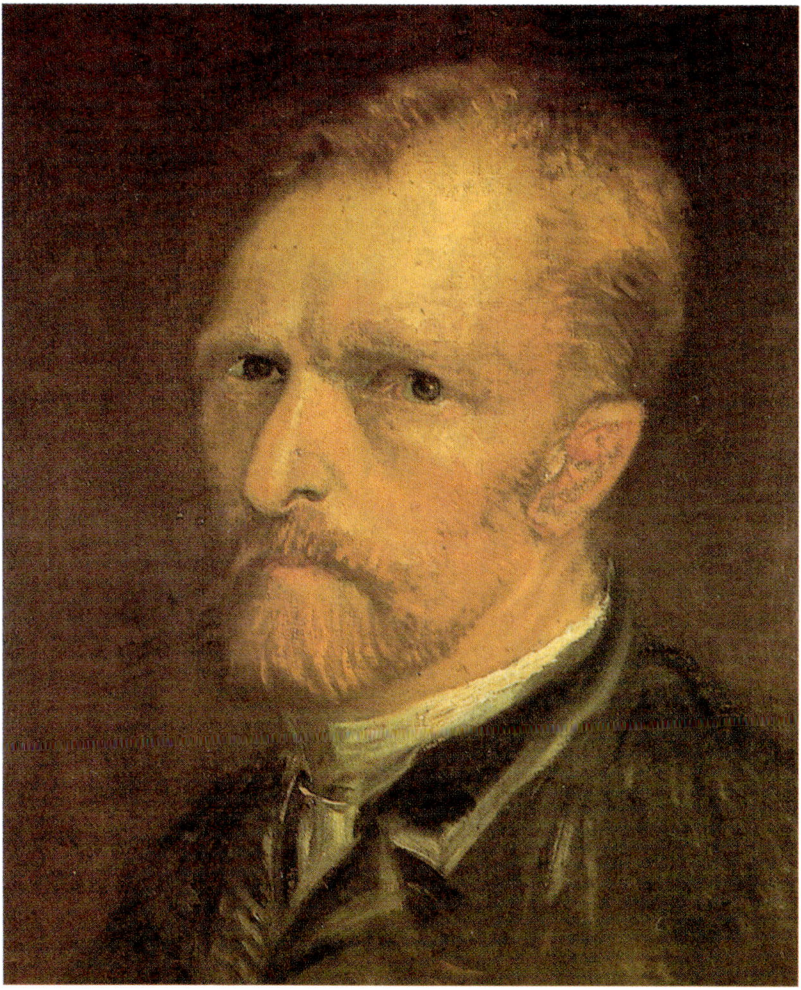

He reduced the world to its smallest symbolic denominators, focusing on objects until they atomised, penetrating them until they rendered their very essence. They trembled under the shock, vibrating as if inhabited by the energy of Vincent's own passion, objectified to the point of total disintegration.

The representation of human misery was only a portion of Zola's literary universe. His vision of society was larger than life, whereas Vincent's was microscopic, revealing the material of which reality was composed, infused with all the energy of life itself. Both his destiny and the fascination of his art was in the revelation of the inner mysteries of existence.

Vincent's appreciation for Zola was that of a young man who still had much to learn of the world around him. But the goal of both the aspiring artist and the accomplished writer was the expression of an aesthetic of realism such as that of Courbet. It was thus that Zola found himself at the centre of the Médan Group, constituted by a handful of young writers such as the Goncourt brothers, Henry Céart and above all, J.K. Huysmans.

Van Gogh was naturally drawn to this new current of realism, which was still considered unacceptable by a society which preferred the comfortable illusions of the Academy painters. As both the hostage and the incarnation of the Establishment (and historically, that of the church and state) this all-powerful institution acted as a rampart against representations of reality which did not conform to its own pre-established conventions. Painters like Courbet were simply rejected out-of-hand for their "proletarian" vision of a world which bourgeois society refused to recognise.

If the new realism had opened a breach and was progressively forging a place in art for the representation of the real world, Van Gogh - like the Biblical Fisher of men's souls - was already inhabiting it.

True to his uncompromising spirit, he would represent reality it as it was, while endowing it with dignity and even nobility. His vision was one of compassion and respect, whereas Zola's - more experienced and tainted by the cynicism of success - was that of the entomologist.

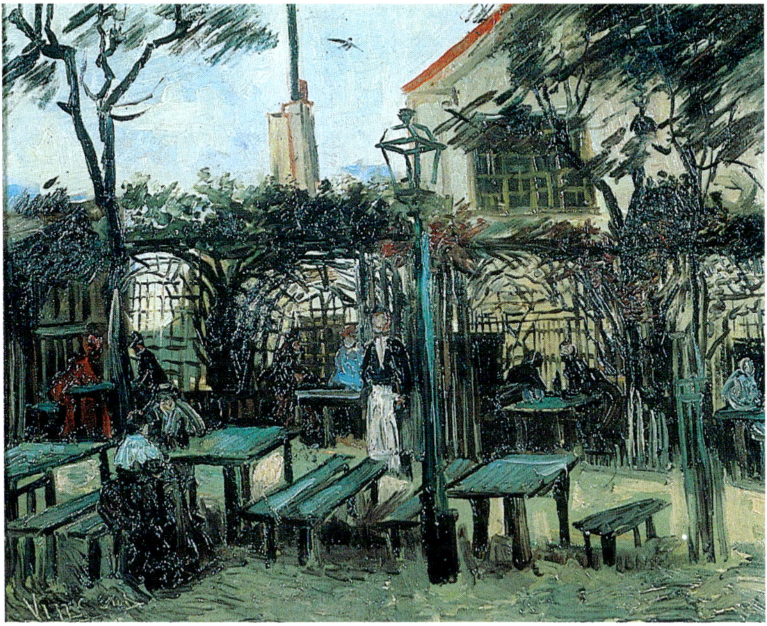

The Guinguette. *Orsay Museum, Paris. A victim of solitude, Vincent haunted cafés as if they were theatres, observing the details of the often unhappy lives of the individuals who frequented them.*

The Gift of Silence

In the countryside of Holland, where the distant horizons merge with the low, heavy sky, each home is a fortress protecting its inhabitants from the assault of the elements.

It is a land which is often marked by silence: not of indifference, but of an intense activity of the spirit and a progressive accumulation of energy that often expresses itself in a passion for exploration and adventure for Holland was long a country of navigators.

Vincent would not take to the sea upon the legendary vessels bound for distant and exotic ports that fuelled the dreams of poets. The ocean he would navigate was within him, as were the raging elements and the immense universe whose stars were like fleets of celestial ships. His ambitions were more grandiose than those who dreamed of conquering the oceans, for it was existence itself that he would explore.

The words of the Bible would prepare him for the voyage that would carry him, navigating as if upon a drunken boat, toward his final and tragic apotheosis. He would wander the cities and countrysides of four countries in quest of himself, observing the glorious eloquence of nature, sharing the lives of the poor and identifying with the most difficult conditions of his fellow-men.

He began his journey humbly and with humility, in the shadows of dimly-lit peasant homes in Holland and Belgium, where ordinary objects expressed the lives and activities of their inhabitants. Vincent would capture their power and inner force, endowing them with a moral significance and quasi-sacred dimension.

Under his brush, objects dissolved in the fragmented expression of their own existence, in the fusion of their substance. They shed their domestic quality and became the visible traces of an epic journey which abolished distance and challenged habitual vision, transforming the commonplace to reveal a dimension beyond ordinary reality where consciousness becomes united with archetypal symbols and primitive forces.

The Impressionists had developed a style of painting which immobilised time, capturing the instant in all its ephemeral rapidity. Vincent invented an art fuelled by passion, totally expressive of his emotions, his ideals and his personal vision of reality. It was an art forged within the silence of an extreme solitude, a desperate and exalted effort to transpose the world to canvas in all its richness and multiplicity. For Van Gogh, the silence of the object became sign, and painting a confession.

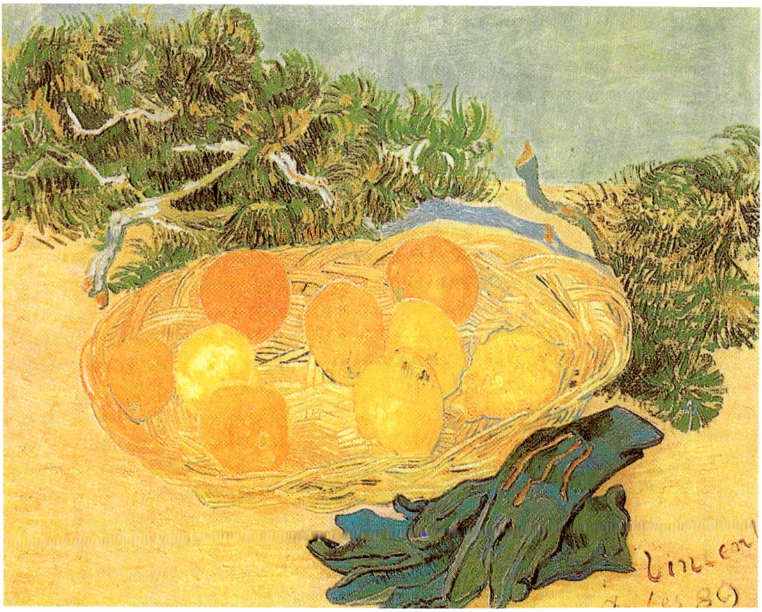

Still Life with Lemons and Blue Gloves.
The Mellon Family Collection, Upperville (Virginia).
Even the most insignificant objects in Vincent's works are charged with personal meaning. Obeying the cycle of change and transformation, their presence exudes a sense of ineluctable mortality.

The Example of Millet

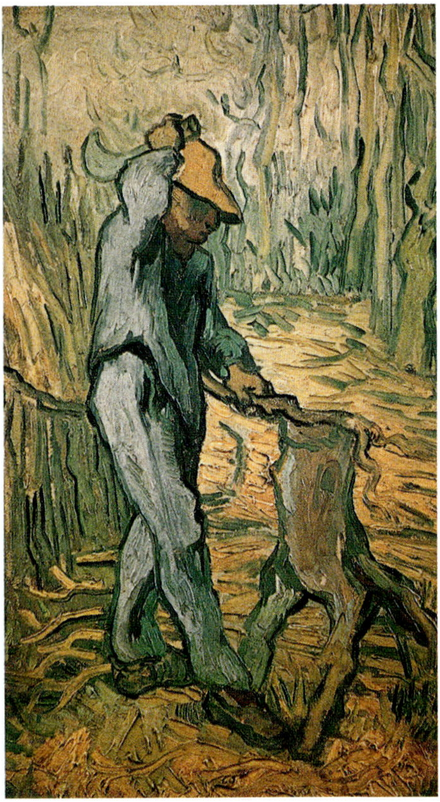

The Woodcutter. *Rijksmuseum Vincent Van Gogh, Amsterdam.*
The man has practically become one with his task, transcending his individual condition to attain a universal significance.

In the beginning, Vincent studiously imitated Millet. The Barbizon painter was enjoying great success and it was easy to obtain reproductions of his most popular works. His art was a constant source of inspiration for Vincent, who yearned to portray humanity's suffering played out against the solemn beauty of vast landscapes, mirrors of man's noble efforts to render his land fruitful.

For Millet, the earth was the theatre of man's struggle with the environment. His painstaking daily labour fascinated him, as it did Vincent, and it was thus that the young artist became the self-proclaimed disciple of an older artist whose place in history had already been acquired.

The author of paintings which became popular icons, Millet was born in 1814 and died in 1875. Unlike Courbet by the extreme simplicity and purity of his style, works such as *The Gleaner* and *The Angelus* attained a degree of popular success that went far beyond the closed circle of the Academy, touching a wide and appreciative public.

Millet's works gave expression to popular stereotypes without denaturing them by the official artistic canons of the period. His

The Siesta. *Orsay Museum, Paris. The sleeping couple are rendered with the same precise brushwork as the golden cushion of hay and surrounding grass upon which they recline. All of nature seems to be basking in the summer's heat, as unseen but omnipresent, the sun infuses the scene with its vibrant energy.*

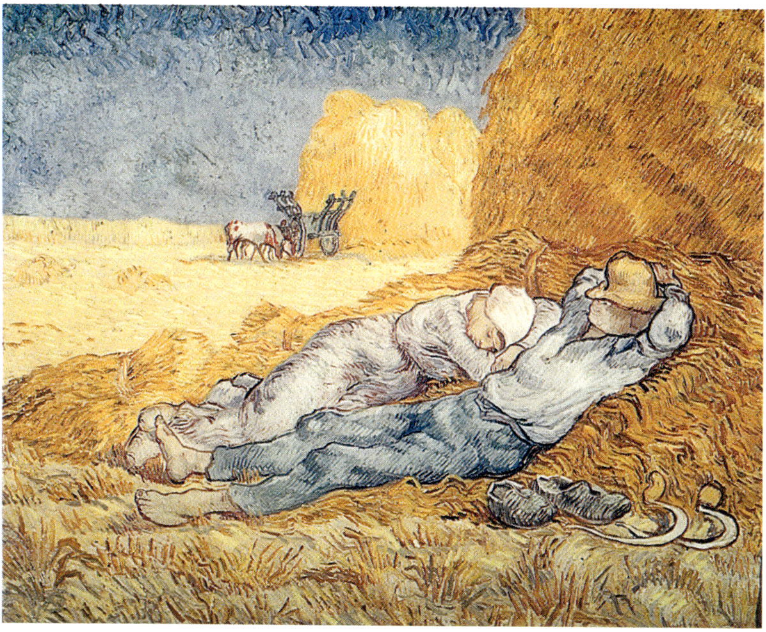

paintings displayed a mastery of technique and subtlety of execution that were considered as being the perfect representations of a real - if idealised - universe, rendered accessible and universally comprehensible even to those who had no special knowledge of art.

Vincent was aware that Millet represented something more than a model simply to be imitated or a source of themes with which he was already intimately familiar. It was Millet's approach that interested him, and particularly his manner of directly addressing the spectator's feelings and emotions.

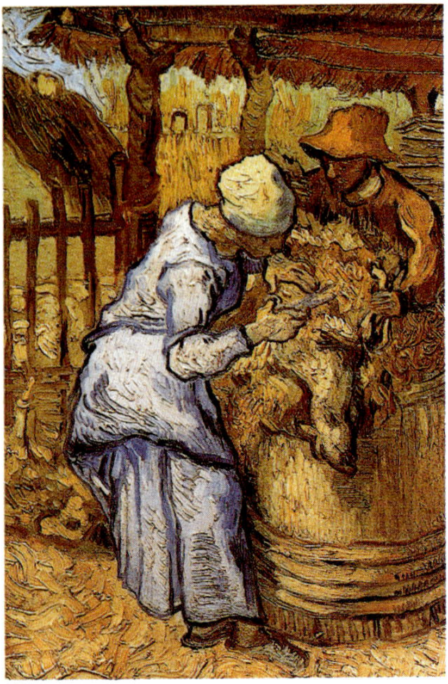

The Sheep-Shearer. *Rijksmuseum Vincent Van Gogh, Amsterdam.*
The long periods spent living in the countryside familiarised Vincent with the daily gestures of rural life, which he portrayed with authenticity and power.

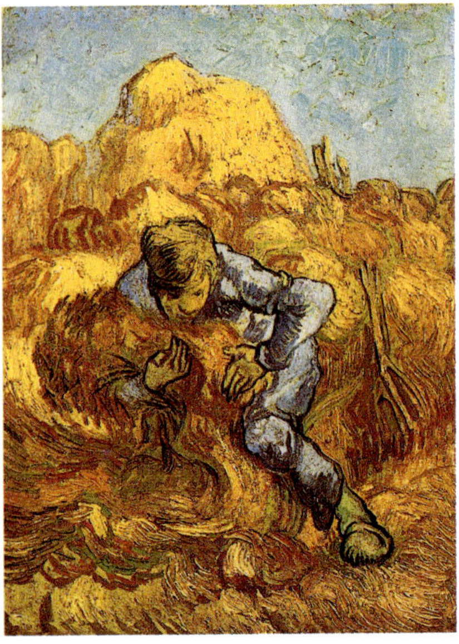

In 1881, Vincent executed a somewhat amateurish version of Millet's *Sower*, in which he nevertheless succeeded in capturing the work's spirit and emotional content, for it spoke of the same melancholy solitude and isolation of the rural environment in which he was living. Only the regions were different, for Millet had inhabited Barbizon, which at that time was surrounded by small traditional farms. As in similar areas in Belgium and Holland, life there was conditioned by an incessant struggle to survive, necessitating an instinctive knowledge of nature and the seasons.

Vincent's fascination for Millet continued throughout his life. During his Provençal period in the south of France, he did dozens of versions of his paintings, working from prints that he had brought with him from Paris. His admiration went beyond the simple recognition of an artistic debt, for despite the originality of his own subjects, he continually returned to Millet as to a source, progressively reshaping his style into his own.

He would retain Millet's rhythms and the flowing lines that highlighted and defined his subjects in their daily gestures. At the same time, he portrayed them as being so intimately connected to the land that like ancient agricultural divinities, they seemed to have sprung from the very soil they inhabited. It was this quality that differentiated Vincent's art from that of Millet: the revelation of the deep and long-forgotten forces that shape the servants of the earth into reflections of its own image.

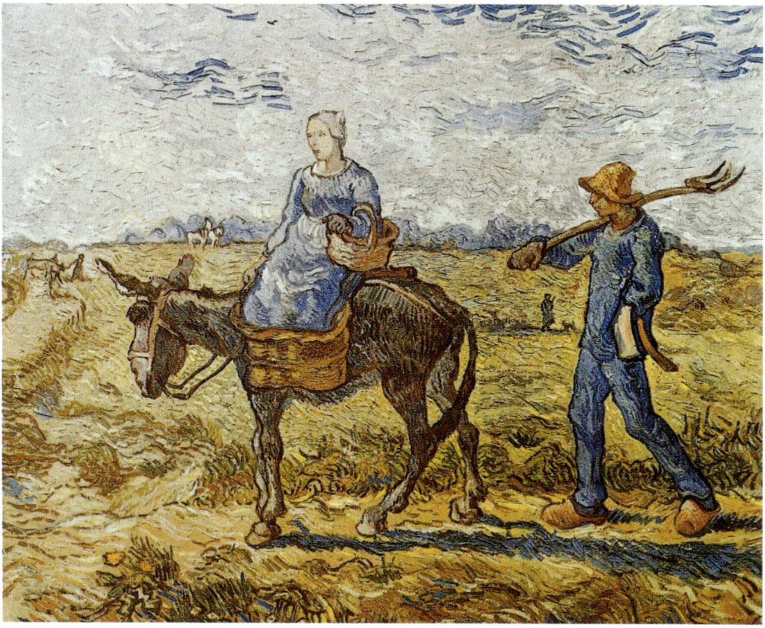

The Sheather. *Rijksmuseum Vincent Van Gogh, Amsterdam.*
The movement is that of a dancer in the midst of the sumptuous ballet of life.

Leaving for Work. *Non-Extant.*
Similar in spirit to Millet's works, the scene echoes the Biblical story of the flight into Egypt.

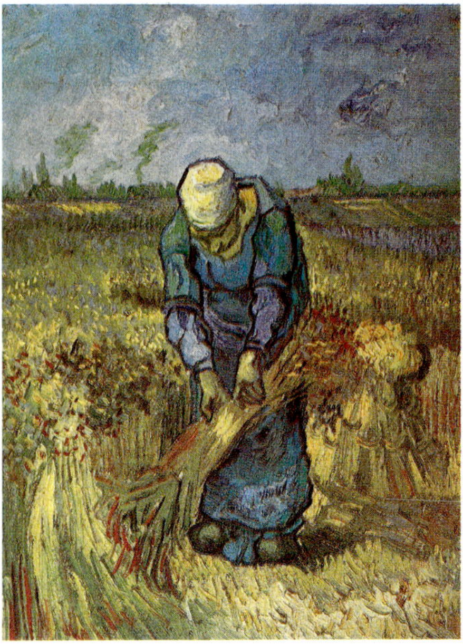

Peasant Sheaving Wheat. *Rijksmuseum Vincent Van Gogh, Amsterdam.*
The sheaver is at one with his task, merging with his universe.

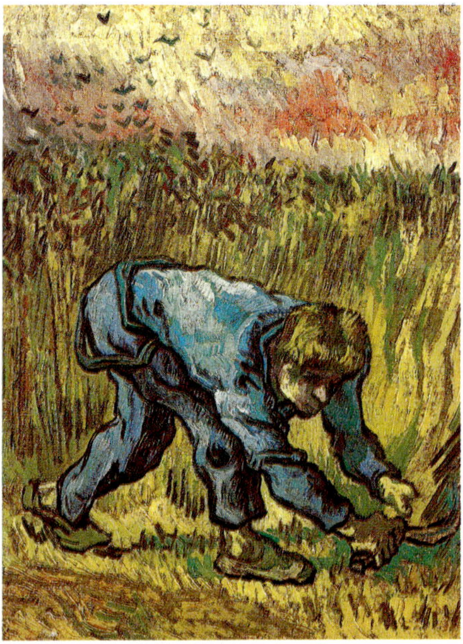

The Reaper. *Rijksmuseum Vincent Van Gogh, Amsterdam.*
The stooped posture of the reaper is that of a man plunging toward the very source of life as if in quest of its nourishing force. By the intensity with which he expresses even the most banal gestures, Vincent endows the peasant's labour with the dignity of a sacred rite.

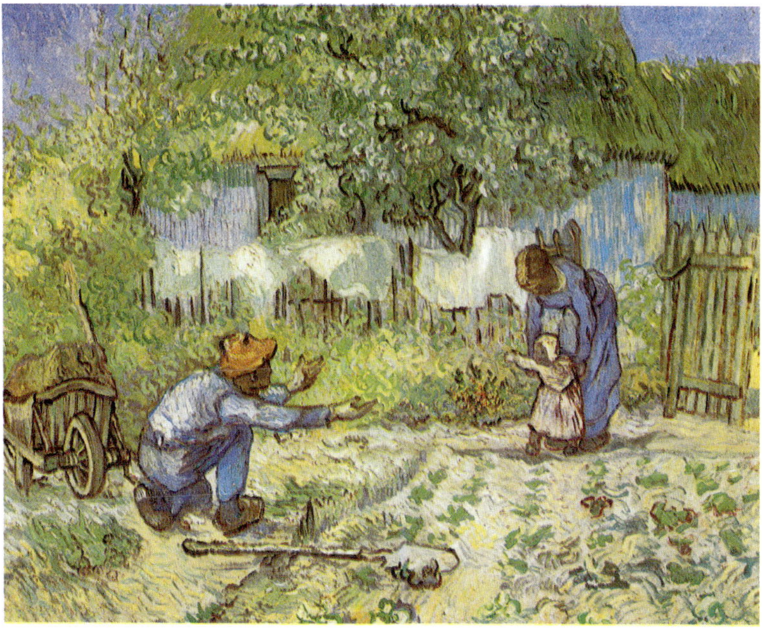

First Steps. *The Metropolitan Museum of Art, New York.*
Vincent, who would never possess a home and family, was particularly sensitive to the simple pleasures offered by both. His love for his nephew was intense and sincere: that of a solitary man who would never marry and have children of his own.

The Peasant Ethic

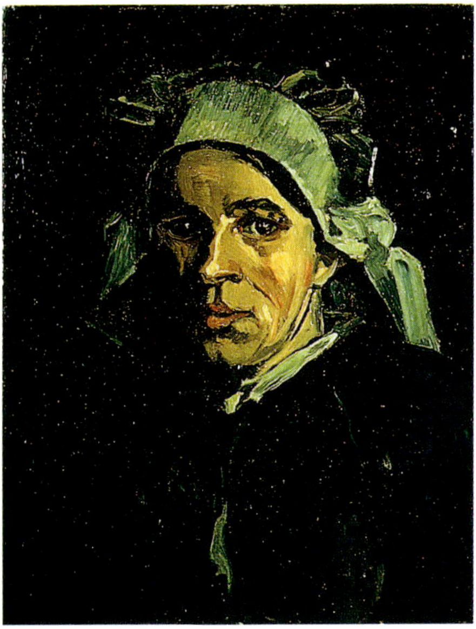

Peasant Woman with White Bonnet.
Rijksmuseum Vincent Van Gogh, Amsterdam.
Vincent's portraits were at opposite ends from the accepted artistic canons of the period: his manner translated the force and authenticity of his subjects, revealing their inner truth.

After acquiring political power and consolidating its newly-acquired wealth in banking and finance, the bourgeoisie of the nineteenth century began seeking moral justifications for its dominance.

The Church had provided repressive codes that imprisoned individuals in a pre-ordained order. The ruling classes promoted an idealised vision that exalted the merits of the agrarian world. Rural France had remained extremely traditional, untouched by the forces of industrialisation which had created the urban proletariat. This new and economically oppressed underclass was constrained to participate in a frantic race for the acquisition of material goods which, since they were generally unattainable, were a constant source of frustration and anger.

The bourgeois vision of the fertile earth and its loyal servants was offered up in the form of ready-made moral lessons to the young, while also providing the means of dampening their increasing desire to abandon the land and emigrate to the cities.

After inheriting the artistic remains of the tradition of the ancient fertility goddesses, the celebrants of the cult of the grandeur of agrarian life willingly abandoned its representation to academic painters whose patently artificial images of Flore and Demeter were the direct descendants of the neo-classical revival, a distant echo of the period when Marie-Antoinette played at being a humble shepherdess with the court of Versailles as her supporting cast.

When not occupied portraying the heroes of ancient wars or themes inspired by classical mythology, the academic painters of the period adopted a realistic style heavily influenced by bourgeois morality to better convey the reality of peasant society from the safe distance of their studios.

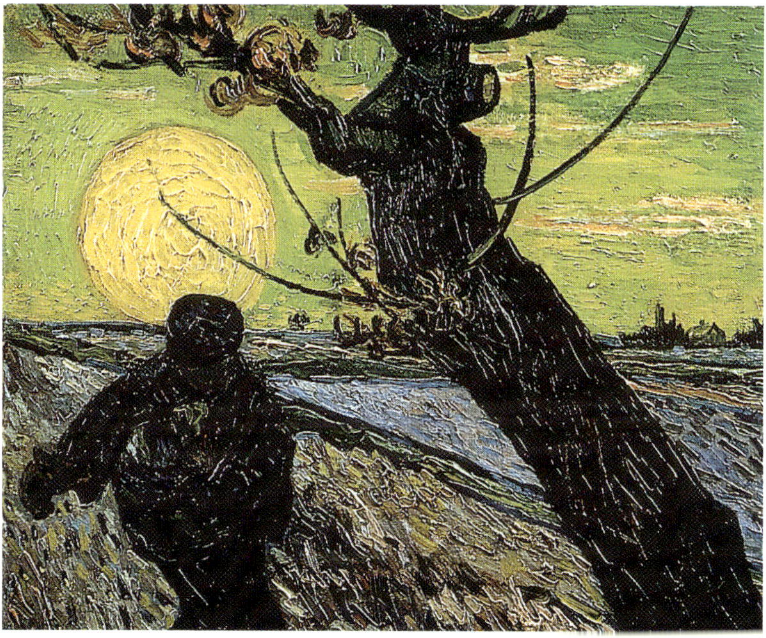

The Sower. *Rijksmuseum Vincent Van Gogh, Amsterdam.*
The theme of the sower traverses all of Van Gogh's work like a constant. Rendered in heavy earth-tones and thick brushwork in his early works, the treatment progressively lightens and gains in dynamism. Here, man, tree, earth and sky are juxtaposed in a masterful expression of the unity of nature, rendered in a manner which recalls Japanese art.

Having survived gentrification by the aristocracy, the representation of agrarian society by nineteenth-century painters was certainly more realistic but still hopelessly out of touch with reality by its persistent delusions concerning the inherent nobility of peasant life.

This type of art was far from being a vector of the proletarian struggle, even if a painter like Courbet occasionally attempted to express the brutal realities of a system which crushed individuals and rendered their dreams unrealisable.

Other painters of the period, such as Jules Bastien-Lepage, Leon Lhermitte, Julien Dupré, Rosa Bonheur and Jules Breton, attempted to portray the agrarian

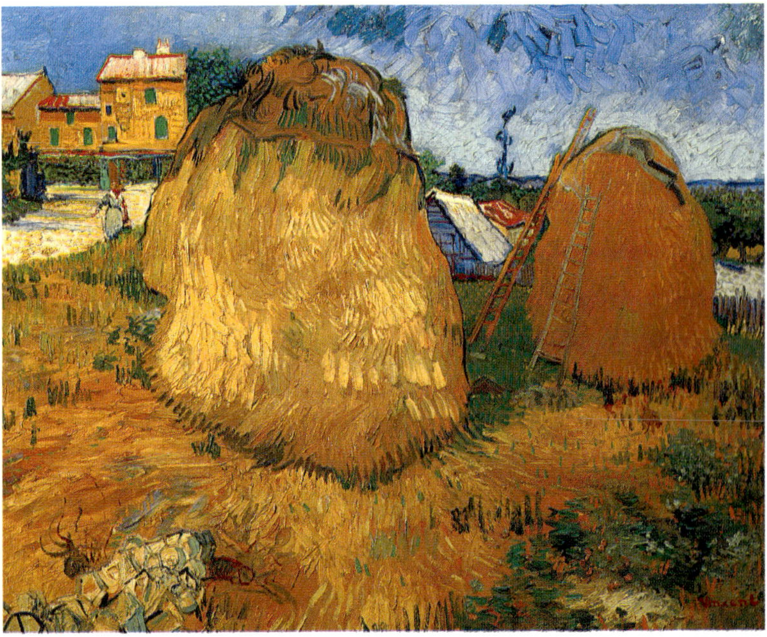

Haystacks in Provence. *Rijksmuseum Kröller-Müller, Otterlo.*
Dominating the foreground, the massive piles of hay seem inhabited by a life of their own. The forces of nature vibrate with tellurian energy. Sky and earth seem traversed by a cosmic vibration; the balance of the haystacks is precarious: the deceptive tranquillity of the scene is pervaded by a strange sense of impending menace.

world with a modicum of realism. Although their works were well-executed, aesthetically pleasing and well-accepted by the public, they were also marked by an idealisation which totally masked the oppressive nature of peasant life. The epitome of the style consisted in the celebration of its most attractive aspects, while conveniently ignoring the toll that it took on the very people they were portraying.

For these artists, all peasants were strong and of noble countenance, their women healthy and beautiful, and their everyday gestures generous and harmonious, filling the cosmos - and the artist's canvas - with a magnificent homage to the fertility of the soil and inherent nobility of those who laboured it.

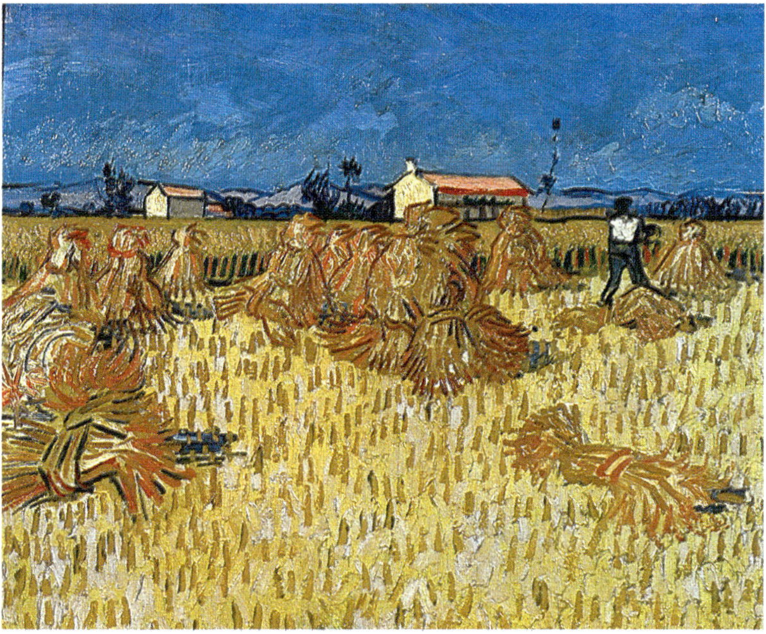

Harvest in Provence. *Museum of Israel, Jerusalem.*
The treatment has here been reduced to the essential. The luminous fields and contrasting cobalt blue sky are rendered in energetic brush strokes whose vivacity infuse the vast panorama with an innate dynamism.

As the benevolent master of the well-traced furrow and natural poet of the bountiful earth, the peasant was seen as the guardian of a tradition that the bourgeoisie contemplated with obvious satisfaction and great peace of mind. It was a vision faithful to the spirit of the French Revolution, which elevated the peasant to the stature of a popular hero: the embodiment of natural wisdom and an innate sense of justice, proudly cultivating the fields of a fraternal and egalitarian nation. Jean-Jacques Rousseau would construct a philosophical system around this concept, unshaken by doubt and untroubled by all evidence to the contrary.

An ideal point of convergence uniting religious fervour and the mystique of peasant society was the historical figure of Joan of Arc. Of humble peasant origins, she had long occupied a privileged place in the popular imagination. By her combined qualities of virginal saint, courageous warrior and simple country girl, she re-emerged in nineteenth century as a force of social cohesion.

Millet, who had the merit of painting directly from life and actually experiencing - rather than imagining - the reality of peasant existence, would remain a touchstone in Vincent's quest to portray the lives of these people as they really were. Refusing to blindly idealise their existence, he instead gave full expression to their reality, endowing it with dignity and significance.

Vincent's style perfectly corresponded to his subjects during his Dutch and Belgian period. His brushwork was thick and textured, and as dark and heavy as the autumn soil. The raw power that it expressed was intended to pierce the veil of indifference covering the eyes of those ignoring the reality of the world that Vincent was portraying, whose intimate contact stimulated his creative drive, nourished his art and forged the originality of his style.

Painting by painting, the style evolved in complexity and tech-

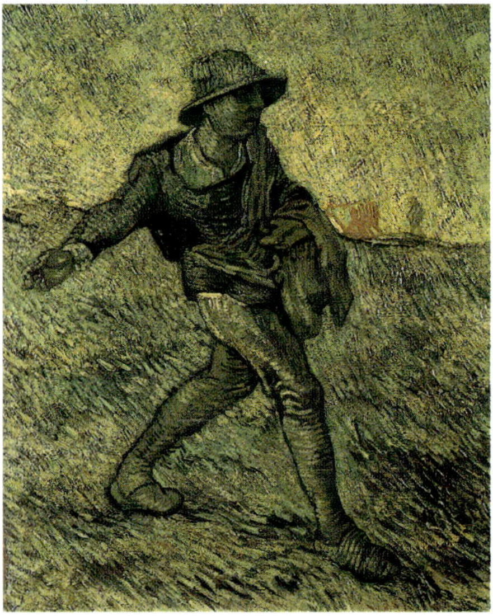

The Sower. *Rijksmuseum Kröller-Müller, Otterlo.*
Millet's influence is once again evident here, but Vincent's nervous brushwork contrasts strangely with the static pose of the sower and the foreshortened horizon. An unusual treatment of a highly traditional subject.

nique. The encounter with Impressionism was decisive: his palette exploded with light and colour, his brushwork with new energy. After the years spent patiently refining his craft, it was a style that finally corresponded to the measure of his artistic ambitions.

He had gone beyond a realism based on pure observation and had attained an manner charged with an energy generated by his boundless passion for life. His quest for realism had not disappeared: it re-emerged, transformed into signs of fire.

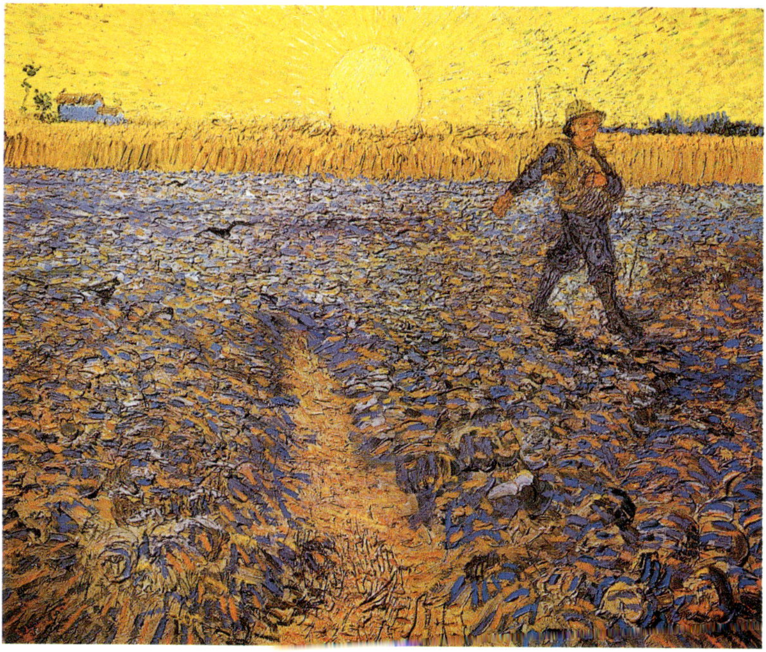

The Sower. *Rijksmuseum Kröller-Müller, Otterlo.*
An expression of the profound solitude of a man dwarfed by the space which he occupies, striding over an earth which swallows him like a thirsty desert.

The Shoals of Passion

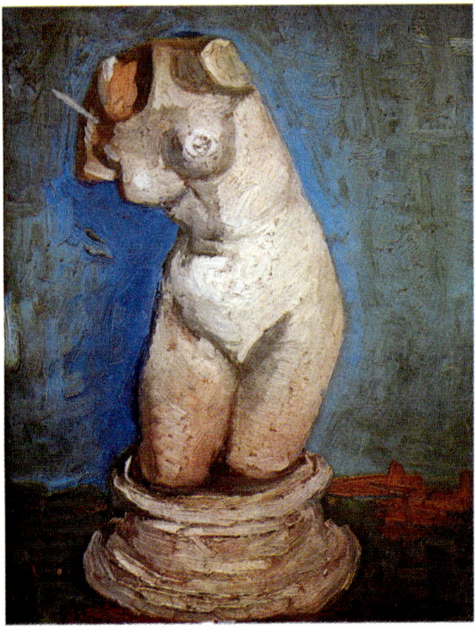

Statuette. *Rijksmusuem Vincent Van Gogh, Amsterdam.*
Vincent occasionally executed conventional and even academic studies. Despite the traditionalism of the subject, his treatment infuses the static plaster statuette with a strange life all of its own.

Female nudes are practically absent from Van Gogh's works: he had been raised in a pious family where sexual desire - and desire in general - was repressed.

To express desire, one must be able to admit it. When repressed, it becomes a distant memory charged with loss, regret and the lingering pain of an impossible fulfilment. Vincent himself confessed that the only real moments of satisfaction and satiety he ever knew were provided by art: creation became a way of re-channelling desires whose expression had early been forbidden and which forever remained sublimated.

His nudes were rare, and lacking in feminine grace and seduction. They indicated a refusal, an absence marked by loss and pain, for his relationships with women were tortured and his love for them unrequited. He was successively rejected by his landlady's daughter in London and his cousin Kate in Etten; the only woman to ever live under his roof was Sien, the pregnant, alcoholic prostitute that he had rescued from the streets.

Vincent took her in, and with her, all of her problems. He never spoke of love when attempting to

Reclining Nude. *Private collection.* *In the straight-laced Calvinist atmosphere that pervaded Vincent's childhood, sexuality was repressed. His relationships with women were affected by the rigidity of his upbringing, forever marking him with the distant reserve of the neurotic. In Paris, he would cryptically remark that "The women I discover here among the people produce a strange effect upon me. I'd rather paint them than possess them, but to tell the truth, both would please me...".*

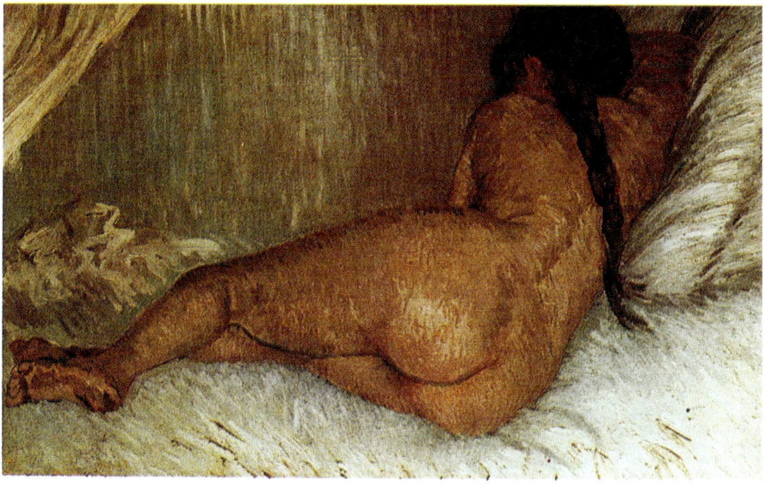

justify his actions before his scandalised family and acquaintances, but of the moral necessity of saving her from a life on the streets. And although it is uncertain whether they ever became sexually intimate, Vincent captured all the pain of her existence in *Sorrow.* For the rest, he was reduced to frequenting bordellos.

Of these nocturnal adventures nothing appeared in his art, contrary to the richly sensual works of Degas, Toulouse-Lautrec and Gauguin. The latter, who was often Vincent's companion during their nightly debauches in Arles, unabashedly gave himself over to the pleasures of the flesh with a veritable harem of women of easy virtue, for he was supremely self-confident, extremely sensual and possessed all the natural authority with women that Vincent lacked.

Even more than the warm conviviality of the bordellos, he preferred the late-night cafés where he would sit alone and in silence, observing the sad spectacle of humanity playing itself out before his eyes.

Confronted by frank sensuality,

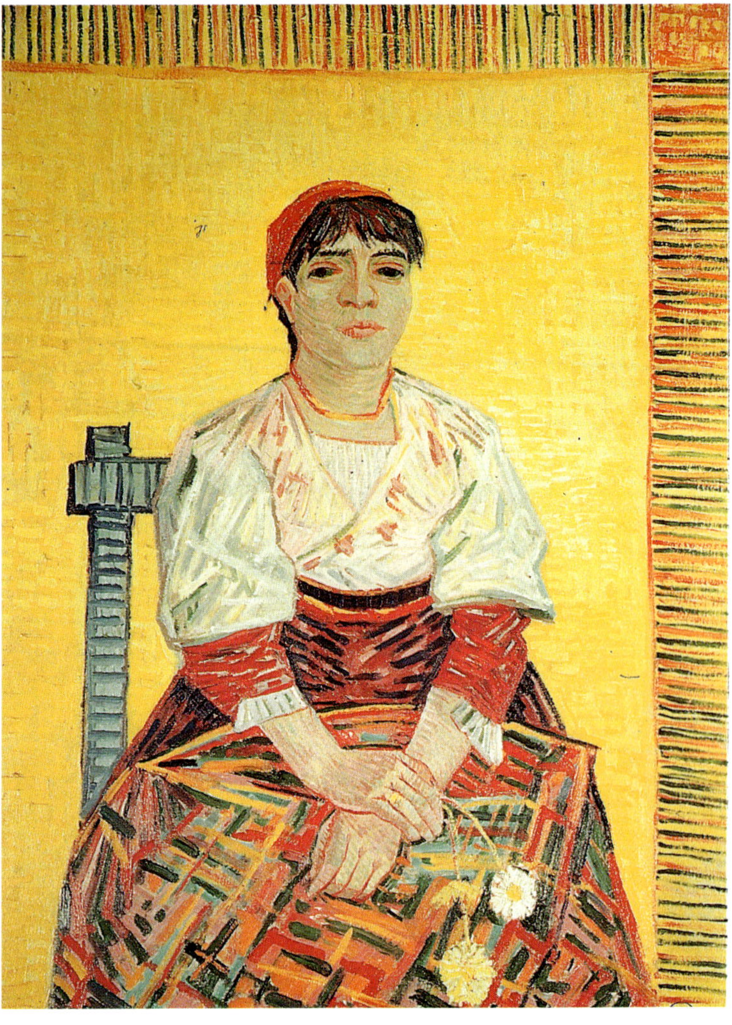

The Italian Woman (*also known as* La Segatori). *Orsay Museum, Paris.*
The manager of a Parisian bistro and briefly Vincent's mistress, she is portrayed stiffly and with a curious immobile rigidity, broken only by the bright vivacity of her multicoloured skirt and the contrasting yellow tones of the background.

he felt only shame and inadequacy, and when - after an argument with Gauguin - he cut off his ear and presented it to a local prostitute, it was an act of contrition, a ritual of self-punishment for having failed to live up to the masculine ideals of sexuality that his friend so perfectly embodied.

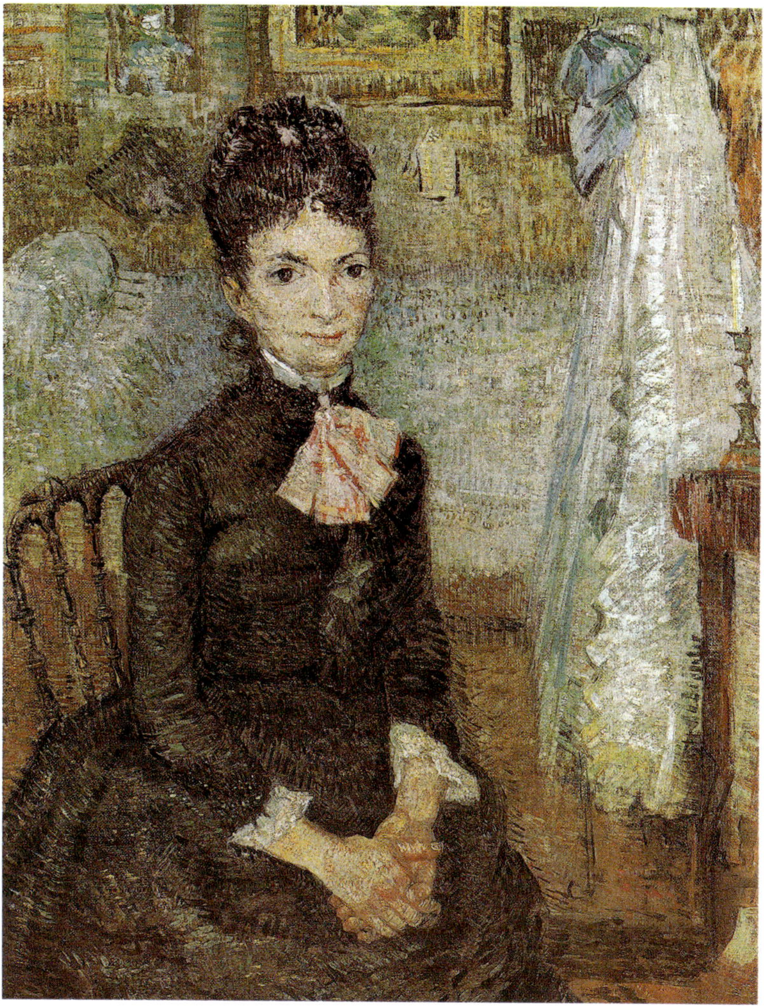

Woman and Cradle. *Rijksmuseum Vincent Van Gogh, Amsterdam.*
Here, it is as if Vincent compensated for the absence of a home and family by painting their idealised images. The habitual nervousness of his brushwork has given way to a more expressive and tender manner, suggestive of the style of Berthe Morisot.

Colour-burst: Rubens

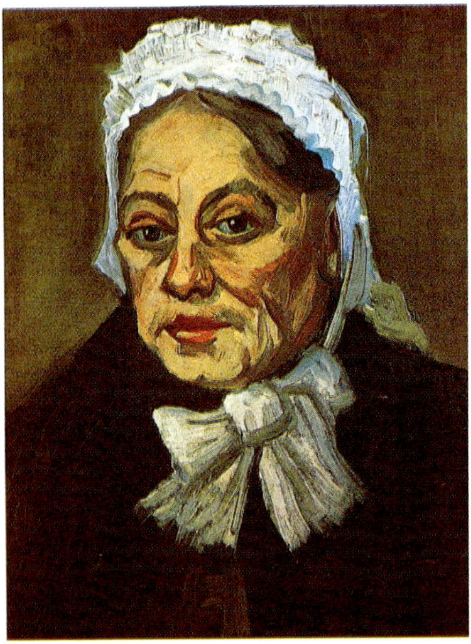

La Nourrice (The Wetnurse).
Rijksmuseum Vincent Van Gogh, Amsterdam.
With her peasant stolidity, the woman is closer to the primitive forces of the earth than the gentle atmosphere of the nursery. As seen by Van Gogh, this symbol of childhood appears as a manifestation of the generosity of nature itself.

In November 1885, Vincent fled the stifling atmosphere of his father's presbytery in Nuenen and moved to Antwerp, at that time a regional centre of the arts. By a strange coincidence recalling the theory of "objective chance" of the French Surrealist André Breton, his lodgings were located on the Longue Rue des Images ("the Long Street of Images").

In a letter to Theo, Vincent described his room: "My studio is quite liveable, especially after I tacked a series of Japanese prints to the wall. I love seeing them there, and I'm so happy to have a place where I can work inside when the weather is bad. The little bedroom is nice, and not at all depressing. In settling in, I spent a few more francs on a stove and lamp. I'm sure that my stay here will be anything but boring....".

The pragmatic tone of the letter and its repeated references to decoration and furnishings reveals Vincent's need for a place of his own where he could work in relative peace and comfort. Despite the turbulence of yet another large city (he had also briefly lived in the Hague, London, Paris and Amster-

Fourteenth of July in Paris. *Jäggli-Hahnloser Collection, Winterthur.*
A subtle explosion of colours similar to the chromatic range employed by Manet or Monet when treating similar themes.

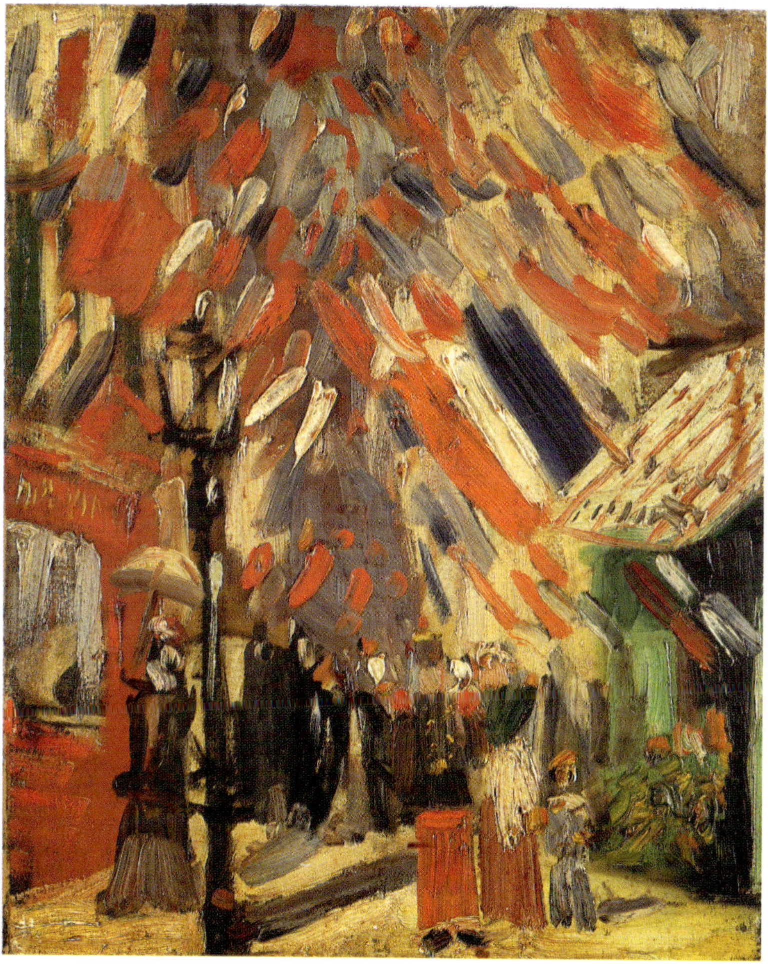

dam), Vincent finally seemed ready to settle down and begin his apprenticeship as a painter. His style was still influenced by the Academy, but he was lucid enough to recognise that there was still much to learn. Turning his back to the more superficial pleasures of the city, he haunted its museums and discovered the works of Jordaens, Van Goyen, Ruysadaël and above all, Rubens.

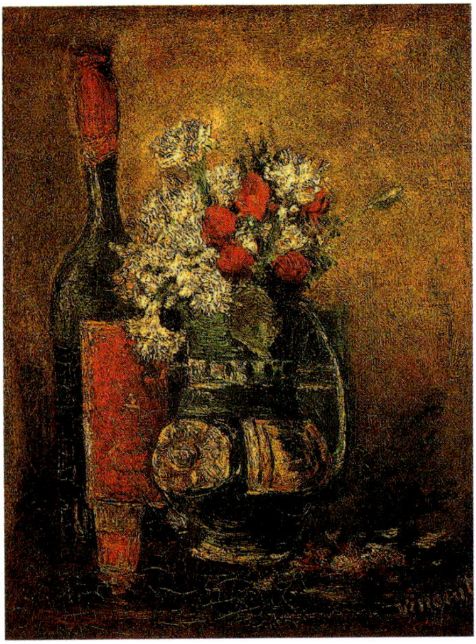

Flowers and Bottle. *Rijksmuseum Kröller-Müller, Otterlo.*
An unusual alliance of objects and flowers, whose rigidity and compactness are the expression of Vincent's personality, even as they reveal an intimate vision of his domestic environment.

Vincent was fascinated by his rich palette but disapproved of his subjects and manner: the plump cherubs surrounding the fleshy classical goddesses with their rosy skin, sensual hips and full breasts were far-removed from the ingrained asceticism and poverty of his own universe. The exuberance of Rubens was at the antipodes of Vincent's conception of life and art, yet his power of expression was undeniable.

The encounter with Rubens stimulated Vincent's creative energy which had begun to stagnate in the raw soil, dark landscapes and human misery of the peasant society which had for so long been his unique source of inspiration.

Vincent had a deep-seated need for an art which expressed his own sense of humanity. He sensed that the example of Rubens would permit him to renew his creative drives without abandoning his objectives, on the condition of integrating certain aspects of the latter artist's manner, rather than his subjects.

His discovery of Rubens was a decisive event which transformed his conception of light and the chromatic range of his palette rather than his style. Rubens had adopted a style which was perfect for celebrating all the sheen and supple softness of the female body. His sense of internal dynamism and use of sumptuous decor was totally foreign to Vincent, who sought to give expression to a far different vision. All he lacked was the means of doing so, and it was through the influence of Rubens that he finally succeeded.

A comparison between the radiant sensuality of Rubens' *Portrait*

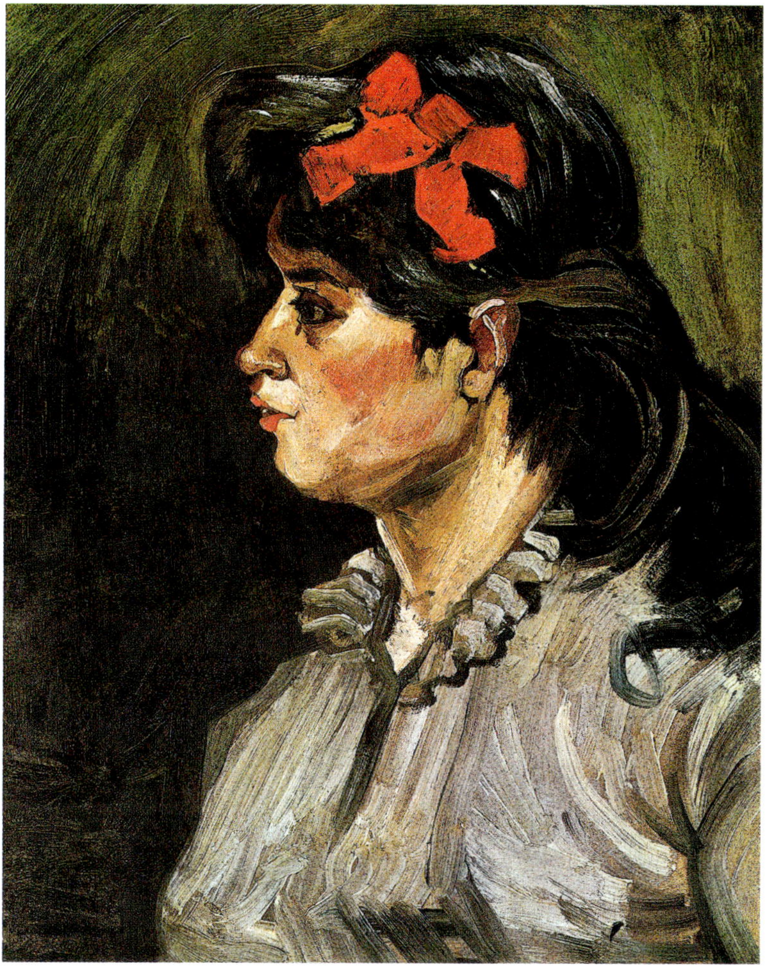

Portrait of a Woman. *Algred Wyler Collection, New York.*
Vincent constantly returned to the same themes. As he gained in self-assurance, his portraits became more expressive, surpassing in quality his earlier efforts. Ultimately, he became the master of a style of his own creation, with which he expressed the very soul of his subjects.

of Helen Fourment and Van Gogh's *Portrait of a Woman* reveals all that separates the two artists. In painting his wife's portrait, Rubens never forgot that he had also painted that of a queen: Marie de Medicis. Something of the same grandeur, formality and sense of distance between the artist and his subject was carried over to the second painting, whereas Vincent - true to his habit of choosing humble, common people for his portraits - adopted a much more intimate tone. Here the subject is a flesh-and-blood human being, a nearly tangible presence. Distance has been abolished, for there is nothing in her social position or way of life which is far from ordinary reality. In painting the common man (or woman), Vincent expressed the rich, natural and innocent beauty of humanity. And even if in their humility they were unaware of their precious gifts, their expressions often reveal the pleasure they felt in sitting for their portrait.

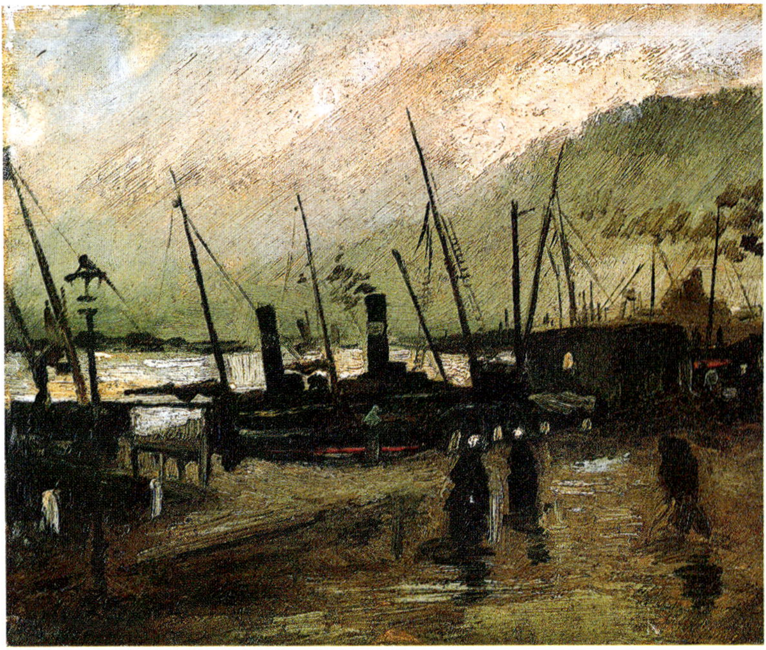

Antwerp Quai. *Rijksmuseum Vincent Van Gogh, Amsterdam.*
In a study executed with thick applications of pigment and influenced by traditionalism, Vincent's personal touch is nevertheless present. The work communicates the brooding atmosphere of the port under the dark rain-streaked skies.

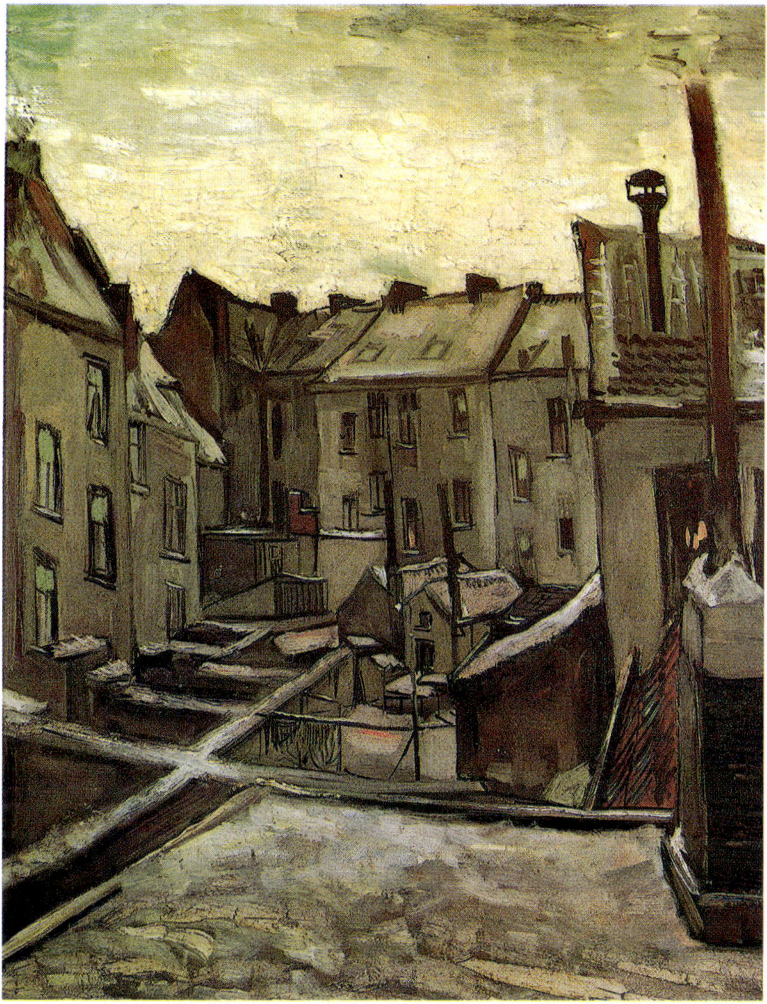

Antwerp Under the Snow. *Rijksmuseum Vincent Van Gogh, Amsterdam.*
Using firm, ample and supple brushwork, Vincent has masterfully structured space as if it were the walls of a prison, expressing all of the ambient pessimism of the scene. For Van Gogh, representations of reality were often marked by sadness and solitude.

Self-Conquest

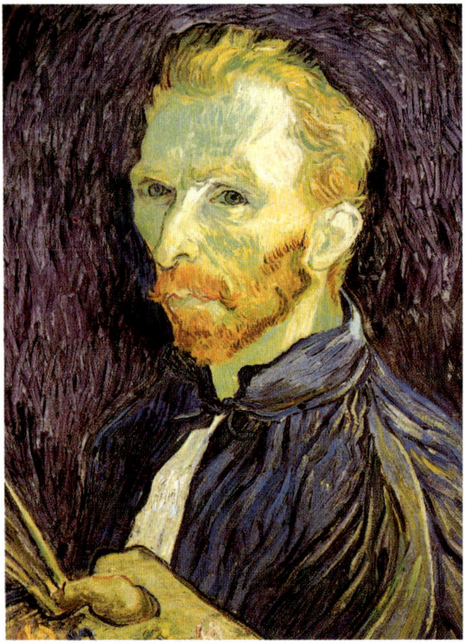

Self-Portrait. *John Hay Whitney Collection, New York.*
Vincent's habitual lack of self-indulgence with his own image is once again evident in the unadorned sharpness of his features and the intensity of his expression.

Although Vincent's mental balance was often precarious, there were also certain periods during which he attained a relative stability.

He had come close to a mental breakdown during his exhausting cohabitation among the peasants and social outcasts for whom misery and injustice were the daily lot. Totally devoted to their cause, touched by a sense of fraternity, he encountered hostility, incomprehension and rejection. By his choices in life and art, his nonconformity and fierce, uncompromising faith in humanity, he progressively cut himself off from others. Even his own family was incapable of offering the understanding and acceptance which he so needed.

He progressively found himself isolated and discouraged, lost in his own inner conflicts, alienated from society, his family and himself. Not surprisingly, his resolution to devote himself entirely to art increased in direct proportion to his growing sense of isolation. What began as a vague attraction progressively became an inner necessity, nearly an obsession. Vincent never did things halfheartedly, and once his choice was made, he invested in it totally.

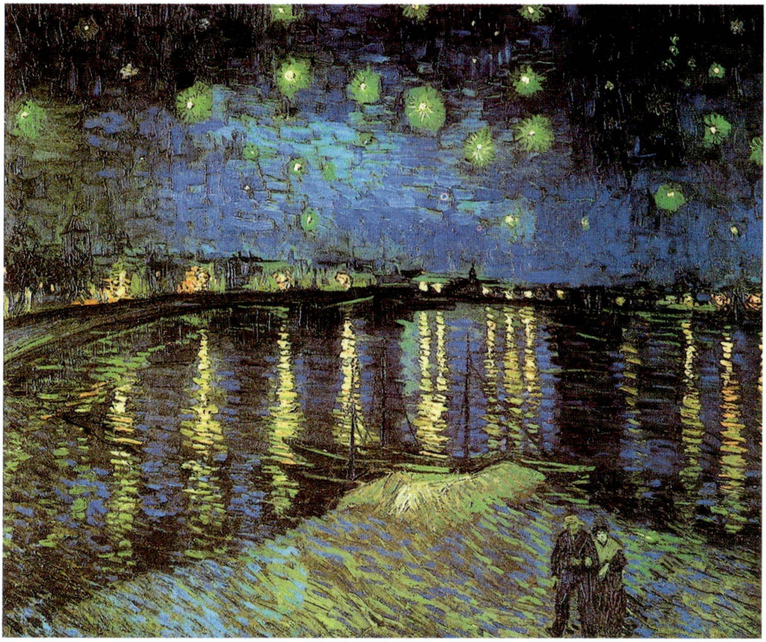

Starry Night on the Rhône. *Orsay Museum, Paris.*
Exhausted by his confinement, Vincent's yearning for liberty expressed itself in a fascination for scenes of space and night. Here, he renders darkness nearly palpable in the explosion of the myriad points of light.

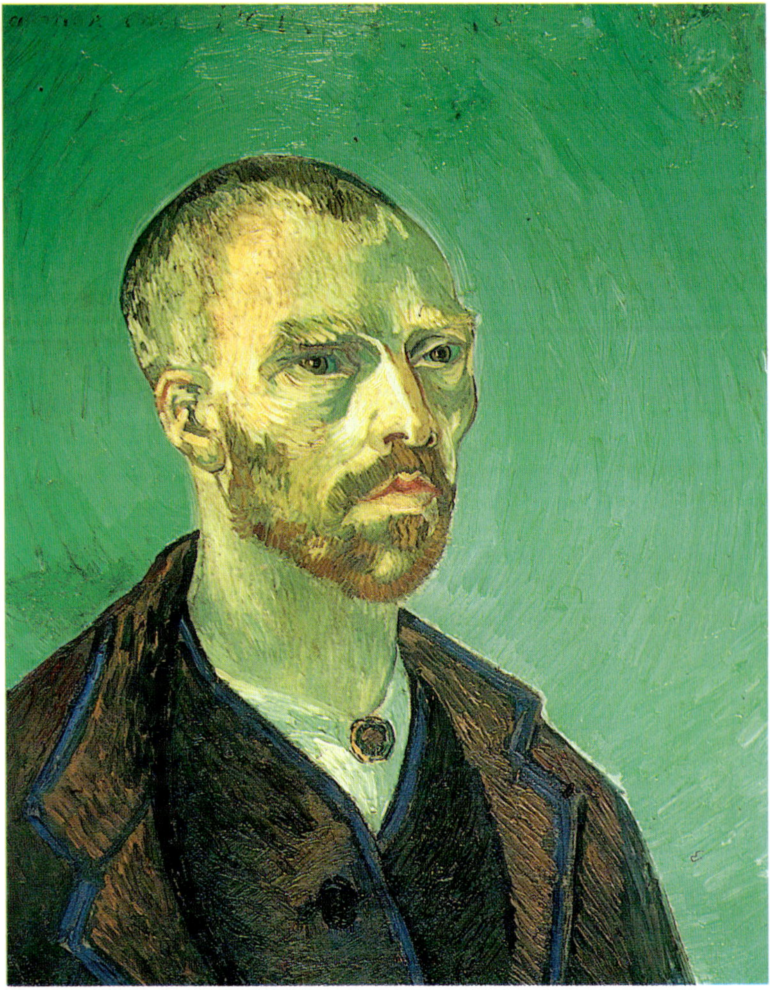

Self-Portrait. *Fogg Art Museum, Harvard University, Cambridge (Massachusetts). In the expression of his subjective reality, Van Gogh portrays himself in a manner suggestive of both monk and prisoner.*

Submerged in psychological pain, deeply wounded by the rejection of his family and the women he had loved, he turned to art as a substitute for all that life had denied him. It is possible that his pursuit of a creative activity and his progressive mastery of technique gradually calmed his tortured spirit. After years of doubt and failure, the period from 1880 to 1890 was his richest and most creative, during which he produced an incredible number of magnificent paintings. They were among his best works, a veritable testament to the beauty of the world, rendered in a manner of which only he was capable.

Yet, even if his private demons were temporarily pacified, they were never totally tamed: their presence was reflected in the lines of his prematurely aged face, whose features had hardened into those of a man forever trapped in the wilderness of his own soul.

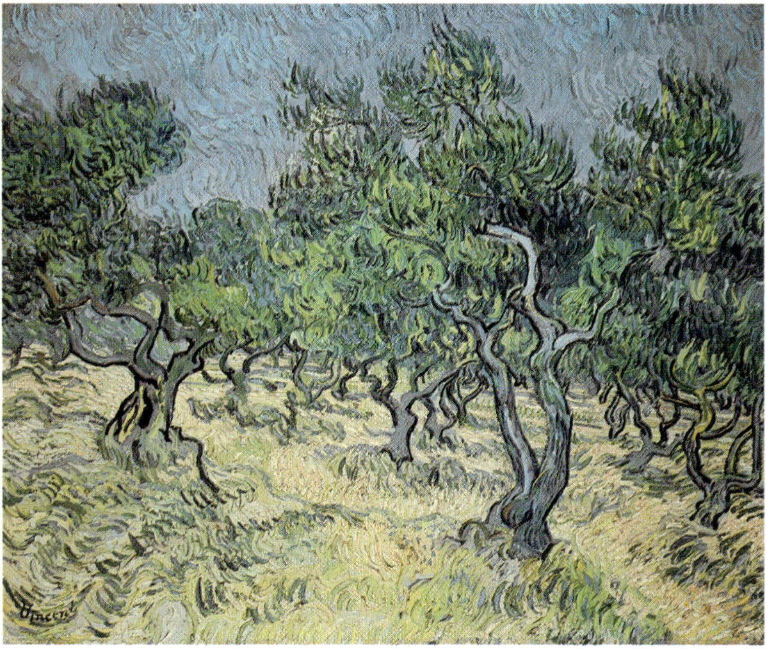

Van Gogh's mastery of his art was also the painstaking conquest of the despair waiting like an enemy deep within the minds of all lucid individuals. The time was no longer of doubt, but for going beyond artistic and personal limits to a clear and luminous vision of reality itself.

Olive Trees. *Rijksmuseum Kröller-Müller, Otterlo.*
It is as if the deepest forces of the earth have knotted the branches of the trees whose fruit possess rich symbolic connotations. In an act of self-identification, Vincent has painted a vision of a nature tortured by the forces of life.

The Luminous Quest

The City of Light

Paris in the latter-half of the nineteenth century was one of the most culturally active capitals of Europe. It would also be the theatre of a crisis provoked by the leading painters of the period, and among them, the most modern.

In 1886, the eighth and what was to be the last Impressionist exhibition was organised at the Maison Dorée, creating what was to be the disintegration of the movement. Encouraged by Pissarro, Seurat presented *La Grande Jatte.* The painting marked the emergence of a rival group of artists whose technique of *pointillism* refuted many of the accepted principles of the Impressionists.

By a fatal coincidence, 1886 was also the year that Zola published *l'Oeuvre,* a fictional account of a failed artist named Claude Lantier that created an immense scandal in the art world. Rumor had it that Lantier was based on Manet - or more probably Cézanne - who had been a boyhood friend of the author. Since Zola had originally been one of Impressionism's most enthusiastic advocates, the book was an additional blow to the unity of the movement. Visitors to Zola's residence in Médan also spoke of the notable absence of Impressionist art on his walls, for the celebrated author had a clear preference for the overblown works of the Academy painters.

Practically at the same moment, Félix Fénéon, a talented young writer known for his acidic style, launched a series of articles attacking the "naturalism" of the Impressionists in favour of the more "scientific" technique of colour and representation of the new movement led by Seurat.

Parisian literary and intellectual circles were rocked by the publication - due in large part to Verlaine - of Arthur Rimbaud's brilliant *Illuminations.* Having precociously attained his summit of glory while still a teenager, Rimbaud abandoned writing and vanished into eastern Africa, where he spent the remaining years of his life in poverty, illhealth and exile.

Mallarmé, another rising star in

the galaxy of Parisian poets, was introduced to Monet and Renoir by their mutual friend and fellow-artist, Berthe Morisot. This meeting of minds grew into a select circle of cultured and kindred spirits which regularly gathered on Tuesday afternoons in the poet's apartment on the rue de Rome. The group provided the impetus for the Symbolist movement, a new literary and artistic current that would soon captivate an entire generation.

Following the Franco-Prussian War, anti-German sentiment was running high; the works of Richard Wagner, who had died in 1883, were still rarely performed, and when the Opéra-Comique of Paris attempted to stage *Lohengrin*, the popular uproar was so great that it had to be cancelled.

Other foreign playwrights and novelists nevertheless began to find favour with the public. Ibsen's works were cited in critical essays, while the novels of Dostoievski and Tolstoy - both socially engaged writers - were tremendously popular.

Paris was also a city of more earthly pleasures, many of which were found in the neighbourhood of Montmartre. There was the Divan Japonais on the rue des Martyrs and the Cabaret des Assassins (later the Lapin Agile) and the Chat Noir, regularly frequented by young avant-garde poets and artists such as Toulouse-Lautrec, whose paintings were exhibited there. Van Gogh was also a client, for the Chat Noir was on rue de Laval, the same street on which Vincent's brother Theo lived.

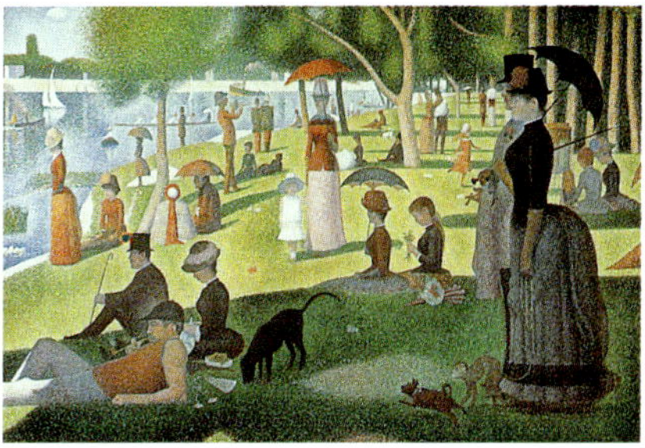

Georges Seurat: A Sunday at the Grande Jatte. *The Art Institute of Chicago (Illinois). Here, reality is expressed in a totally new artistic idiom. With Pointillism, Seurat had developed the foundations for a scientific approach to painting based on the relationships between primary colours. It was at opposite ends from Vincent's passionate and highly subjective manner which announced an art of pure expression.*

Gustave Caillebotte: Paris Under the Snow. *Musée du Petit Palais, Geneva. Caillebotte's regard is that of the city's permanent inhabitant, whereas Vincent's, more transient and furtive, was that of a man whose eyes were already fixed upon other and more luminous horizons.*

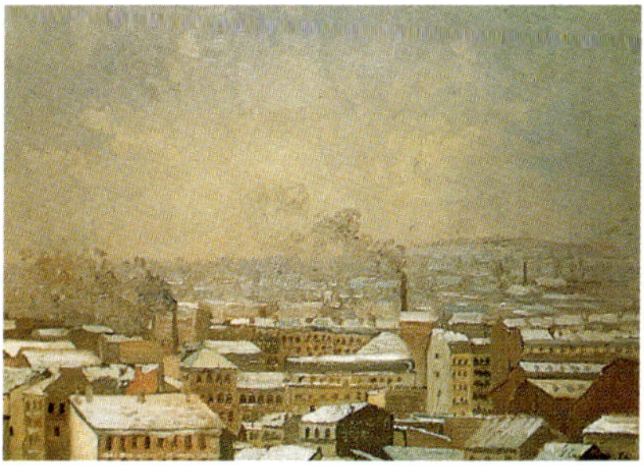

The Paris Period

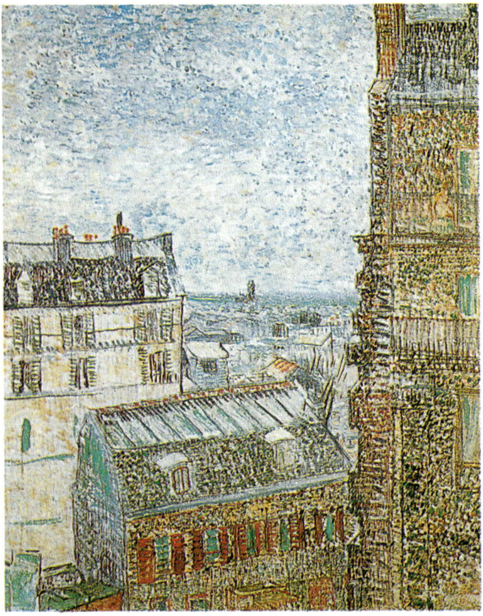

View of Paris From Vincent's Room on Rue Lepic. *Rijksmuseum Vincent Van Gogh, Amsterdam.*
During his brief sojourn in Paris, Vincent discovered the special charm of Montmartre. Its summit offered a vast panorama of the city, whose perspectives he rendered in the Pointillist manner.

The mystique of a city is essentially due to those who inhabit it: the individuals who have chosen it as the place where their dreams and ambitions are transformed into often exceptional realities.

The period author Gustave Coquiot, a familiar of Parisian streets, described the city as follows: "There's something at once chaotic, incredible, marvellous and definitively unique about this city, and all of it is concentrated in a handful of buildings and avenues. When you hear the word 'Paris', it evokes nothing less than a magic circle. It is the centre of the universe, an oasis of wonders, a fabulous caravan, a voluptuous Mecca."

In the latter half of the nineteenth century, Paris was a cosmopolitan, international and extremely sociable city. During his two brief stays in 1874 and 1875, Vincent was too absorbed by his job at the Goupil gallery to appreciate all of the new sights, emotions, adventures and encounters that the city offered. One of his main pastimes was reading. His letters to Theo were filled with frequent references to authors such as Michelet,

Erckmann-Chatrain, Renan and Heine. There were also the visits to the Paris museums: Sundays were often spent at the Luxembourg or the Louvre. It was in the Salon Carré of the latter museum, under a painting by Delacroix, that he met Theo after his arrival in 1886: "The more that I think about it, the more I believe it's the best decision," he explained, attempting to justify his desire to live in Paris.

He had come to study painting, and briefly followed courses at the Atelier Cormon, where he became friends with Toulouse-Lautrec and Emile Bernard. Vincent had also been working on his own, principally doing studies of flowers which he executed in brilliantly luminous colors.

After a short and disappointing period at the Atelier Cormon, Vincent searched for inspiration in the streets, chiefly in and around Montmartre, where he was staying after moving in with Theo at 54 rue Lepic.

The semi-rural atmosphere of Montmartre was accentuated by its comparative lack of urbanisation. A patchwork of vegetable gardens and vacant lots covered portions of the hill. Its crest - from which the factories and smoke-

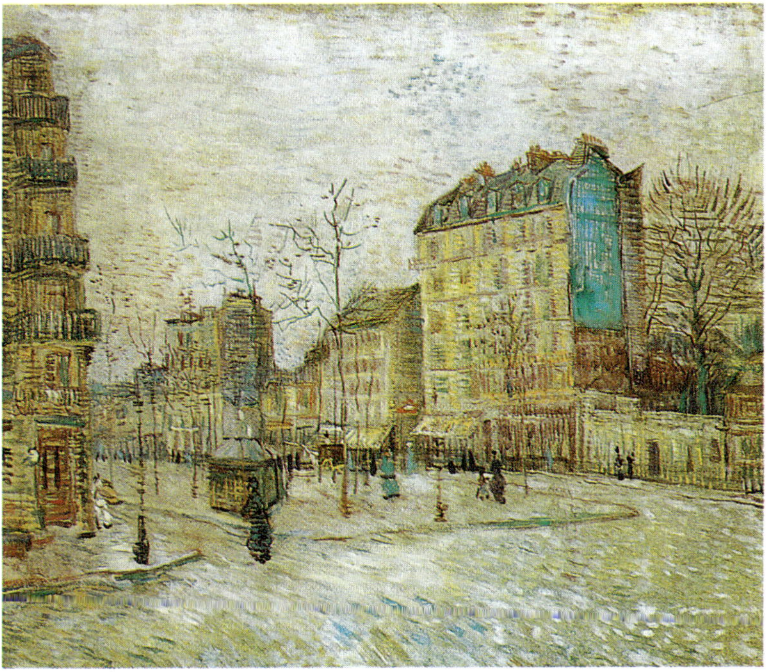

Boulevard de Clichy. *Rijksmuseum Vincent Van Gogh, Amsterdam.*
The Impressionists had already explored the figurative possibilities offered by an urban environment. Van Gogh's vision of the city was often marked by a strange absence of a precise sense of place.

stacks of the industrial zones of Saint-Ouen and Saint-Denis could be seen in the far distance - was dotted with the silhouettes of the huge windmills which had formerly served to grind wheat into flour. It was thus an altogether picturesque and colorful neighbourhood, and the perfect place for an artist like Vincent.

As a free man in Paris, Vincent became a regular visitor to its museums and exhibitions, where he became familiar with the works of contemporary artists. All of the current artistic currents of the period could be seen in Paris. Bracquemond, Guillaumin, Berthe Morisot, Camille and Lucien Pissarro, Odilon Redon, Schuffenecker, Seurat and Vigon had all participated in the ill-fated Eighth Salon of the Impressionists. The Fifth International Exhibition of painters and sculptors, organised by the Petit gallery on the rue d'Uzès, presented the works of Monet and Renoir, while in the Tuileries Gardens the Second Exhibition of Independents gathered painters such as Angrand, Cross, Duboit-Pillet, Pissarro, Seurat and Signac. The latter artists represented the forefront of the Pointillist movement, which was emerging as the successor to Impressionism.

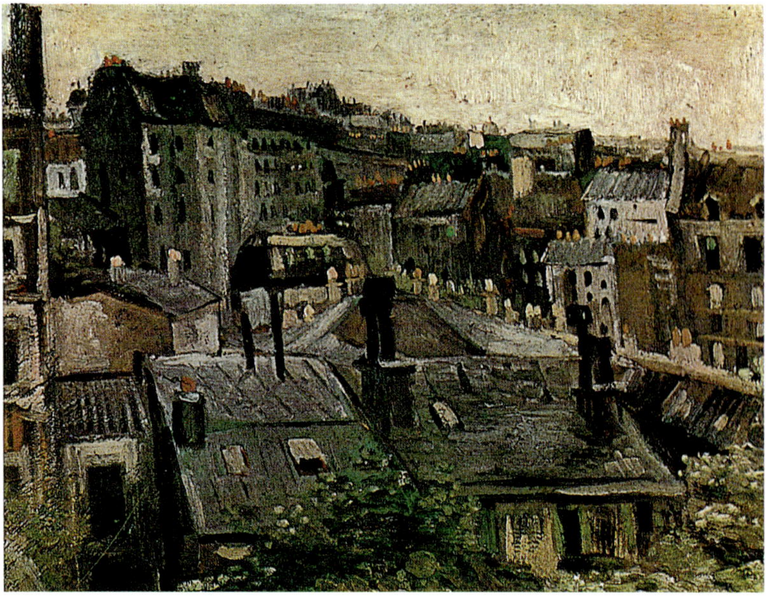

View of Paris. *Rijksmuseum Vincent Van Gogh, Amsterdam.*
The manner is somewhat vehement and cursory, as if crushed by the weight of the buildings succeeding each other to the horizon.

The decline of the impressionists had been marked by rivalry and internal conflicts. Although Vincent had not entirely abandoned the themes and manner of his earlier period, he was nevertheless attentive to the possibilities offered by the style.

The works he executed in Paris were radically influenced by new and sometimes conflicting elements which he analysed, experimented with and progressively integrated into his style. Essentially solitary despite his friendship with fellow-artists such as Lautrec, Angrand, Emile Bernard and Signac, Vincent gradually emerged from the shadow of his own past. Paris represented his artistic rebirth, for he succeeded in mastering much of his natural instability and channelling his passion into serving his creative drive.

Around him, art was being transformed by the conflicts between the Impressionists and the new currents which were both structuring pointillism and preparing the ground for the emergence of the Symbolists. Vincent participated in neither movement, investing only in the development of his own style.

In Vincent's time, the mainstream Impressionists were known as the *grands boulevards* artists,

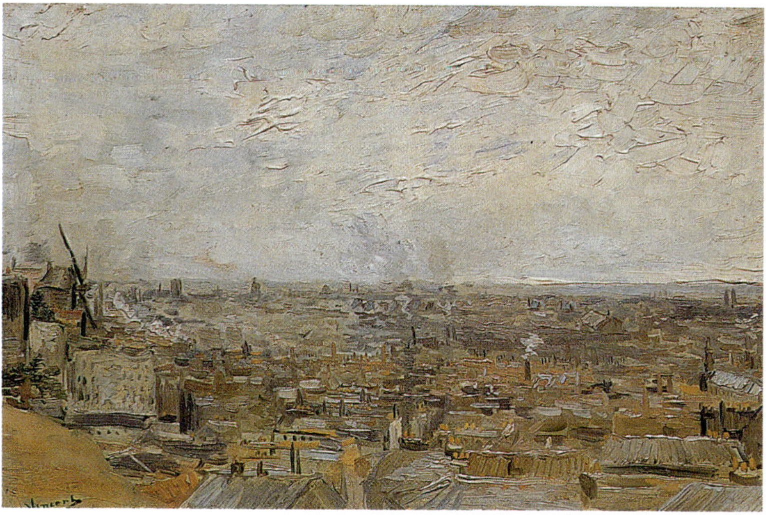

View of Paris From Montmartre. (*also known as* The Rooftops of Paris). *Kunstmuseum, Basil.*
Habituated to open spaces and the omnipresence of nature, Vincent's cityscape is like an ocean of rooftops stretching to the horizon. In its suggestion of hidden life, he renewed with a characteristic typical of the Drenthe period.

in reference to their first exhibition at Nadar's and their triumphal acceptance into the select group of artists represented by the Boussod and Valandon Gallery on boulevard Montmartre. Artists of lesser renown were known as the *petit boulevard* painters, since many of them - including Toulouse-Lautrec and Anquetin - lived or had their studios in the small streets of lower Montmartre.

Despite his difficult character and unsociability, Vincent appreciated talking about art and succeeded in making friends with several of his fellow-painters. After years of isolation, he found himself suddenly projected into the heady Parisian art world just at the moment that Impressionism was being challenged by the Pointillists and the Pont-Aven painters, led by Paul Gauguin.

Theo did as much as he could to make his brother's name known in Parisian art circles. He introduced him to the independent art merchants in the neighbourhood around rue Saint-Georges who were willing to take the risk of promoting painters ignored by the bigger, well-established galleries. Although often closer in spirit to bric-a-brac dealers, they nevertheless regularly attracted knowledgeable collectors in search of new talent.

Vincent's works were often exhibited in the back-rooms of their shops. There was Delarebeyrette, with whom Vincent shared a boundless admiration for the painter Monticelli, and Theo's neighbour Portier, whose clients included wealthy collectors such as Camondo, Singer and Rouart. Promoted energetically by Portier, Vincent found himself in the company of artists such as Degas, Monet and Pissarro.

Other dealers belonging to this parallel world of art merchants included "Papa" Thomas and "Father" Martin, of whom Zola wrote: "Located on rue Lafayette, he was a small dealer of the old school, simple, direct, unassuming and democratic. He would visit painters in their studios, frowning as he inspected their works, stop in front of one and make as if to go on. Business was bad, but after all, he was willing to do what he could for the artist... 'How much for that one, sixty francs? Eighty five! You can't be serious... I'm not that rich... It'll never sell... No, I'm not bargaining with you! Of course you're a great artist, but I've so many paintings I don't know where to put them.' And he ended up by getting the painting for forty francs. What is more, he already knew exactly who he was going to sell it to. His stock-in-trade were artists whose reputations - as well as their prices - were still reasonable. He was a good man, very clever, and a real connoisseur."

Martin would appear under a different name in *l'Oeuvre*, Zola's novel about the Paris art world. He had started out in a shabby bric-a-brac shop at 20 rue Mogador. Despite these humble beginnings, many of his clients were wealthy and distinguished. Among them, Count Doria, Henri Rouart and Alfred Sensier, who ironically referred to themselves as the "Circle Mogador." Martin would also become the temporary director of the first Impressionist exhibition, for by that time, he had moved to 29 rue Saint-Georges and was a neighbour of Renoir.

Vincent and Signac, who often painted together on the banks of the Seine at Asnières, were invited with Seurat to expose their works at the Théâtre Libre on rue Pigalle. Antoine, the organiser of the exhibition, confided to Paul Alexis: "I have between sixty and eighty square meters to decorate in the rehearsal hall. I also plan to invite other young artists - the ones who paint or sculpt marvellous works that are never exposed.... They can exhibit them here, where they will be seen by any number of important people; the exhibition may be modest, but it should also be profitable. I've already got a list of princes and millionaires who have reserved, and whenever a painting strikes the fancy of these people, they buy it....". Unfortunately for the artists who exhibited, this was not the case. Antoine went on to organise a small exhibition in the offices of the *Revue Indépendante,* thanks to the influence of Felix Fénéon.

Vincent's persistent dream of an artists, collective led him to organise an exhibition of Emile Bernard, Anquetin, Toulouse-Lautrec, A.H. Koening, Guillaumin and his own works at the restaurant Le Chalet du Grand Bouillon, 43 avenue du Clichy. Although sales were disappointing, Vincent strengthened his ties with the other painters. He was introduced to Seurat and in an exchange of paintings renewed his friendship with Gauguin, who had returned from a voyage to Martinique.

The exhibition terminated in a falling-out between Vincent and the restaurant owner. The same thing had happened earlier with Agostina Segatori, who ran the Tambourin café at 62 boulevard de Clichy. Vincent had first met her in January 1887; she became his mistress and before they separated in July, hosted an exhibition of his collection of Japanese prints attended by his friends Emile Bernard and Anquetin.

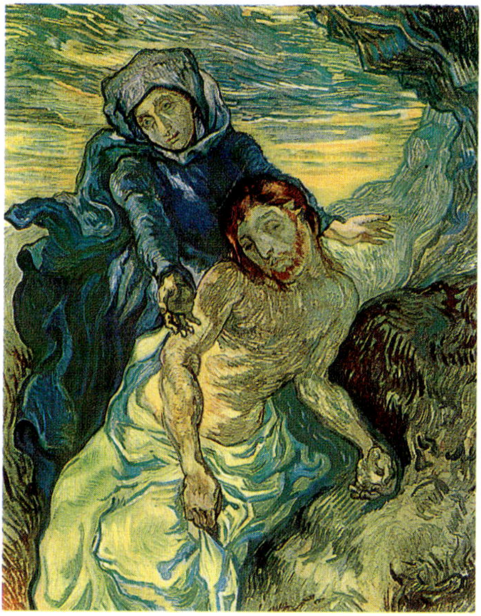

Pieta *(after Delacroix). Rijksmuseum Vincent Van Gogh, Amsterdam. Vincent could not fail to be attracted by this classic religious theme, expressive of profound compassion.*

The Windmills of Montmartre

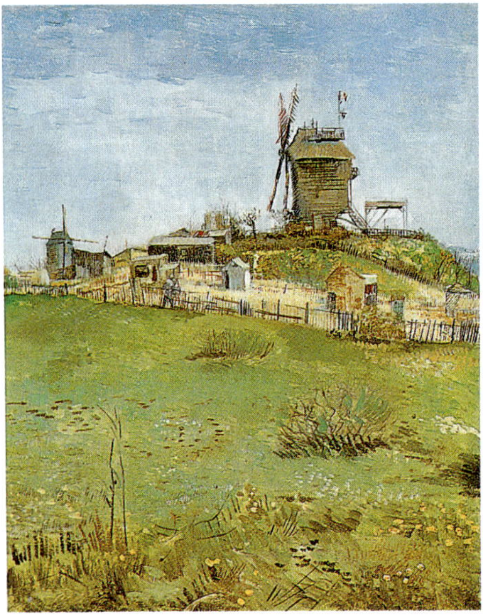

The Moulin de la Galette. *Carnegie Institute Museum of Art, Pittsburgh (Pennsylvania).*
Transformed into a cabaret and surrounded by non-descript buildings and vacant land, the souvenir of one of Montmartre's great windmills, engulfed by change. Vincent was strongly attracted by zones of transition whose atmosphere evoked a vanished past and uncertain future.

In the eighteenth century, the village of Montmartre counted seven hundred families. It was a population composed of day-labourers, millers, wine-growers and small tradesmen.

The hill was dotted with the remains of approximately twenty-five windmills, many of which had belonged to the ancient Abbey of Montmartre which occupied the summit of the hill, at that time covered by fields and vineyards.

By Vincent's time, there were also a number of cabarets and bistros that contributed to the particularly convivial atmosphere that Montmartre was known for, a tradition which continued through the nineteenth century, during which the great windmills were progressively converted into dance-halls and cabarets. On Sundays, the charm of the neighbourhood attracted throngs of Parisians in quest of amusement and adventure; according to Ponsard, "more skirts were lifted than wheat ground into flour."

Montmartre's gentler, more picturesque aspects inspired a number of contemporary artists, and particularly the Impressionists. Their canvases sang with its poetry, depicting all the warmth and colour of its dance-halls and bistros and the pleasure of the encounters they offered, while Vincent's paintings testified to the desolation hidden under the apparent charm and gaiety.

Although Montmartre would long maintain its semi-rural character, the quarter that Vincent discovered and which he would often represent in his paintings was gradually being urbanised as

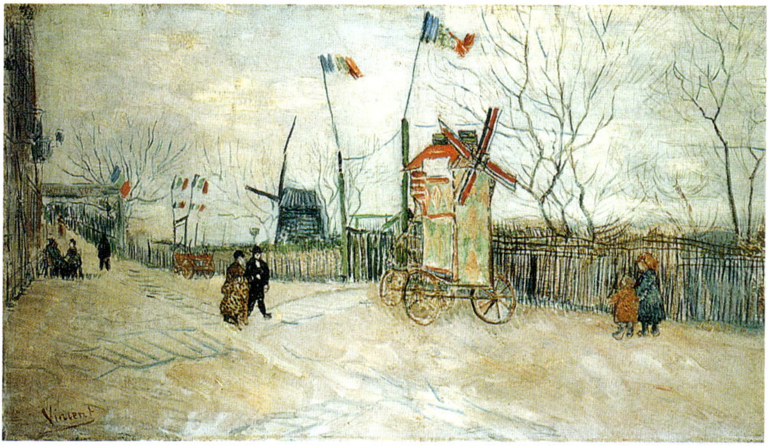

Festival in Montmartre (A Corner of Montmartre) *Rijksmuseum Vincent Van Gogh, Amsterdam.*
An ephemeral vision of festivities touched by emptiness and pathos.

the city advanced. As construction continued, the formerly open fields were reduced to gardens, and later, to small parcels of vacant land. Here and there, great irregularities appeared in the denuded slopes of the hill, revealing the traces of ancient rock quarries.

Van Gogh's paintings of Montmartre were marked by a subtle organisation of volumes and space, perfectly suggestive of its strangely desolate quality during this period of transition. Rather than accessing Montmartre by the busy Parisian boulevard which ran below its southern flank, Vincent preferred the northern approach which offered an anarchic landscape of empty lots, private homes and industrial buildings. The overall effect of this mutilated zone was of the very sort that appealed to Vincent's tortured spirit, so prone to self-destruction and the denial of pleasure: in the midst of both a city and a neighbourhood undergoing growth and renewal, he chose to represent all that had been left behind in paintings which spoke of solitude, despair and hopelessness.

Vincent was also drawn to the vast panorama offered by the

summit of the hill. His *View of Paris from Montmartre* is touched with all the grey melancholy of the city. Its heavy, smoke-blackened atmosphere echoed the current of deep pessimism voiced by many of the writers of the period, such as Zola, Verlaine and Rimbaud.

In time, Vincent turned away from both Montmartre and Paris, drawn to areas in which the city and its periphery came together in a sort of no-man's-land, preferring this space of uncertainty to that which was already imprisoned within its own limits, activities and predictable future.

He would often haunt the banks of the Seine, following the river to the outlying villages of Clichy, Asnières and Gennevilliers. As the open spaces that separated them from the city diminished, they began to dissolve into an undifferentiated and desolate landscape of factories, vacant lots and grey working-class neighbourhoods.

The Seine was no longer the natural frontier between Paris and its periphery: a series of new bridges - painted by Vincent as well as artists such as Monet and Caillebotte - linked them to the capital. And as the distances between them diminished, so did their special character and atmosphere.

Vincent was drawn to these zones of transition, often choosing modest restaurants and public gardens as subjects. But the scenes lacked joy and were marked by a strange sense of solitude. Only the physical decor seemed to possess any intrinsic reality; his treatment of the human element during this period was furtive, hesitant and ill-defined. Summarily rendered, they

The Moulin de la Galette *Rijksmuseum Kröller-Müller, Otterlo.*
The silhouette of the former windmill rises above the buildings surrounding it. Renoir portrayed the festive sensuality of its dance-hall, whereas Vincent painted it from the exterior as a spectral apparition in a pale city.

had nothing of the self-confident and well-dressed appearance of city-dwellers, and if their unmistakable lack of sophistication harked back to his earlier manner, Vincent had all but abandoned the concept of the inherent nobility of the common man for that of the dehumanisation of the proletariat.

The apartment that Vincent shared with Theo on rue Lepic was a symbolic milestone between the numbing atmosphere of the city and the discovery of new artistic horizons. But before approaching them, he would once again traverse the desolate zones of misery so familiar to him, and which were his private hell.

As if following a legendary path of initiation, Vincent accomplished the successive steps of his voyage toward the light, each of which was marked by a painting.

The conquest of light was not only the quest of the artist, it mobilised the energy of the man, who drew upon it to achieve a more personal goal. For Vincent, the shadows of the great windmills of Montmartre were only the distant reflection of his native Holland: unconsciously, he was preparing for his ultimate journey to a region whose promise was both rebirth and oblivion.

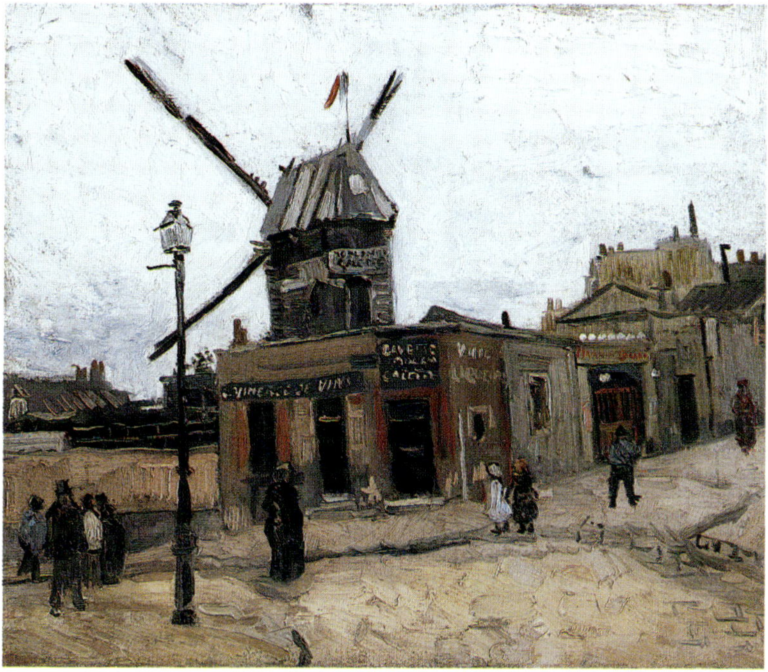

La Butte Montmartre. *Rijksmuseum Kröller-Müller, Otterlo.*
The traditionally placid and semi-rural quarter of Montmartre had not yet been invaded by the modernity of Paris. Vincent captured its more nostalgic aspects before its total destruction.

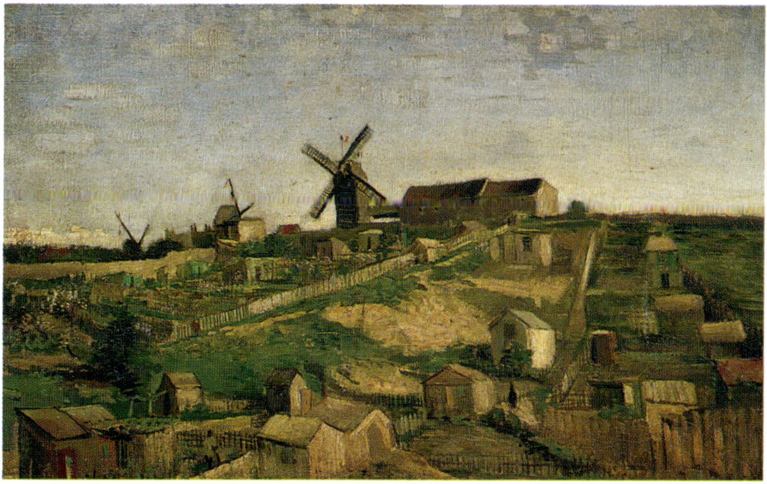

A Vision of the Abyss

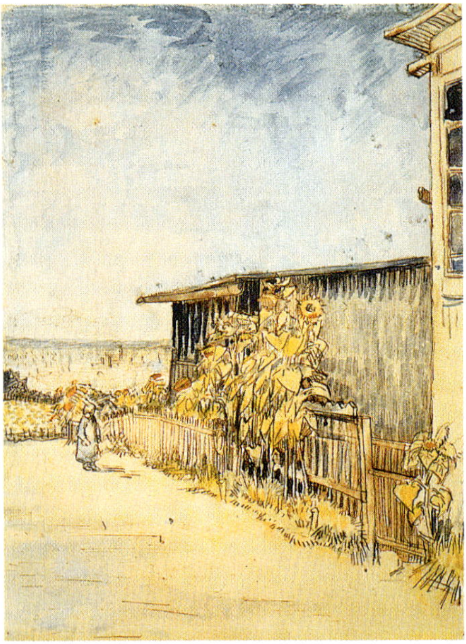

Shed with Sunflowers. *Rijksmuseum Vincent Van Gogh, Amsterdam. Vincent perceived the poetry of nature's indomitable presence even in unlikely places such as this. Here, echoed by the presence of the young child, a patch of sunflowers are quietly thriving in their modest surroundings.*

The representation of the darker side of existence was also an artistic fashion of the period. If the Impressionist's expressed this in a lighter, far less dramatic manner, other artists were attempting to capture the terrible beauty of the urban wastelands on the outskirts of Paris.

The writer J.K. Huysmans took long walking-tours in the poor neighbourhoods of south-eastern Paris and became the apostle of the painter Raffaelli, whose works "evoked the sad charm of shabby cabarets, the ragged rows of poplar-tress lining the endless streets that disappear into the horizon beyond the city limits. In seeing the exhausted passers-by marching through this superbly ugly landscape, all of the ancestral misery of the place rose up before me. Raffaelli has demonstrated the originality of his vision in all its multiple aspects. His admirably gloomy scenes reveal all the human distress of these poor wretches. Here, in the exhaustion of broken rag-pickers sifting through heaps of refuse or carrying their bundles; there - and despite the artist's habitual melancholy - in the sudden flashing laugh, the irrepressible and joyous manifestation of nature, a flock of cackling hens and a donkey. And all of this bathed in sunlight, lu-minous and charming, as in his painting of Asnières with its stunted little trees, the archetypal drovers, modest officials, street-sweepers - perhaps the double of some Jean Valjean - all rendered with astonishing vivacity and truth."

Van Gogh admired the authenticity of Seurat's paintings of the working-class suburbs, his portrayal of large, open spaces and the distinctive geometry of industrial architecture. He was also drawn to the social consciousness of Luce, the poet of the working-class and openly engaged in their struggle, as well as Signat, with whom he painted zones in transition from the fading charms of the countryside to the cancer of progressive industrialisation.

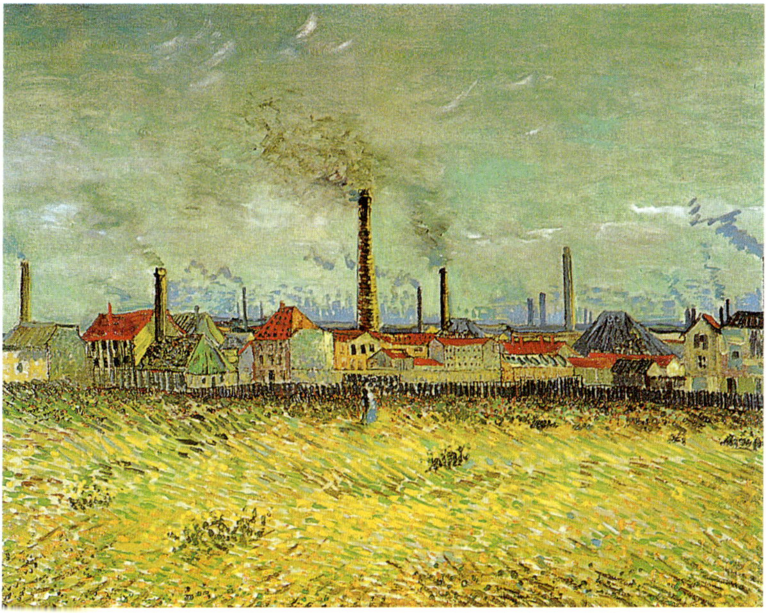

Factories in Clichy. *The Saint Louis Art Museum, Saint Louis (Missouri).*
The Impressionists were among the first artists to portray the industrial landscapes that existed on the outskirts of Paris. Here, Van Gogh captures their bleak atmosphere in a resolutely modern manner.

Guillaumin's paintings had celebrated the dark lyricism of the no-man's-land ringing the periphery of Paris. His vision of the desolate industrial landscapes of Charenton and Ivry echoed the bitter poetry of Verhaeren and the cycle of *Villes Tentaculaires.*

The spirit social realism which had inspired Vincent's scenes of peasant life in Holland was transformed by his experience of Paris. Here, the human element was generally reduced to a minimum, crushed by the soulless weight of the city.

On the Banks of the Seine. *Rijksmuseum Vincent Van Gogh, Amsterdam.*
As a subject of choice, the Seine was the theatre of the beginning and end of the Impressionist movement. Vincent would also paint it, contributing his highly personal vision to the multitude of works that the river and its surroundings inspired.

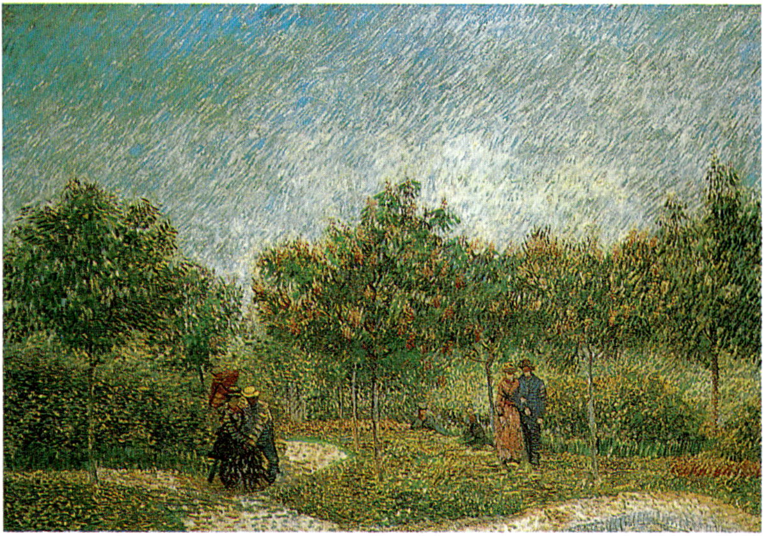

The Voyer d'Argenson Gardens in Asnières: The Lovers. *Rijksmuseum Vincent Van Gogh, Amsterdam.*
One of Van Gogh's extremely rare love scenes. The representation of the public garden is harmonious, even if the lack of finesse is suggestive of a certain distance between the artist and his subject: Vincent's lack of real empathy for the two lovers.

The Bridge at Courbevoie. *Rijksmuseum Vincent Van Gogh, Amsterdam.*
Amply described in period literature and art, the banks of the Seine were the universe of the common man and simple pleasures. Vincent would also make a brief incursion, inspired by subjects such as the skiff passing under the graceful arches of this bridge that linked Paris to the Grande Jatte.

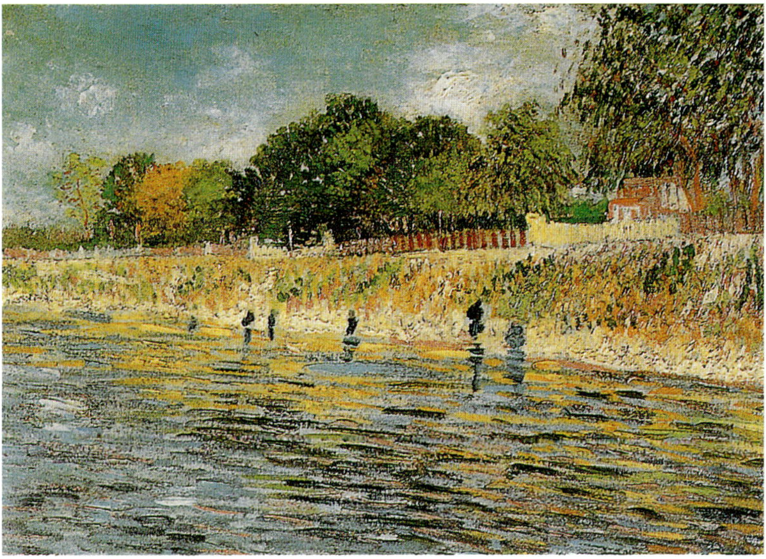

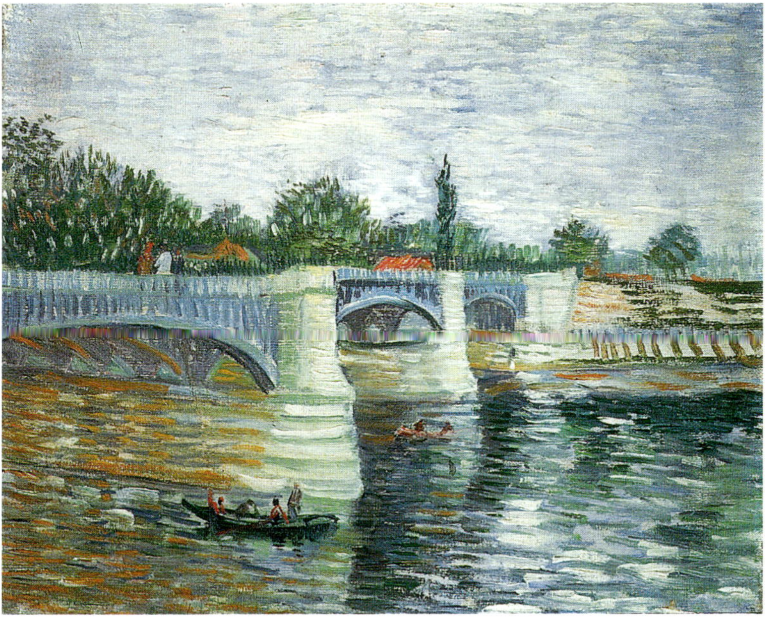

At 'Papa' Tanguy's

Five square meters of space, plus two smaller adjoining rooms on rue Clauzel: this was both the shop and living-quarters of Papa Tanguy. The son of an impoverished Breton family who had emigrated to Paris, Tanguy had successively worked as a butcher and house-plasterer before finally opening an artist's supplies shop in lower Montmartre.

He had started out at 14 rue Clauzel before moving across the street to number 9; his neighbour Guy de Maupassant was comfortably installed at number 19 on the same street - in a discreet bordello. The neighbourhood counted several of these establishments, as well as a countless number of charming and available young women who on any particular evening could be found, suitably powdered and dressed in the full gowns of the period, offering themselves - for a price - to the stray Englishman in quest of local colour or the naive provincial out for a night on the town. It was a world straight out of the pages of Henri Murger's *Scenes de la Vie de Bohême,* populated by glittering butterflies preying upon fleeting sentiments.

Paris was a city whose reputation for brilliance and easy pleasure was belied by the disdain with which it treated those who refused to enter into its endless round of furtive pleasures and ephemeral satisfactions. Both Maupassant and Zola would describe this universe, drawing fine character studies of the vipers who inhabited it.

The neighbourhood was also a veritable hot-house of artistic activity, and each of its streets was home to genius. There was the rue des Martyrs, where the legendary Géricault lived at number 23; the Théâtre Libre, 96 rue Blanche; the Lugné-Poe Theatre which staged Zola's *l'Oeuvre,* 28 rue Pigalle; the studio of Gustave Moreau, frequented by the cream of the new generation of painters, 14 rue La Rochefoucauld; Gauguin's birthplace, 56 Rue Notre-Dame-de-Lorette; the studio of Delacroix - a shrine for young artists, two doors away at number 58; the Goupil gallery, 9 rue Chaptal; "La Nouvelle Athènes," a celebrated artist's

Portrait of Tanguy. *Ny Carlsberg Glyptothek, Copenhagen.*
Vincent has captured Tanguy's inner nature, touched both by fantasy and a reserve verging unsociability but nevertheless firmly attached to his ideas and ideals. His determined and unyielding features reveal all of his basic kindness as well as the tenacity with which he confronted existence.

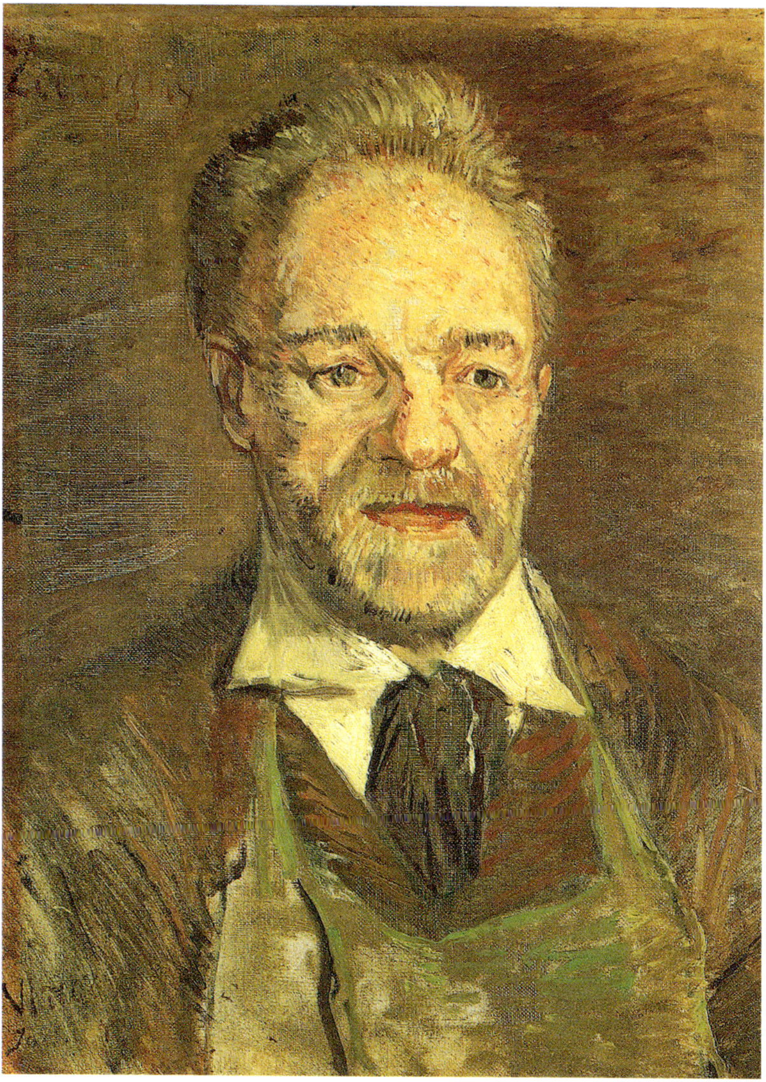

café, 9 place Pigalle; Renoir's studio, the birthplace of the Impressionist movement, 35 rue Saint-Georges; the residence of the Goncourt brothers at number 43 of the same street; Emile Zola, 21 *bis*, rue de Bruxelles.

A true art-lover and endowed with an infallible instinct for talent, Tanguy opened his shop in the middle of all this intense artistic activity, where he sold a new and revolutionary product: paint in tubes, rather than the powdered pigments which had to be carefully diluted and mixed by the user before attaining the desired shade and consistency. His timing was perfect, for artists were starting to leave their studios and paint in the open air. Only the academic painters remained confined in their studios, surrounded by their admirers and sundry hangers-on. For the Impressionists and an entire new generation of young artists, the studio was wherever they set up their easels, which increasingly was outdoors.

Motivated by his love for art and a sincere kindness toward those who practised it, Tanguy exchanged his tubes of colour for the works of painters too poor to pay for them. His tiny shop on rue Clauzel soon became an informal meeting-place for both artists and collectors.

Tanguy's love for painting was equal to his affection for painters: he was always there when they needed him, helping to solve their problems, defending them against the daily difficulties of life which often condemned them to an existence of misery. His love for art and artists was touching in its humility and almost religious in its quiet fervour.

Vincent's striking portrait of *Le Père Tanguy* reveals a rugged, square-jawed visage, homely but placid features and an honest regard framed by a short beard. At opposite ends from the fashionable art merchants whose calculated sociability served purely professional objectives, Tanguy was a product of the same popular classes whose simple and innate virtues Vincent identified with.

Tanguy, like *Le Facteur Roulin* ("The Postman Roulin") and the other men and women who Vincent would later portray in Arles, was the type of person that perfectly corresponded to his own temperament: scrupulous, attentive, generous and passionate, but with an underlying need for love and understanding.

Despite the efforts of Theo, Vincent was totally excluded from the world of established galleries and collectors. His abrasive personality had provoked clashes on more than one occasion, and with the exception of his brother, the only person he could really depend on for moral and even material support was Tanguy. It was by his ongoing help and encouragement that Vincent was able to continue painting and develop himself as a veritable artist. For Vincent, the word was associated with an almost religious fervour far beyond the mere activity of creation. This dimension was naturally ignored by a society turned inward upon its own pleasures, blind to the idealism and uncompromising rejection of mediocrity of an artist such as Vincent. If like religion, art can be said to possess its share of saints and martyrs, Van Gogh can be considered as both.

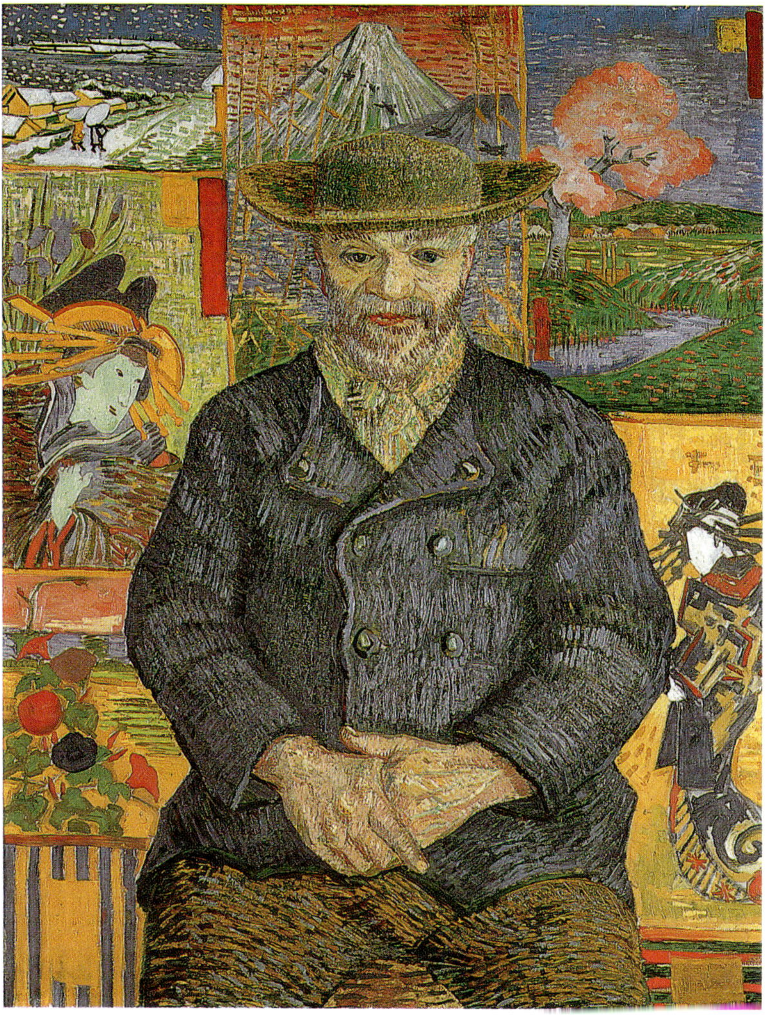

Le Père Tanguy. *Rodin Museum, Paris.*
By his reference to Japanese art and a masterful economy of line, Vincent has gone beyond simple figurative art and achieved the grave beauty of an icon.

Japanese Influences

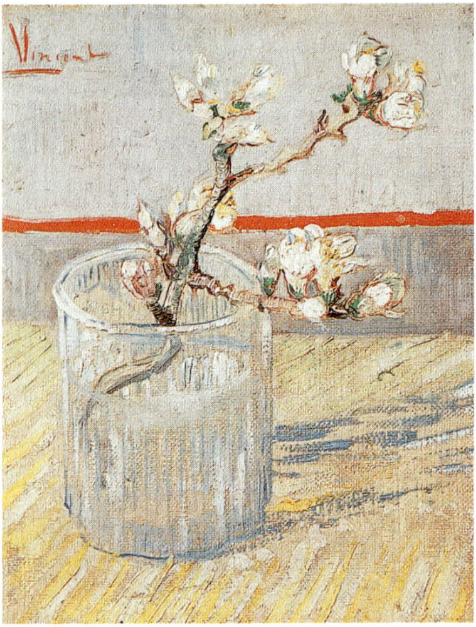

Still Life: Sprig of Almond Blossom.
Rijksmuseum Vincent Van Gogh, Amsterdam.
The art of endowing even the most insignificant objects with meaning. Vincent's masterful rendering of a simple almond branch in flower expresses all the graceful force of nature's renewal.

In 1818, a four-volume edition entitled *Le Japon, ou moeurs, usages et coutumes des habitants de cet empire* ("Japan, or the Morays, Practices and Customs of the Inhabitants of that Empire") was published by Nepveu Editions in Paris. Illustrated with fifty-one engravings, the work marked the beginning of cultural exchanges between Japan and the Occident. Over the following years there were an increasing number of voyages and expeditions, as well as arrivals of works which progressively found favour with the public and whose stylistic elements profoundly influenced nineteenth-century art.

In Germany, Dr. Siebold's col--lection of Japanese art was probably one of the finest in Europe; by 1837, it had become the basis for the museum named after him in Leyden, Holland. Other works began turning up in auctions, and it soon became fashionable to possess one's own collection of Oriental art. Members of the best Parisian society frequented specialised shops such as La Porte Chinoise, 36 rue Vivienne, whose regular customers were the Goncourt brothers; Au Céleste Empire, 55 rue Vivienne; Desoye, 220 rue de Rivoli; Chinoiseries et Japonaiseries, 19 rue Le Peletier; Malinet, 25 quai Voltaire; and the celebrated Bing, articles de Chine, which opened its doors at 19 rue de Chauchat in 1885.

The writers of the period were among the most enthusiastic collectors. Baudelaire proudly showed off his "superb collection of magnificently-coloured Japanese prints" to the painter Zacharie

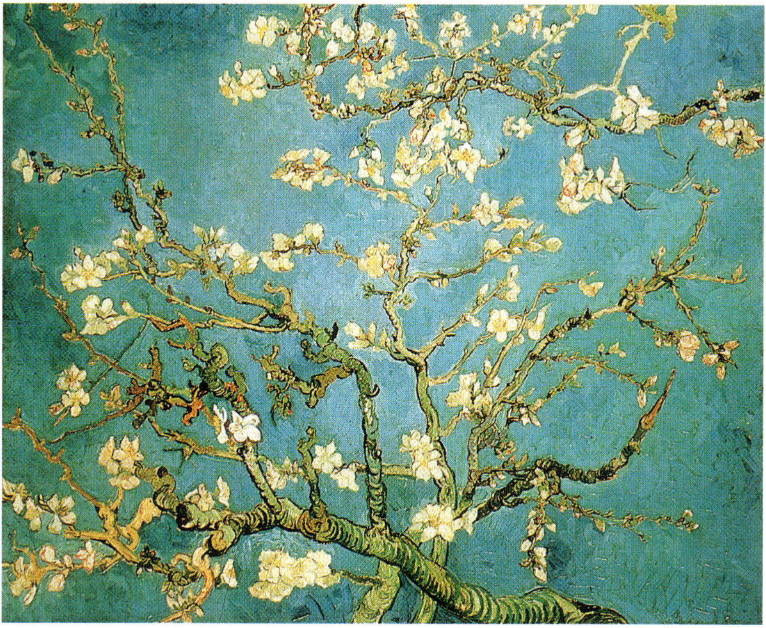

Almond-Tree Branch in Flower.
Rijksmuseum Vincent Van Gogh, Amsterdam.
With an innate decorative sense, Vincent deploys the branches in a harmonious pattern by suppressing the laws of perspective and extending the natural imits of the canvas. A delicate and haunting rendition of nature's joyous symphony of life.

Astruc; Alfred Sensier initiated the Barbizon painters Millet and Théodore Rousseau into the mysteries of Oriental art; Champfleury illustrated his book *Les Chats* with works by the Japanese master-engraver Hiroshige, while Judith Gautier chose the illustrations of Yamamoto for her *Poèmes de la libellule.* The newspaper *l'Etendard* published an article by Astruc about the famous writers and artists of the period who collected Oriental art. The list included Diaz, James Tissot, Alphonse Legros, Bracquemond, Fantin-Latour, Manet, Monet, the Goncourt brothers, Champfleury and Philippe Burty.

Following a series of voyages to the Far East, Cernuschi organised exhibitions which helped popularise Japanese art; the movement gained additional notoriety during the several World Fairs which were held in Paris.

Japanese art would also greatly influence the future Impressionists. At their first exhibition in 1874, Astruc presented his *Poupées japonaises;* Manet painted motifs of Japanese prints into the background of his *Portrait of Zola* and other references appeared in the works of artists like Whistler *(The Princess in the Land of Porcelaine)* and Monet *(La Terrasse de Sainte-Adresse* and *La Japonaise).*

Japanese art also became fashionable in England, largely thanks to Whistler who used Japanese motifs in decorating the Peacock Exhibition for the patron of the arts Thomas Jeckyll. In northern Europe, Carl Larson and Anders Zorn introduced the movement into Sweden.

In the spring of 1887, Vincent organised an exhibition of his collection of Japanese prints at the Tambourin café, run by his mistress Agostina Segatori; in the same year, Pierre Loti published his enormously popular *Madame Chrysanthème.*

As early as 1885, Vincent was already thinking about Japan as he roamed the docklands of Antwerp: "I've often walked here, exploring the waterfront. The contrast is so strange, especially when one comes from a land of moors and sand and a peaceful, unchanging peasant village. This confusion, this unfathomable, shifting fog... this landscape is so extravagantly, unbelievably, typically, Japanese." And in another letter: "My studio is fairly liveable now that I've tacked up my collection of Japanese prints that I like so much. You've certainly seen those small engravings of women in their gardens or at the seaside, and those prints of horsemen, flowers and the gnarled boughs of the hawthorn-tree."

Ultimately, it was in the Midi that he would give expression to his fascination for Japanese art. For Vincent, this region in south-eastern France represented the perfect surrogate for the distant Orient: "Even if it's more expensive to stay in the Midi, look at it this way: I love Japanese art, we've all been influenced by it - all of the Impressionists have - but no one is going to Japan, for the equivalent of Japan is the Midi itself. I believe that it represents the entire future of contemporary art."

Vincent was also attracted to the spirit of Japanese art: "You see a philosophical and intelligent man spending his time - doing what? Studying the distance between the earth and the moon? Not at all. He is contemplating a blade of grass. But this leads him to begin drawing plants, and then seasons, sweeping landscapes, animals and finally, man... One can't immerse oneself in Japanese art without becoming happier and more joyous: we have to get back to nature, despite our education and our life in a world governed by convention."

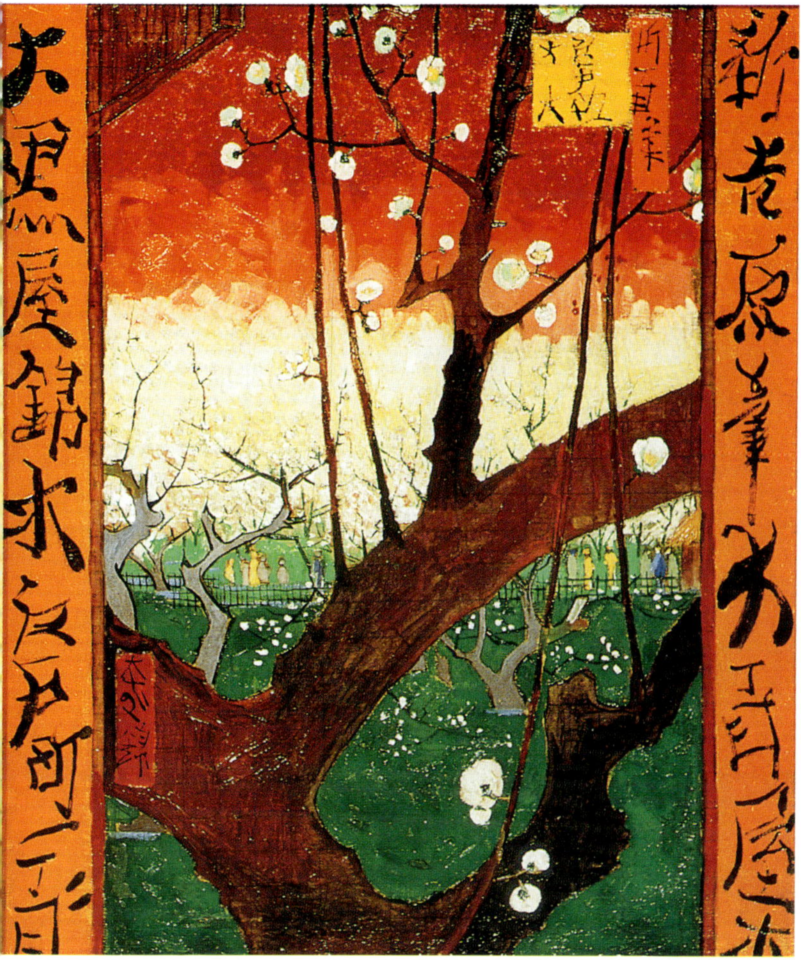

Japonaiserie: Plum Trees In Blossom.
Rijksmuseum Vincent Van Gogh, Amsterdam.
Perhaps for more than any other artist of the period, the influence of Japanese art is visible in Van Gogh's work. It became determinate during his stay in Arles, providing an additional stylistic possibility and further extending Vincent's range of expression, already heavily influenced by pointillism and Impressionist art.

Self-Portrait

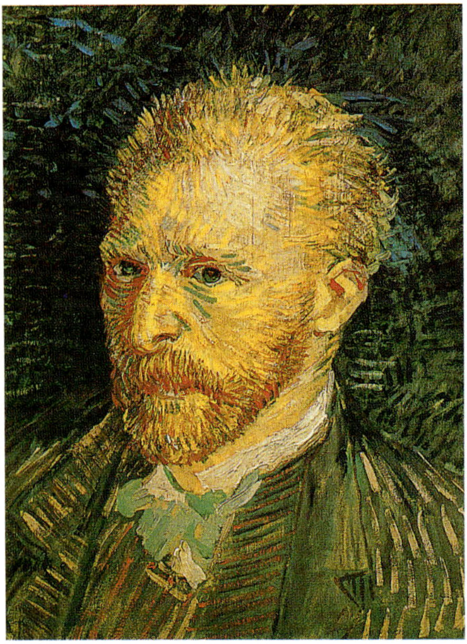

Self-Portrait. *Orsay Museum, Paris.*

And what to make of Vincent's self-portraits, with their impression of a man looking at himself in a mirror as if trying to decipher the message of his own features: has he finally let drop his mask, or struggling against the irreparable outrages of age and time, is he attempting to capture this instant for eternity? Like some modern-day Narcissus, is he in thrall to his own reflection?

It was for a very different reason that Van Gogh portrayed the ravaged image of his own face - and which made him return to it again and again: he often had difficulties in finding models to pose for him.

His face taut with sufferance but radiating inner dignity, Van Gogh's self-portraits constituted a gallery of poignant testimonials to self-honesty. Here, revealed simultaneously, was a man who knew he was unattractive, a human being and artist whose existence was composed of solitude and rejection, and the genius too proud, too fierce and too immense to comply with artistic conventions. For a man incapable of striking the usual poses in both art and life, the conventions governing portrait-painting were simply too far-removed from his imperious desire to push art to the limits of its expressive potential.

In the early self-portraits, his brush is still heavy and the palette sombre. His image is practically bourgeois and his clothing reassuringly conventional. With the passage of time and experience, the palette progressively lightened and there was more expressive liberty in his brushwork. In 1887, the famous wide-brimmed straw

Self-Portrait with Easel. *Rijksmuseum Vincent Van Gogh, Amsterdam.*
Vincent rarely represented himself before the easel. In general, he preferred poses in which allusions to his personal life were absent, with the exception of the ever-present anguish revealed in his eyes.

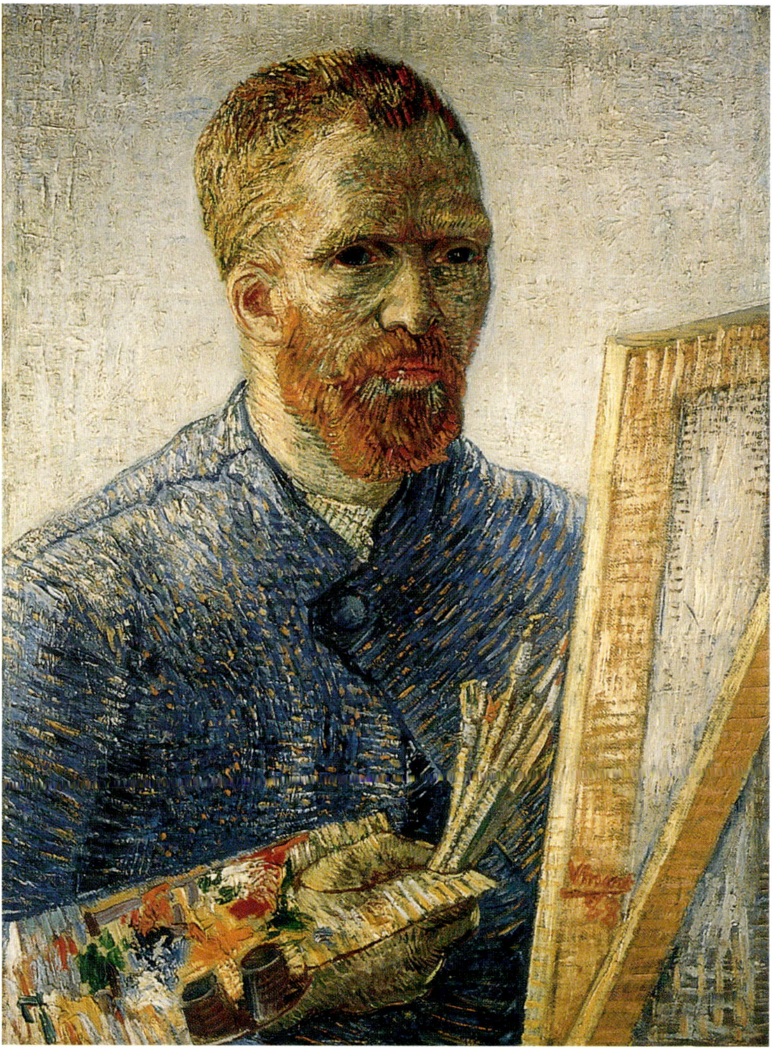

hat appeared - a necessary protection from the sun when painting outdoors. The jacket hugs his body tightly, and nothing in its style or cut suggests that he is a painter. Despite the dominance of yellow, the tone is subdued yet charged with the tension of his indomitable energy.

In the Midi, the brushwork accelerated, racing across the canvas and bursting into swirling lines and tortured arabesques: in the space of only a few months, a new artist and a new manner had been born. His self-portraits displayed an unchanging constant: the head and bust were tightly framed; later, the Nordic features of his visage were accentuated and the unconventionality of his clothing was more pronounced. Ultimately, the metamorphosis was complete.

In his later portraits, Vincent revealed himself as he really was: a proud, fiercely idealistic individual, as uncompromising with himself as he was with others, whose art had taken on a life of its own, burning with white heat as if fuelled by his own inner fire.

The successive transformations seen in his self-portraits are those of a man whose existence was intimately rooted in his art. They express the ongoing development of a creative force that nothing could stop - except the fatal reverberation of a pistol-shot rolling across the stillness of a wheat-field on a July afternoon.

In January 1888, Vincent had completed his *Self-Portrait at the Easel*. In February he moved from Paris to Arles, where in August he executed another, more modest version. A year later he would paint the tragic *Self-Portrait with Severed Ear*. And eighteen months after that, he would be dead.

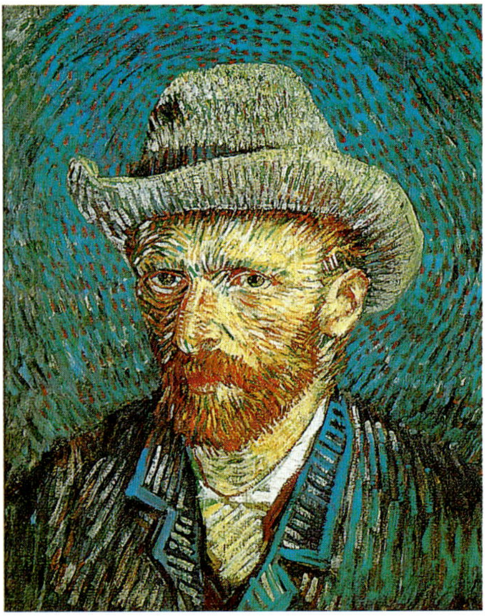

Self-Portrait with Felt Hat. *Rijksmuseum Vincent Van Gogh, Amsterdam. Vincent's frequent portrayal of distinctive touches such as this hat was perhaps the reflection of the doubts of a man uncertain of his real identity in society.*

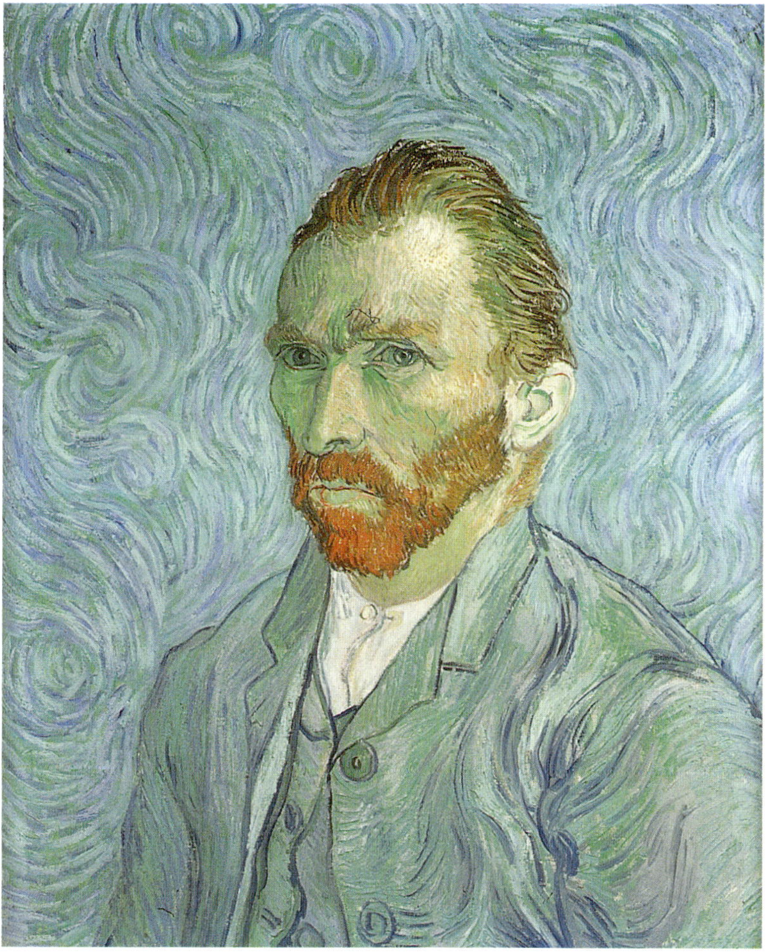

Self-Portrait. *Orsay Museum, Paris.*
Upon a background of flame, like the landscapes painted in the heat of his passion, a race against the fatal moment which he sensed was waiting for him in the near future.

The Celebration of the Common Man

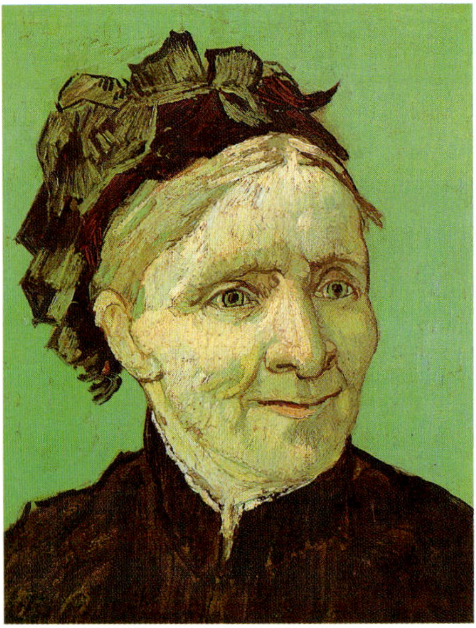

Portrait of the Artist's Mother. *Norton Simon Museum of Art, Pasadena (California).*
A rare reference to a member of his immediate family.

In his letters to Theo, Vincent spoke of his desire to support himself by his art. His idea was to specialise in portraits, which in his opinion were the surest means of assuring himself a modest but steady income.

The habitual clients for portraits were the members of the bourgeoisie, upper-middle class citizens proud of their possessions, their physical appearance and the position they occupied in society. For them, the portrait was both a symbolic and very tangible proof of their qualities and station in life. As Vincent remarked, "When sitting for their portrait, they dress up in their best Sunday clothes, in which neither their knees, elbows and shoulders, nor any other portion of their anatomy have succeeded in leaving the slightest wrinkle or bump."

He was irritated by their demands and the artificiality of the situation. Portraits often represented a highly-idealised private and public self-image, but rarely revealed any deeper truths concerning the subject. Even the new and fashionable photographic portraitists used painted backdrops and accessories to create the at-

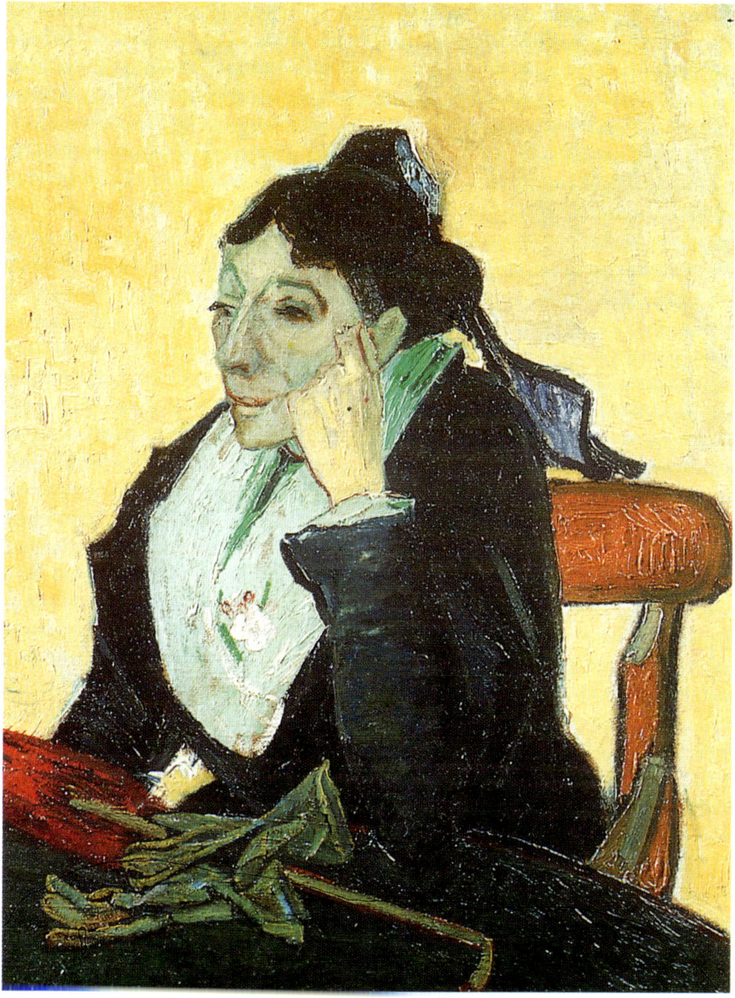

mosphere of dignity and prestige expected by the sitter.

Vincent's desire to reveal inner truth - as well as his disconcerting style and personality - discouraged his potential clients. But when the common people posed for him, it was with the authenticity he demanded: "I want a peasant to look

The Arlésienne (Madame Ginoux)
Orsay Museum, Paris.
Madame Ginoux was the owner of the café-hotel (Café de la Gare) where Vincent first stayed after arriving in Arles. Her family would appear in many of the portraits he painted during this period.

like a peasant; when I paint a whore, I expect her to look like one...I am increasingly convinced that a total reality of the subject is more important than simply capturing the mere physical details..."

Not without reason, Vincent considered that he had pioneered a new approach to portraits: "On the surface, nothing seems as easy as painting peasants, rag-pickers and workers, but there is nothing else as difficult to represent as these ordinary subjects. As far as I know, no school teaches how to sketch or paint a sower, someone spading the earth, a woman hanging a kettle over the hearth, or a seamstress."

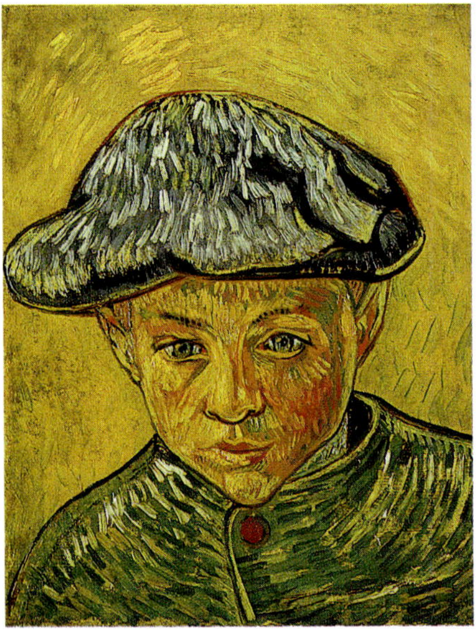

Vincent's rejection of bourgeois existence (and painting) was total: "I often find servant-girls more interesting and beautiful than their mistresses, and workers more interesting than gentlemen. In the common people I find the strength and energy necessary for expressing their uniqueness, which I capture with firm brushwork and a simple technique."

Vincent's natural sympathy for common people facilitated his contacts with them. After the peasants of Holland and Belgium, the working-class inhabitants of Arles posed for him. In the portraits of Mousmé, Roulin and his family, the Zouave, the Arlésienne (Madame Ginoux) and Dr. Félix Rey, Vincent would give free rein to his talent for composing backgrounds, capturing attitudes and expressing the hidden subtleties of the soul.

His attitude was uncomplacent yet kind; the portraits were warm, human, honest and intensely personal: the harsh passion of Agostina Segatori, the good-natured calm of 'Papa' Tanguy, the naive self-importance of Roulin the postman, the quiet authority of his son Armand and the world-weary gaze of Doctor Gachet.

The simple and direct quality of these portraits has something of the immobile grandeur of the religious icon or primitive art. Their presence seems eternal, while the totality of their inner life is expressed with uncommon force. Devoid of artifice and hypocrisy, the subjects reveal their very souls, and if there is occasionally a hint of satisfaction in their expression, it is doubtless from the pleasure of sitting for their portrait.

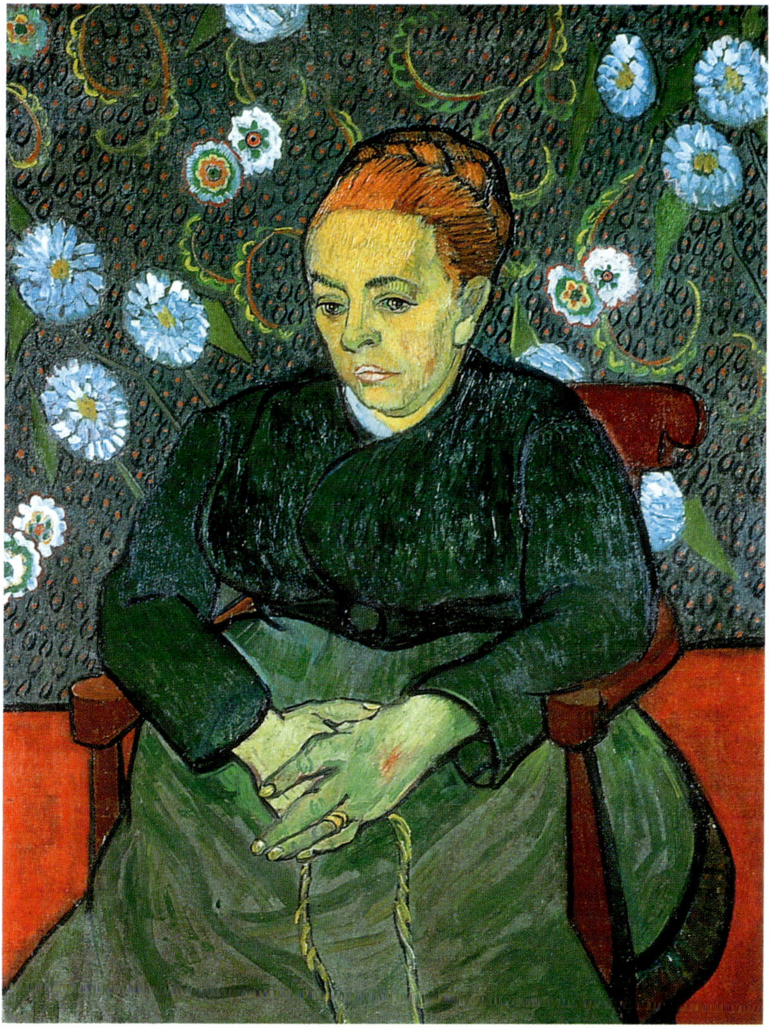

Portrait of Camille Roulin. *Rijksmuseum Vincent Van Gogh, Amsterdam.*
"How completely he understood the sadness, the unknown and the divine in the eyes of the poor madmen and the brotherhood of the sick," exclaimed Octave Mirabeau in reference to Van Gogh. He might have added that Vincent could also express a child's innocence.

La Berceuse (Madame Roulin). *Rijksmuseum Vincent Van Gogh, Amsterdam.*
As in the portrait of Père Tanguy, Vincent posed his sitter against a highly-stylised background of his own invention.

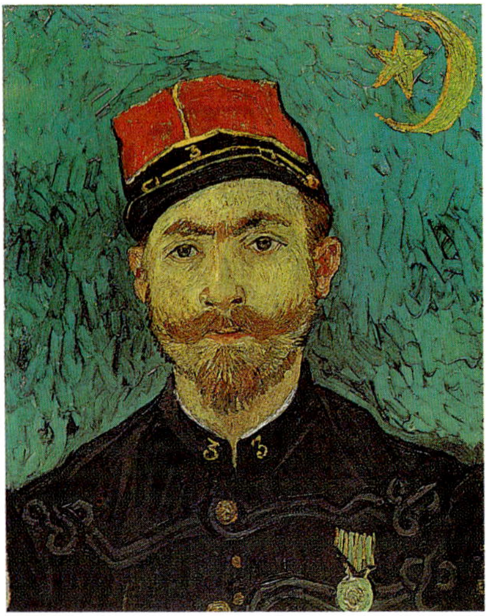

The Lieutenant of the Zouaves. *Rijksmuseum Vincent Van Gogh, Amsterdam.*
Vincent's love for humanity fuelled his desire to become a pastor. Having failed to realise this ambition, his affection for his fellow-man was channelled into his art. His subjects were common people, whose naturalness and authenticity corresponded to his own qualities. Although uncompromising in its honesty, his manner was always tender.

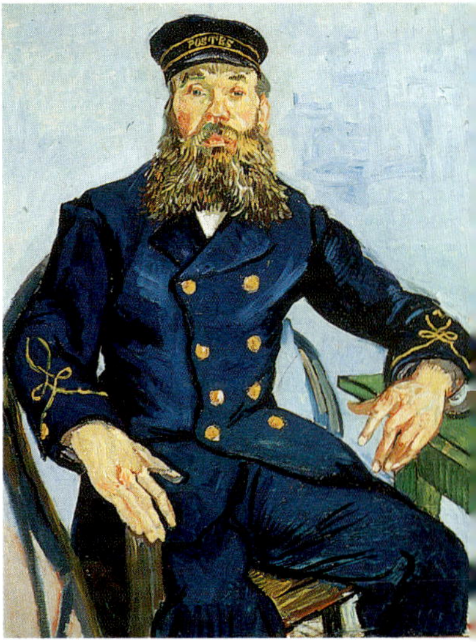

Portrait of Patrice Escalier. *Stavros S. Niarchos Collection.*
Using vivacious and authoritative brushwork to render the distant and dreaming expression of the man leaning upon his cane, Vincent captured all the quiet melancholy of his declining years.

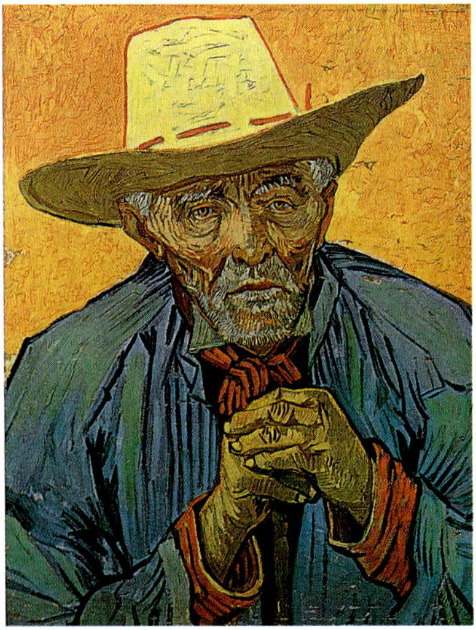

Roulin the Postman. *Museum of Fine Arts, Boston.*
In his portraits of the people of modest condition who were his preferred subjects, Vincent never forget the lessons of humility of his youth. His regard was generous, and respectful of their inner dignity.

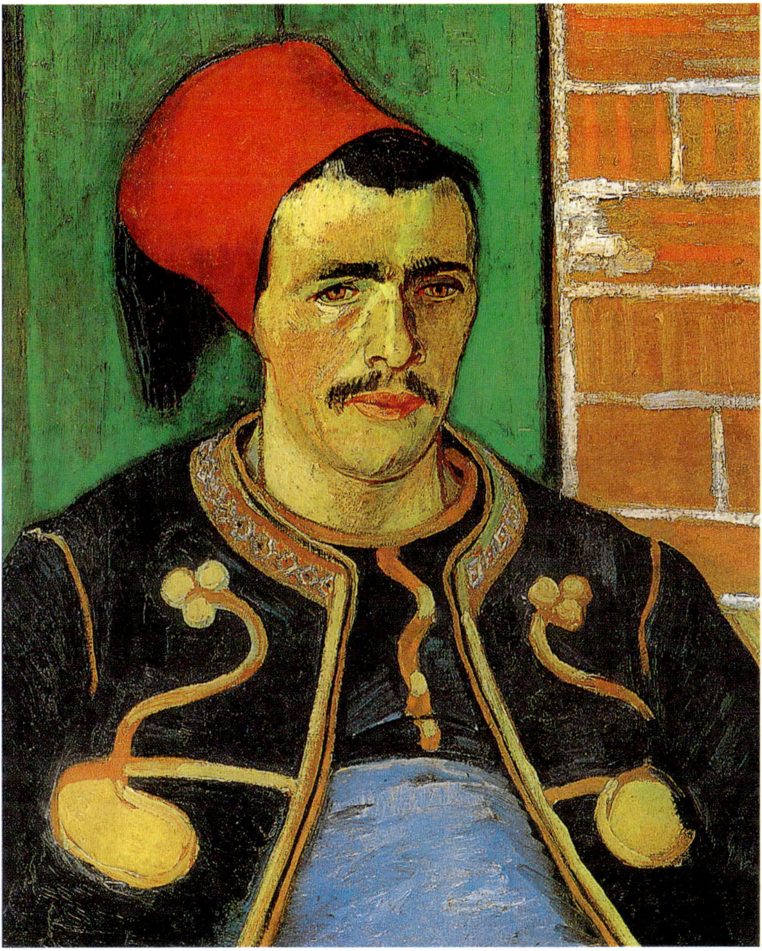

The Zouave. *Rijksmuseum Vincent Van Gogh, Amsterdam.*
"The human visage is what touches my emotions the most...and more than anything else, seems infinite." Beyond the purely decorative touch of the uniform, Vincent expresses a world of emotion in the Zouave's regard.

Tranquillity and Crisis

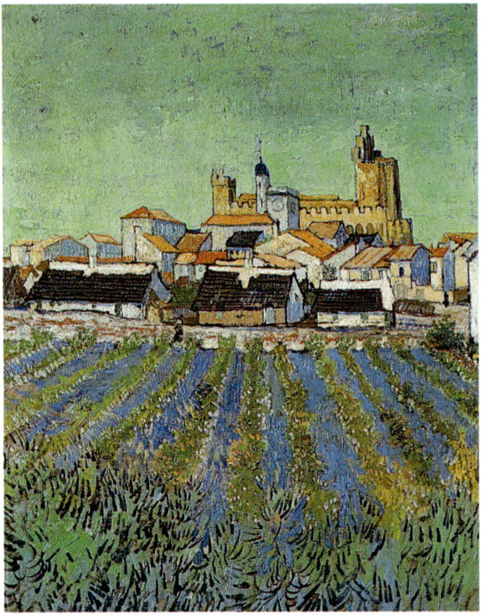

A View of Saintes-Maries-de-la-Mer.
Rijksmuseum Vincent Van Gogh, Amsterdam.
Vincent's visit to the village of Saintes-Maries resulted in several masterful landscapes executed in firm and authoritative brushwork and expressive of the region's exceptional luminosity.

Paris had totally exhausted Vincent; his head was still buzzing with the clamour of the city when he descended from the train "in a land of blue tones and gay colors" on February 20, 1888.

Before arriving in the south of France his experience of nature had been chiefly limited to the austere grey landscapes of the Boringage and Drenthe. His awakening to the possibilities of colour was due to the influence of Rubens and his recent encounter with the Impressionists, but rather than adopting their palette, he reinvented his own.

His enthusiasm for Arles, his delight in furnishing his new lodgings in the Yellow House and his multitude of projects were all signs of a profound transformation in his outlook on life.

One of Vincent's long-standing desires was to create an artists collective, and Arles seemed to offer the possibility of transforming the dream into reality. He invited Gauguin, Toulouse-Lautrec, Emile Bernard and Anquetin; only Gauguin would eventually accept, but the experience of living under the same roof with Vincent proved to be as disastrous as it was brief.

Shortly after Vincent's arrival in February the days began growing longer, heralding the return of the sun-filled luminous skies of Provence. Spring comes early to the Midi, accompanied by a flowering of almond, cherry, apricot, plum, pear and apple blossoms as the trees flame into life. The region's power and beauty impressed Vincent, who declared that it was "as beautiful as Japan by the clarity of its light and the brilliance of its colors. The waterways trace lovely emerald and blue lines across the landscape, like so many ribbons of crêpe-paper. The sun is a splendid yellow, turning as it sets into a pale orange that transforms the landscape with deep shades of blue."

As if stimulated by the increasing luminosity of the season, Vincent accelerated his rhythm: "I apply the paint to the canvas without reworking it. It piles up thickly in some places, and not at all in others, which are left as they are. My brushwork has become rapid and brutal...".

The fifteen works he completed in less than a month reflect both the brilliant luminosity of the Midi

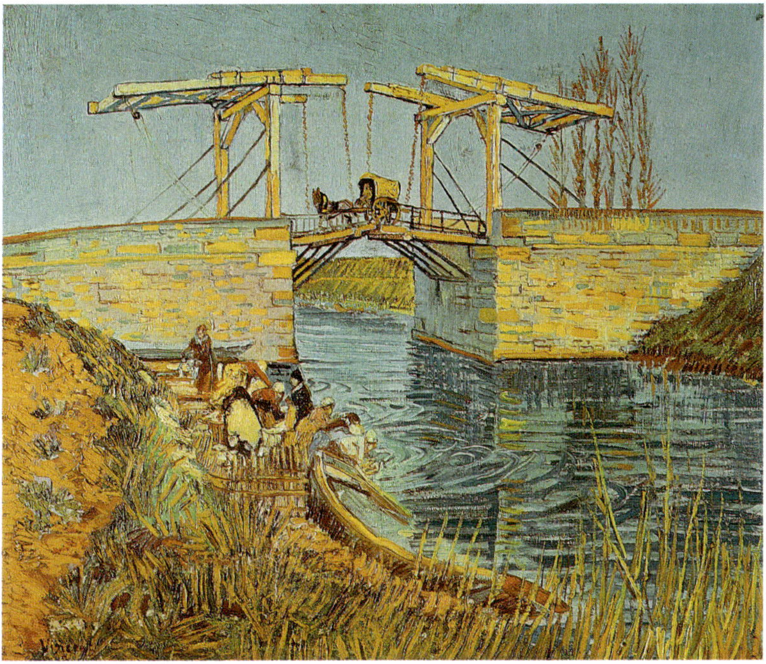

The Bridge at Langlois. *Rijksmuseum Kröller-Müller, Otterlo.*
The bridge, located near Arles, was a typical feature of the region. Vincent's painting captures the hard and brilliant light of Province which backlights the bridge's unusual wooden framework.

and the influence of Japanese art which manifested itself in the vigorous linearity of his compositions.

Although he also employed the techniques of pointillism, he was never limited by its stylistic conventions, which he modified and transformed with his own characteristic energy and aggressiveness. His creative drive liberated as never before, the works of this period display a new and unusual quality of spontaneity and joy.

To economise paint and canvas, Vincent often executed drawings with a sharpened reed and various inks, like the Japanese artists that he so admired.

His quest for subjects led him to explore the countryside surrounding Arles, where he sketched the rippling wheat-fields and vast panoramas from the heights of Montmajour. Perhaps to compensate for the simplicity of his means, some of the drawings are unusually ambitious and monumental in scale.

Fascinated by the scenes stretching below him, Vincent portrayed them in a manner similar to that of the golden age of Dutch landscape painting. The drawings in this series are the result of painstaking observation and a masterful patterning of space into a coherent series of discrete points and limits, giving them a unique quality of a universal vision.

By sheer patience and enormous effort, he developed a stylistic language based on points and arabesques, expressing both the timeless aspects of reality and the intensity of specific instants of human activity. It was a moment of serenity in his tormented life, eloquently paraphrased in the words of Henri Michaux: "In those times, I lost myself in the infinity of the horizon's outstretched arms."

Market Gardens. *Rijksmuseum Vincent Van Gogh, Amsterdam.*
A vast panorama composed of a succession of perspectives. The rolling landscape recedes to the blue horizon, punctuated by references to man's labour and habitations.

The Yellow House. *Rijksmuseum Vincent Van Gogh, Amsterdam.*
Vincent rented four rooms here in June 1888. He dreamed of creating the "Atelier du Midi" - a sort of artists' community, of which Gauguin was the first, last and sole member. Instead of offering the peace and stability of which he was so in need, the Yellow House was the scene of Vincent's desperate act of self-mutilation (the episode of the severed ear) and the symbol of the ultimate failure of his ideals, preceding his internment in an asylum.

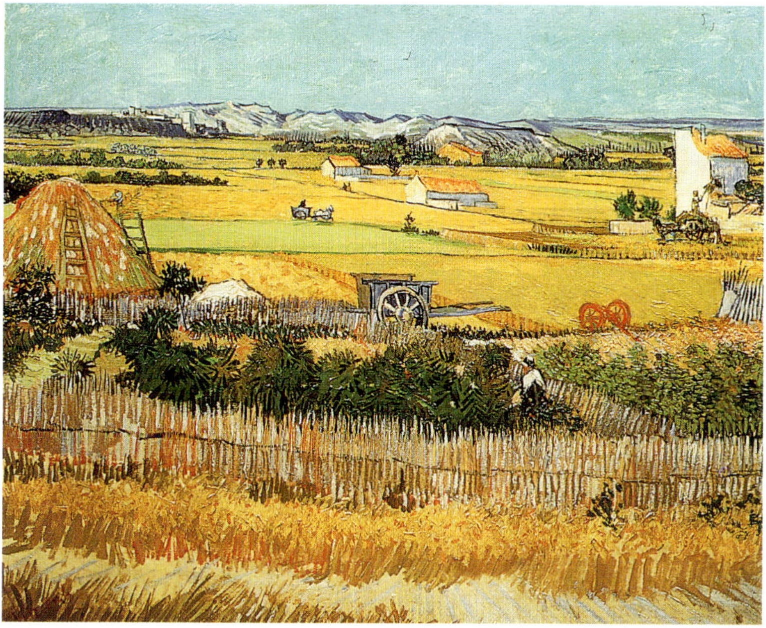

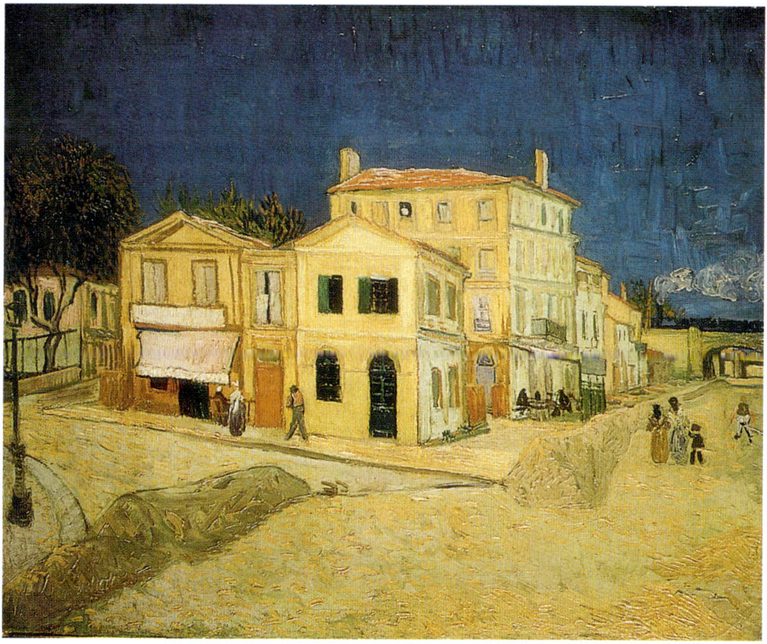

The World as Object

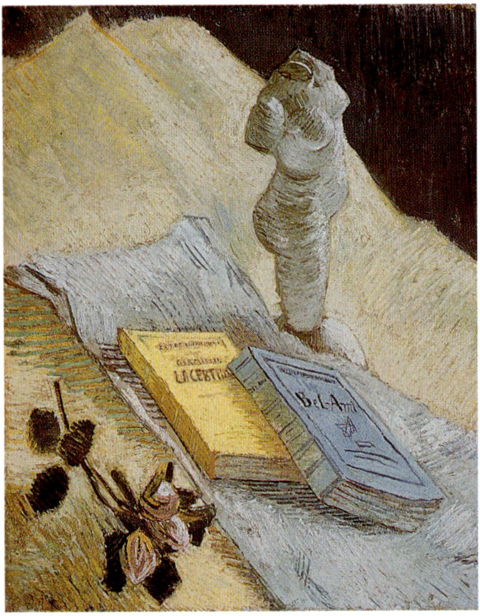

Still Life with Plaster Statuette and Books. *Rijksmuseum Kröller-Müller, Otterlo.*
Viewed from above and diagonally, the objects are disparate, yet united by Vincent's treatment of space and perspective. Symbolically, each class of object may be interpreted as offering an insight into the artist's conception of his own life.

The period in Arles was also marked by a return to still lifes and interior scenes. Their presence is affirmed from painting to painting - from the dark compositions of his early manner to the luminous studies of his maturity, charged with the final logic of his death.

The Yellow Room is like a monk's cell. The sparse furnishings have been reduced to the essential: a narrow bed, two chairs and a rustic table, and for sole decoration the images which are the icons of Vincent's adoration for the art of painting.

Like everything else in *The Yellow Room*, the chairs are strictly utilitarian, devoid of any fantasy and assembled out of rough-hewn wood with modest straw seats whose comfort is summary.

In the painting entitled *On The Threshold of Eternity*, the chair is no longer empty and the man seated in it appears to be at the end of his life and waiting to die. Hunched over in an almost foetal position, solitary and withdrawn, he is like a living illustration of a page from Vincent's diary and an eloquent confession of his deepest fears.

After moving into and furnishing his rooms in the Yellow House, Vincent painted the extremely atypical *Still Life with Cup and coffee-pot*. The work is a

Still Life with Drawing Board and Onions. *Rijksmuseum Kröller-Müller, Otterlo.*
In the representation of these everyday objects, Vincent once again adopted a vertical perspective, as if offering an overview of his life to those capable of decoding the inherent meaning of the articles represented. Significantly - for the painting was executed shortly after his mental breakdown - the book on the drawing-board deals with health problems.

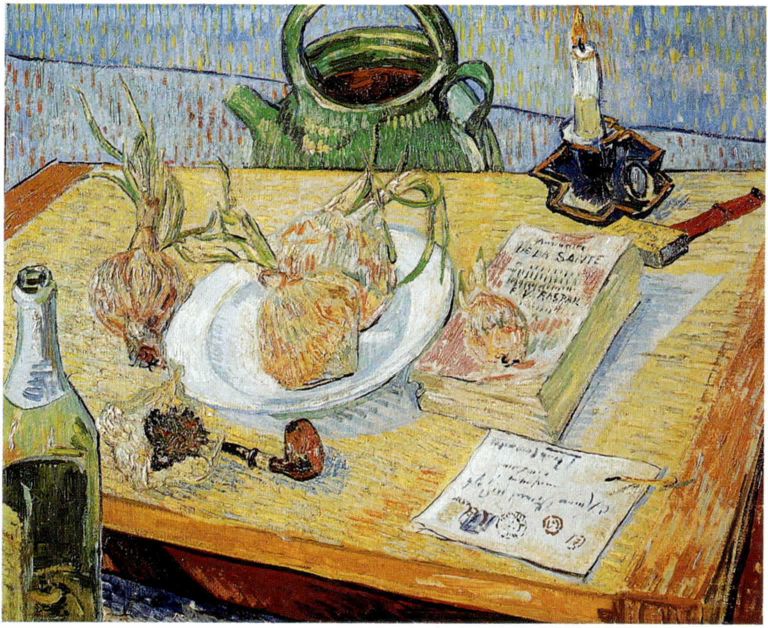

naive celebration of the possessions proper to a life-style which had always eluded him, the affirmation of having a place of his own and the promise of the serenity necessary for his work.

Although the objects appearing in the early works of his Dutch period were determined by local usage, the representations of wooden clogs, pipes, onions, bowls, jugs and frugal meals also provide precious insights into Vincent's daily life.

These were soon followed by a series of basic themes whose realism Vincent infused with a symbolic dimension. Unlike Cézanne, who rapidly passed from the object itself to the representation of its deeper and more abstract structural aspects, Vincent remained in the same current shared by many of his fellow-artists whose works celebrated the forces of nature and the demanding yet bountiful earth.

With the exception of the more dynamic quality of his many floral compositions - an outgrowth of his early interest in botany - Vincent painted the ordinary objects of his daily life. The silent witnesses of his solitude, they also resumed his entire existence: the candle that illuminated his nights, the envelope of his daily letter to Theo, his pipe and tobacco, the simple meals and the books that he read.

The books that appear in his works offer insights into his reading-matter and the allusions to it that appear in his correspondence. The first, executed during his Dutch period, was *The Open Bible* (1885). In *Still Life with Books,* the covers of Maupassant's *Bel Ami* and the Goncourt's *Germaine Lacerteux* appear, while the works of Dickens and H.B. Stowe are represented in *The Arlésienne.* Literary references are also present in *Still Life with Three Books.* In this strange, small painting executed during his Parisian period, Vincent represented the covers of the Goncourt's *La Fille Elisa,* Jean Richpin's *Braves Gens* and Zola's *Au Bonheur des Dames.*

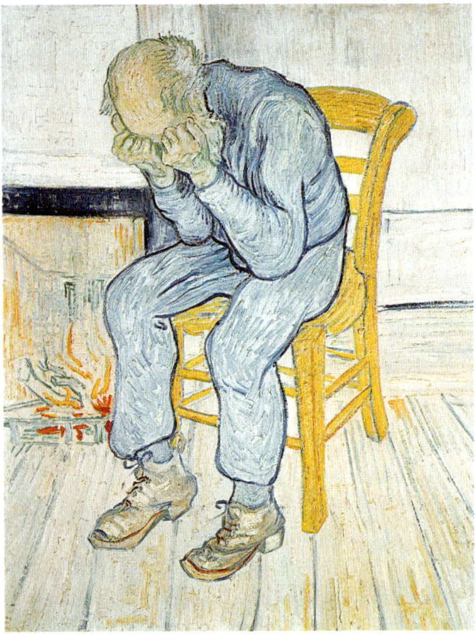

On the Threshold of Eternity.
Rijksmuseum Kröller-Müller, Otterlo. One of Vincent's most powerful and pathetic works. If the model's attitude recalls that of Rodin's Thinker, *his quiet desperation is that of the universe of Dostoievski.*

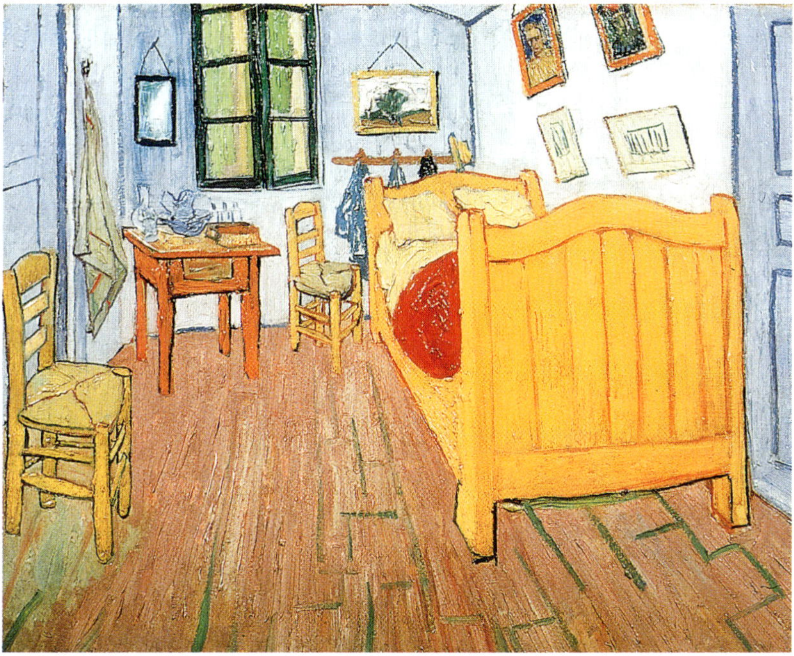

Vincent's Room in Arles (The Yellow Room). *Rijksmuseum Vincent Van Gogh, Amsterdam.*
Both in furnishing and portraying his room, Vincent paid careful attention to the smallest details. By its asceticism, the atmosphere is clearly monastic - a reflection of Vincent's preference for sober and unadorned authenticity.

Café Society

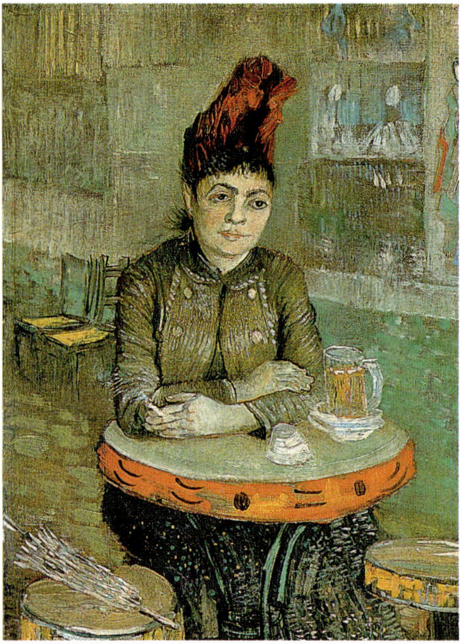

Agostina Segatori at the Tambourin Café.
Rijksmuseum Vincent Van Gogh, Amsterdam.
Vincent was briefly her lover and a regular client of her café, in which he organised several exhibitions.

Cafés were centres of social life during the nineteenth century. They influenced the habits and schedules of their clients, and by offering planned or unexpected encounters, often played a determinate role in their love-life. Reputations were made and undone around their tables, writers frequented them and painters portrayed their interiors. Manet, Degas and Caillebotte captured their excitement and atmosphere, which could vary according to whether one was with friends, family or simply unaccompanied.

Van Gogh, whose domestic life was limited to boarding-houses and rented rooms, frequently haunted cafés, and when he portrayed them, it was always in terms of emptiness and desperate solitude: "In my painting of *The Café at Night*, I represent it as a place where one can destroy oneself, go mad or commit a crime...and all of this in a hellish atmosphere of yellow light that hits you with all the blinding force of a blackjack...".

The same approach can be seen in his *Restaurant Interior* (1887), executed during the summer of his stay in Paris. Here, the modest dining-room is filled with a light which is nearly surgical in its pointillist clarity. There is a bouquet of flowers on each of the tables; all is in readiness to receive, yet the room is entirely empty.

Although filled with customers, the several versions of Vincent's nocturnal scenes of cafés in Arles evoke the same atmosphere of solitude and emptiness. The inte-

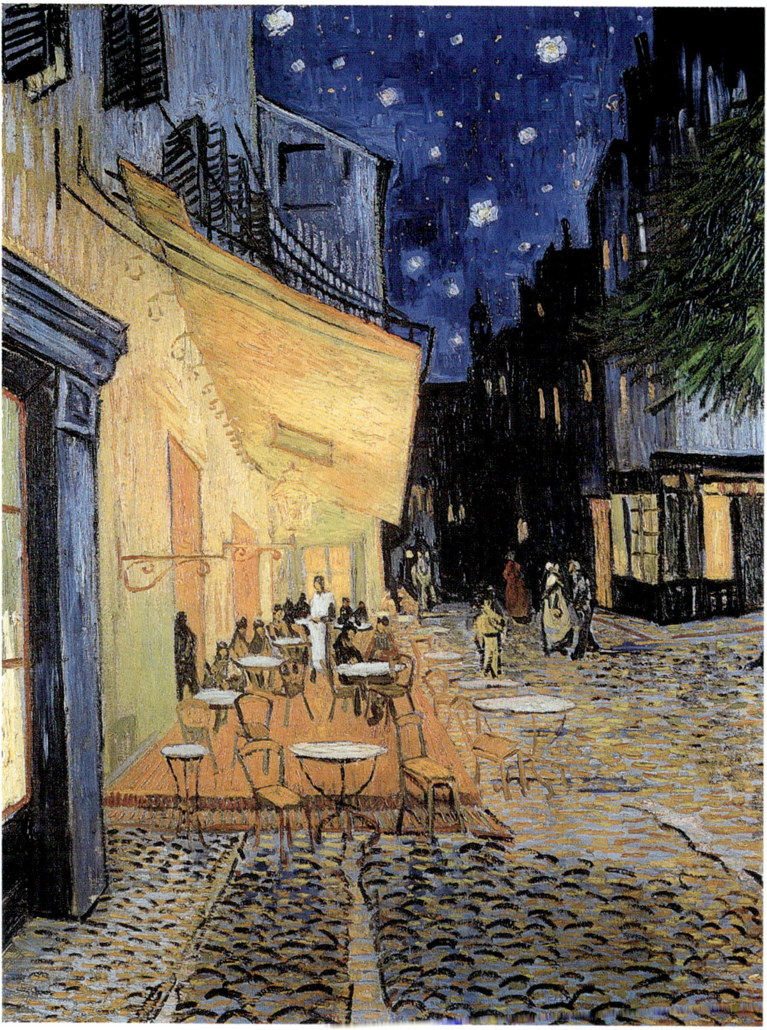

The Café in the Evening. *Rijksmuseum Kröller-Müller, Otterlo.*
Night scenes were still rare at this epoch (Anquetin was probably the first to attempt this). Vincent's vision is an intensely personal expression of reality disintegrating into a series of impressions, floating as if at sea in the warm humidity of a summer's evening.

rior of *The Café at Night* resembles nothing so much as a shelter for the homeless. The clients are summary, distant and spectral. The same lugubrious quality appears in *The Café in the Evening*, whose normally convivial atmosphere has been transformed into that of a place where couples separate, lives are ruined and where all encounters are fatal.

La Sirène, Restaurant at Asnières. *Orsay Museum, Paris.*
Vincent often followed the Seine to the outlying suburbs of Paris, whose riverside cabarets and semi-rural atmosphere he portrayed in paintings such as these.

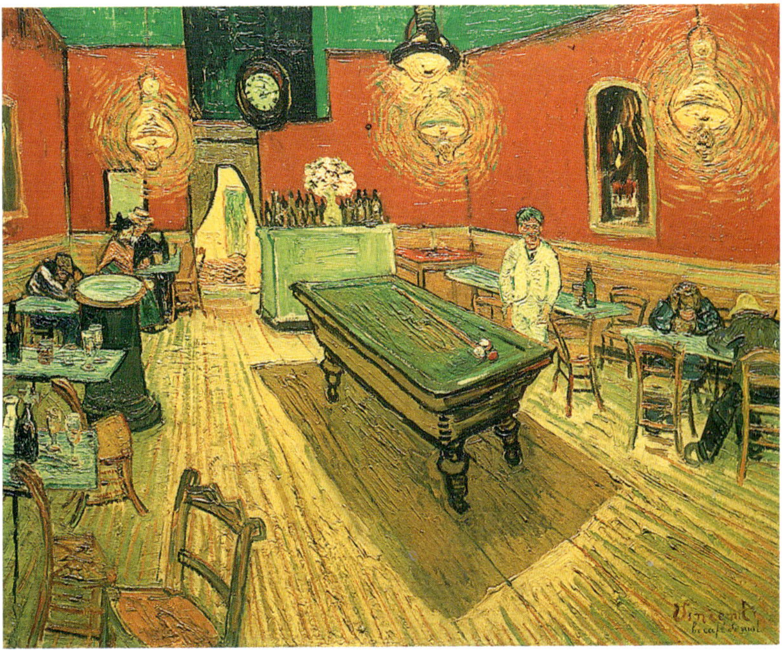

The Café at Night. *Yale University Art Gallery, New Haven (Connecticut).*
A regular client of the establishment, Vincent's painting of its interior is one of his strongest, most pathetic and quietly violent works. Its lugubrious atmosphere expresses all of the loneliness and desperation of society's outcasts.

Restaurant Interior. *Rijksmuseum Kröller-Müller, Otterlo.*
As a bachelor with no permanent address, Vincent was a regular client of modest restaurants such as the one portrayed here, with its simple but charming interior rendered in the pointillist manner.

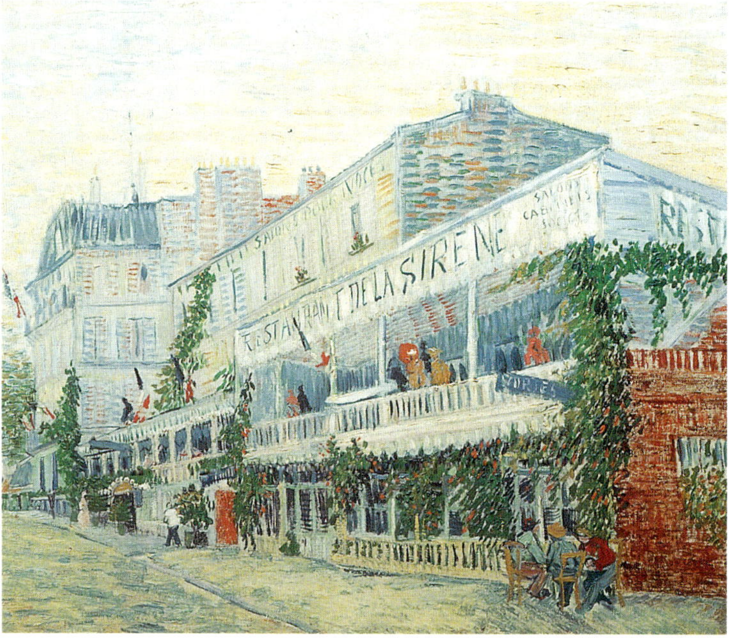
RESTAURANT DE LA SIRENE

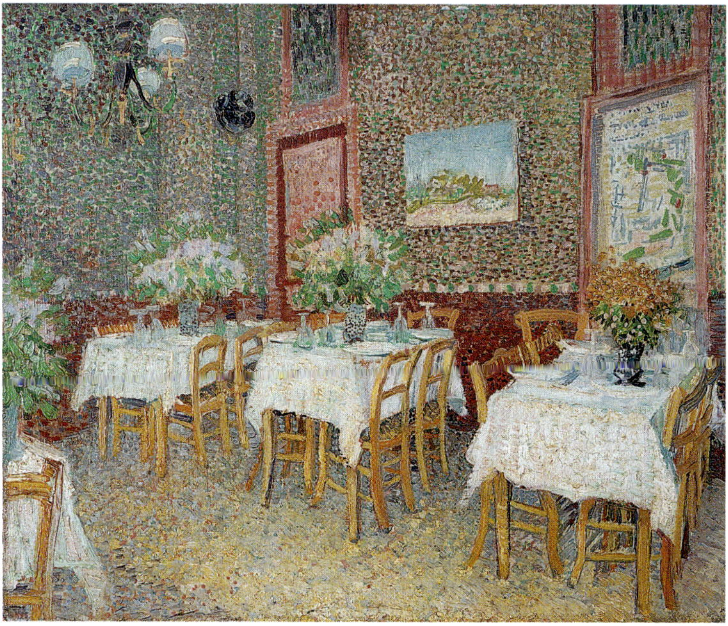

Paradise Lost: *l'Atelier du Midi*

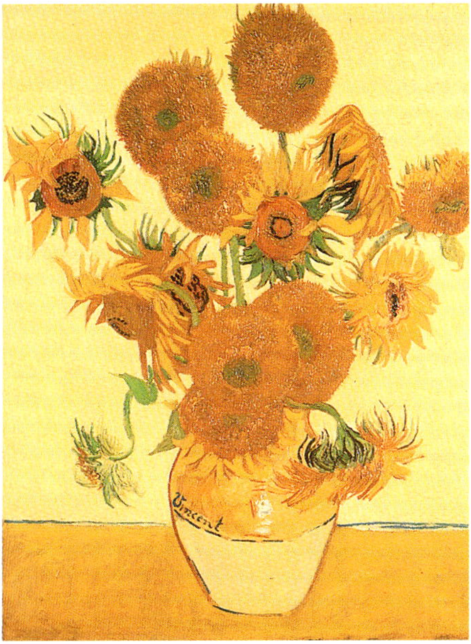

Sunflowers. *National Gallery, London. Vincent elevated this common flower to the status of an icon and a symbol of the sun in all its sumptuous and triumphant glory.*

Often mentioned in his letters to Theo, one of Vincent's fondest dreams was to organise an artists' collective. After moving into the Yellow House in Arles, Vincent took up the idea once again, enthusiastically preparing rooms for the fellow-artists he was planning to invite. After many hesitations, Gauguin accepted. The experience was as short-lived as it was tragic, and given his friendship for Gauguin, all the more crushing.

Gauguin arrived on October 23, 1888. In anticipation of his arrival, Vincent had lovingly furnished and decorated his friend's room around the theme of the sun. The gesture - as well as the symbolism - appeared to be lost on him, for his attitude rapidly became coldly distant.

Among other things, he was archly critical of Vincent's use of thick layers of raw colour in his works. The approach was at opposite ends from his own, for he employed a subtle palette of small quantities of pigment applied to precisely-delineated areas in a manner directly inspired by cloisonnisme.

Subjugated by Gauguin's authoritarian personality and anguished by the idea of his leaving, Van Gogh redoubled his efforts to please, even going so far as attempting to integrate his aesthetic principles into his own works, painting *Promenade in Arles, Memories of the Garden at Etten and The Dance Hall.* At the same time, he copied Emile Bernard's *Breton Women in a Green Prairie,* which Gauguin had brought from Pont-Aven to Arles.

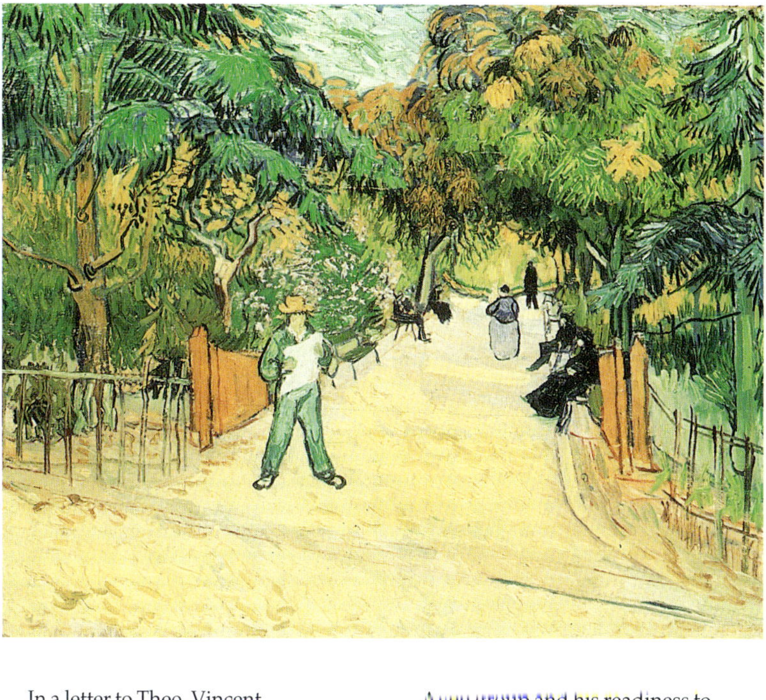

Entrance to the Public Gardens in Arles.
The Phillips Collection, Washington.
Here, the vegetation is represented with all the vibrating energy typical of Vincent's style during this period, as well as a vague menace: the tunnel of tree-branches has a suffocating, almost claustrophobic quality. With each of its figures scattered, isolated and non-communicating, Vincent's garden is a reflection of his own solitude.

In a letter to Theo, Vincent wrote: "Bernard is a young painter - twenty years old at the most - and extremely original. He is attempting to create modern works that possess the elegance of Greek or Egyptian art, the grace of expressive movement and the charm of vivid colors."

The letter indicates Van Gogh's interest in the artists of the Pont-Aven group and his readiness to experiment with new styles, much as if he doubted the validity of his own. It is possible that his only certainty was the passion he invested in his works, for more than anything else, his style was the result of emotion, inner necessity and the force of a highly personal vision which transcended all schools and established currents.

As the tension progressively mounted between the two men, their incessant quarrels and artistic differences began to make it impossible to live and work together. In his supreme self-confidence, Gauguin was certain that he possessed an artistic truth that Vincent had yet to discover, while the latter laboured mightily to impose his own technique and style. The confrontation between two such different and wilful personalities was doomed from the start, and rather than a mutually enriching exchange, their cohabitation degenerated into a sterile routine of daily quarrels and nightly visits to the local bordellos.

Their aesthetic divergence was exacerbated by Vincent's hypersensitive and often stormy personality. He became increasingly aggressive and occasionally menaced Gauguin, who after threatening to leave, attempted to placate him by executing his portrait "painting sunflowers." Rather than being flattered by the gesture, Vincent dismissed the work with a phrase heavy with future signifi-

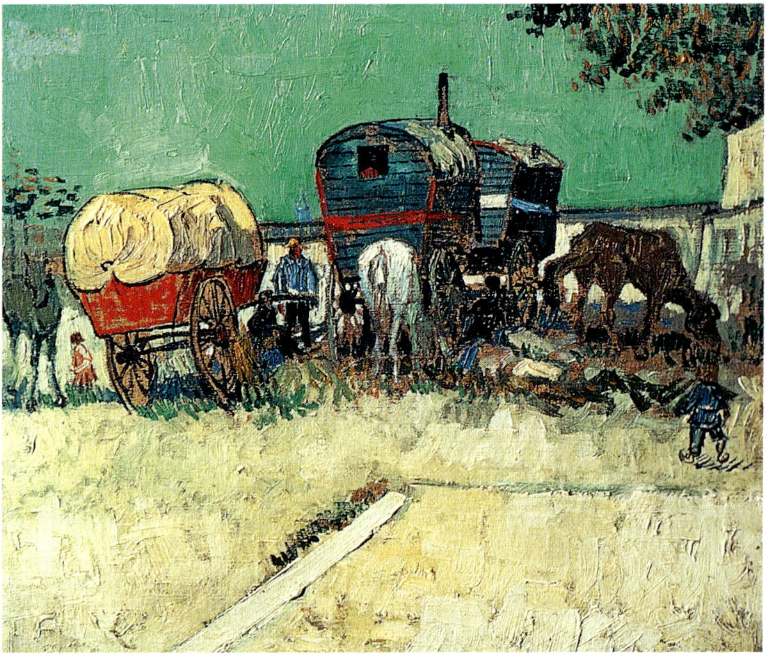

Gypsy Caravans. *Orsay Museum, Paris. Vincent was attracted to these restless travellers with whom he identified in his own ceaseless wanderings.*

cance: "It's me, but I look like a madman."

The tension mounted inexorably until the day that Vincent could no longer contain his anger. But when he finally unleashed it, the target was not Gauguin, it was himself.

Their highly emotional psycho-drama recalls that of Arthur Rimbaud and Paul Verlaine, which terminated by the latter shooting his former friend. But Van Gogh, true to the innate logic of his self-destructiveness, turned his violence against himself. After a final argument with Gauguin, Vincent severed a portion of his ear and carried it like an offering to Rachel, a prostitute to whom he had become attached.

Insofar as Gauguin had remained deaf to Vincent's pleas for understanding and co-operation, his gesture was highly symbolic. The failure of their common life together was insupportable, for it signified both the end of a friendship and a cherished ideal. The shock unbalanced him; in the death of this final illusion, the legend of the mad artist who severed his ear was born.

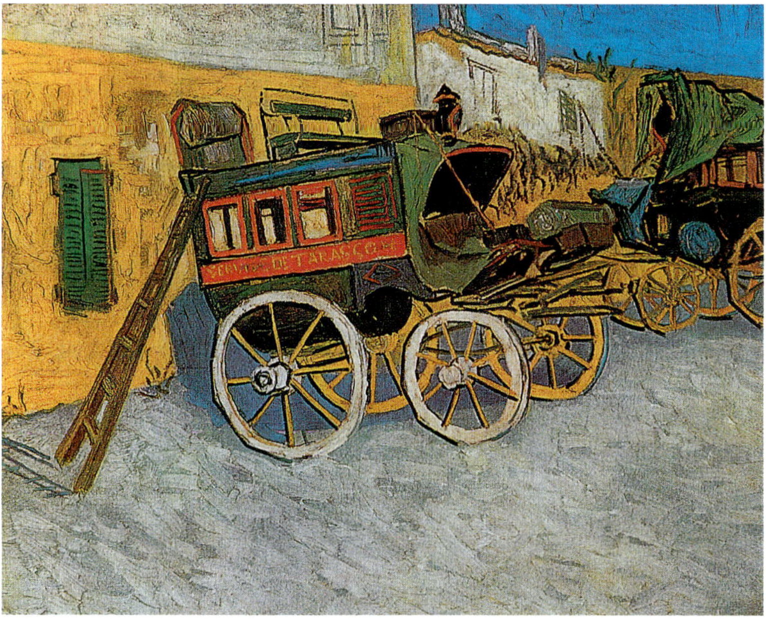

The Tarascon Coach. *The Henry and Rose Pearlman Foundation, New York. Van Gogh's brushwork could be astonishingly precise and controlled. A testament to the discipline, effort and objective realism of which he was capable.*

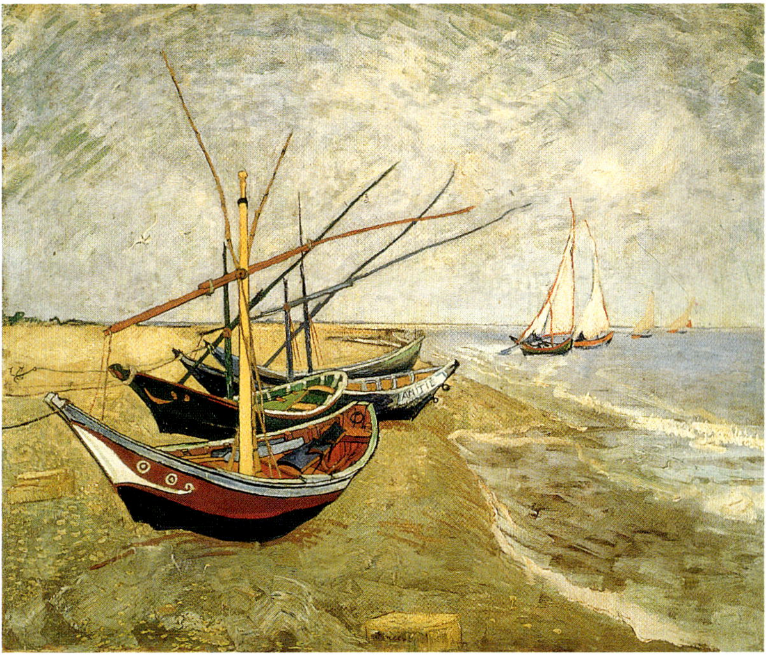

Boats on the Beach of Saintes-Maries-de-la-Mer. *Rijksmuseum Vincent Van Gogh, Amsterdam.*
The call of the sea is often less a discovery than a confirmation of one's deepest desires. Like Rimbaud and Gauguin, Vincent also yearned for distant horizons. As the impotent spectator of his own dreams, he would remain - like the boats portrayed here - awaiting a tide that never came.

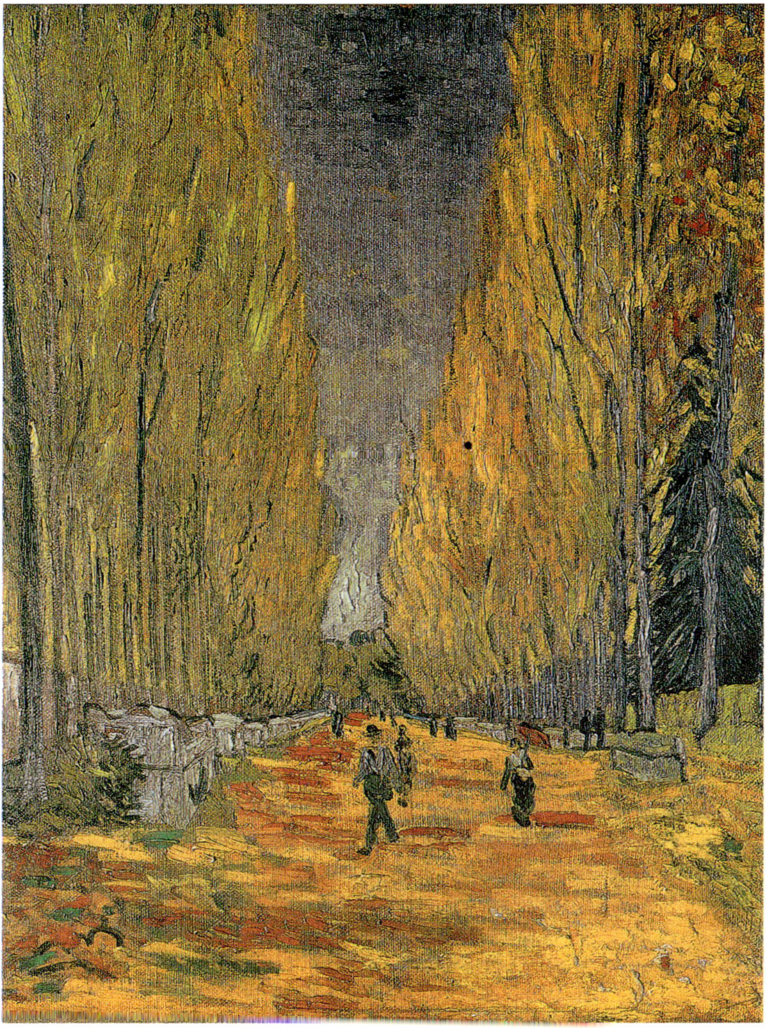

The Alyscamps. *Private collection.*
Along with Gauguin, Vincent painted this ancient tree-lined path in Arles on numerous occasions.

Vincent's Ear, Bataille's Eye

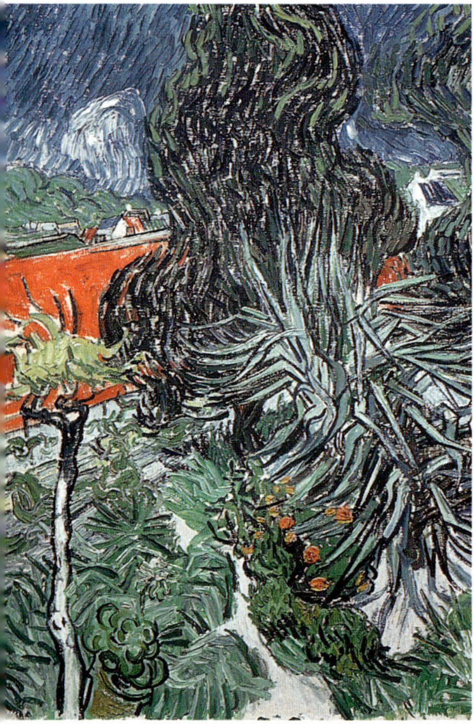

Doctor Gachet's Garden. *Orsay Museum, Paris.*
Executed shortly after his arrival in Auvers-sur-Oise, the painting reflects the chaotic disorganisation of Vincent's mind. Proportion and perspective have nearly been abandoned; all that remains is a terrifyingly direct perception of the force of nature. The tree invades the sky, dwarfing the habitations in its flame-like vertical thrust.

At the same time that his relationship with Gauguin was degenerating, Vincent painted *Chair and Pipe (Vincent's Chair)* and *Gauguin's Armchair.* In the first work, the chair and its straw seat are rendered in the golden yellow tones of the sunlight of the Midi. The pipe and open package of tobacco express the solitary and contemplative existence of the artist, while both objects are dominated by the volumes of the chair and the broad planes of the walls and red-tiled floor. Low and rough-hewn, Vincent's chair is similar to those used in churches, and embodies all of his deeply-rooted asceticism.

Represented in deeper tones of red and green, *Gauguin's Armchair* is positively royal in comparison. The candle, books and illuminated gas lamp on the wall suggest a late-night vigil, as if the room itself were waiting for its occupant. Throne-like and empty, the armchair is an unmistakable reference both to Vincent's esteem for his friend and his conspicuous absence.

Vincent's admiration and affection also contained an element of animosity, for both Gauguin's personality and style were radically different from his own. His approach to painting was more superficially decorative than Vincent's, who pushed his representa-

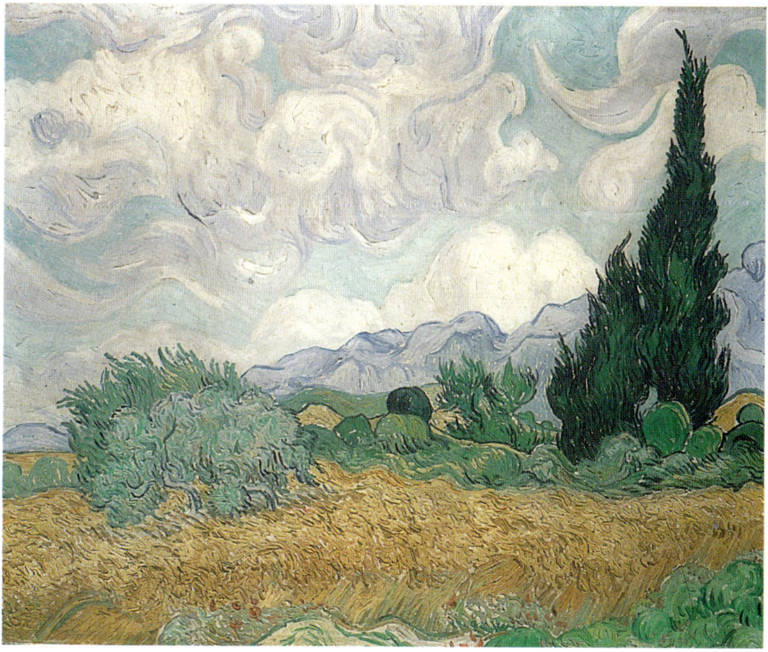

Wheat Field and Cypresses. *The National Gallery, London.*
Designed in flowing arabesques, the turbulent clouds provide a dynamic backdrop to the dark flame of the cypress, leaping skywards as if to escape the tortured and windblown landscape.

tions of reality to extremes in order to reveal its deeper truths.

Following a particularly violent argument with Gauguin, Vincent resorted to an act of great desperation, as if the only way to pierce his friend's carapace of implacable indifference was through an even more powerful act of self-assertion, which in the logic of Vincent's underlying streak of masochism could only mean self-sacrifice.

Georges Bataille commented Vincent's self-mutilation in poetic and psychoanalytical terms, placing it within a context in which reality and mythology merge: "The monstrous ear... abruptly leaves the magic circle in which the rituals of liberation are performed. It departs with the severed tongue and shattered teeth of Anaxarque of Abdera, spat in the face of the tyrant Nicocreon, and those of

Zenon of Elêe, spat in the face of Demylos: both philosophers were subjected to horrible tortures, the first being ground to death in a mortar".

Bataille continues: "Van Gogh had accorded a new meaning to the sun. He no longer portrayed it as part of the decor, but like a sorcerer's dance that slowly stirs the crowd, drawing it progressively into its movement. His paintings became light, explosion, flame, and he also: ecstatic, lost within the shining light, exploding, in flames. As this sun-dance began, nature itself suddenly exploded, the vegetation caught fire and the earth rolled like the waves of the sea and broke apart. Nothing was left of its stability, the foundation of all things. Then, like the sun seen through the flesh of a living hand, revealing the shadows of its bones, Death appeared in a kind of transparence. Brilliant wilted flowers and the haggard depressing face: the Van Gogh of the sunflowers signified the end of the reign of immutable laws, of courts, of all that gives faces their disgusting aspect of being shut, of existing behind walls."

Bataille's flamboyant analysis equated Van Gogh with Prometheus, inhabiting a universe from which order had departed. Only the incandescent stars remained, wheeling in the chaos of the night and unleashing their inner fire - Vincent's swirling stars - upon a silent, immobile earth. And under the furnace of the sun's heat, plants wilted at the very apogee of their growth, drawing upon life with all their vibrant energy and consuming themselves in the fire that both nourished and destroyed them.

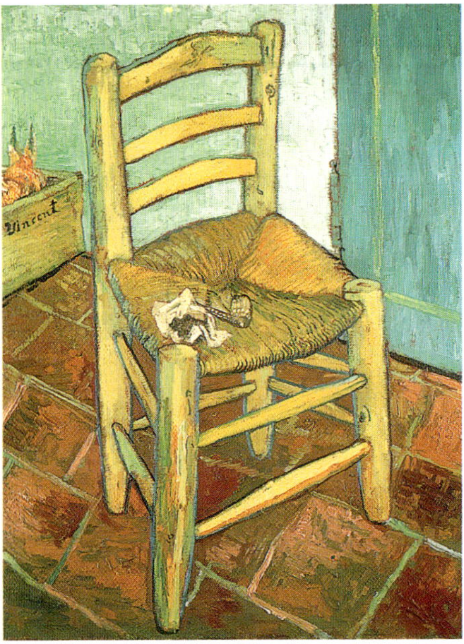

Chair and Pipe (Vincent's Chair).
Rijksmuseum Vincent Van Gogh, Amsterdam.
The echo of Gauguin's Armchair both stylistically and in the portrayal of the objects on their seats, Vincent reserved the more modest of the two for himself, in keeping with his ingrained habit of self-denigration and denial.

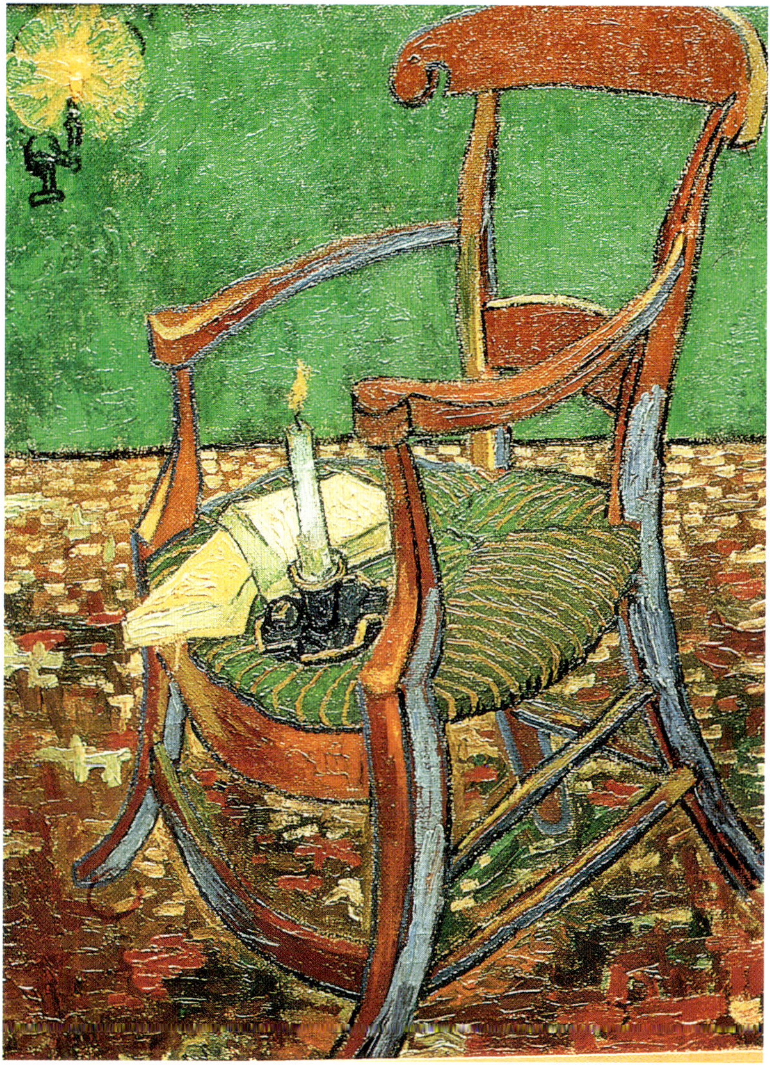

Gauguin's Armchair. *Rijksmuseum Vincent Van Gogh, Amsterdam.*
Painted during the height of their conflicts, Vincent's representation of Gauguin's throne-like armchair with its phallic candle is perhaps an unconscious reference to his friend's imperious and dominating personality. The chair is empty: Gauguin would soon leave Arles, abandoning Vincent to his madness.

The Loneliness of the Long-Distance Runner

More than in any other period of history, the nineteenth century was an age of solitude. The frenetic energy of the French Revolution which had fuelled the Napoleonic Empire was depleted. The bourgeois stasis of the Restoration had engendered Romanticism, an ideal inseparable from death, and alienated an entire generation of artists and writers who had rejected the aesthetic conventions of the Academy.

From Rimbaud, whose rebellion led him to the far horizons of Africa to Gauguin's departure from a moribund Europe in full moral and aesthetic decomposition, the flame of authenticity was carried by the emblematic figure of Van Gogh, whose refusal of mediocrity and suicidal quest for absolutes would influence artists for generations to come.

Vincent's inimitable specificity was rooted in his very existence. Much of his life and artistic vision had been affected by the disintegration of his personal relationships with his family and friends and ultimately, with society itself. His alienation was also the result of an uncommon conscience and an uncompromising moral stance. If the uniqueness of his work was inseparable from that of his personality, this was far from being the case for the most successful artists of the period, honoured by the official institutions of the cultural establishment and whose popularity reflected the conservative bourgeois tastes and self-satisfaction of their public.

As a child of the realism of the Hague School, Impressionism and the Pointillists, he produced a new category of works beyond all norms, conventions and historical continuity. From all these encounters and influences he created his own personal idiom, a language intimately connected to the trajectory of his own soul and style which expressed the hidden mysteries of objective experience.

As no other artist before him, he succeeded in penetrating reality and communicating his vision with the same prophetic clairvoy-

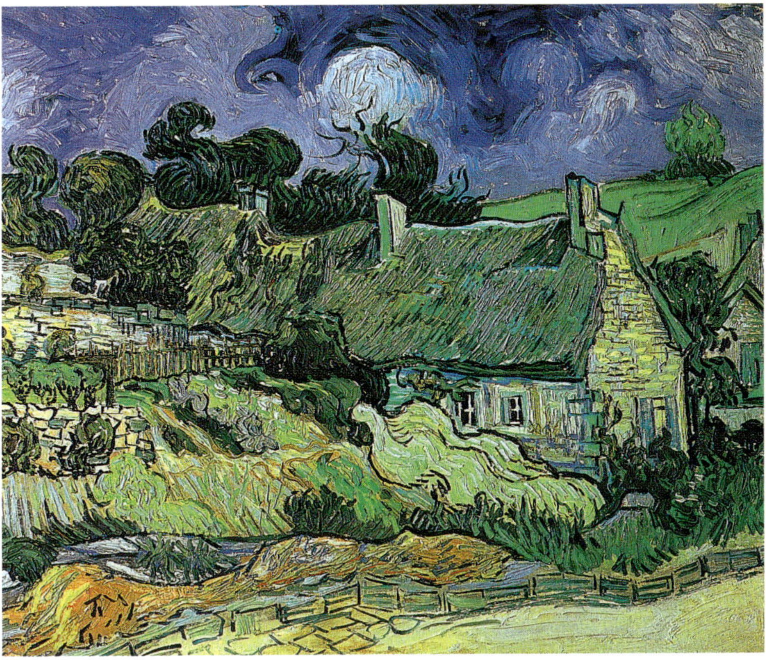

Cottages in Cordeville. *Orsay Museum, Paris.*
Vincent's tortured manner of representing landscapes and architecture that had progressively appeared in his works during his sojourn in Arles continued after his arrival in Auvers. Here, the thatched roofs of the cottages appear to be receding into the chaotic landscape of the hill and garden, buffeted by the tree-tops and swirling masses of clouds.

ance of a Baudelaire or a Rimbaud. In his exploration of the dimension that lay beyond the strictly visible, he chose the heroic path of revealing the profound and intense energies of the universe.

If Vincent could be said to have painted an icon, it would be *The Sower*. Dominating the foreground of the landscape and silhouetted by the enormous late-afternoon sun, the sower emerges like an ancient god.

Van Gogh's expression of reality was no longer that of the merely visible, but of a totality. Artists who un-dertake this quest do so at their own risk, for the vision that it endows is often mortal. For those who survive, the images of what they have witnessed remain as precious testaments to the magic and beauty of the world in which we live.

The Ravine des Peyroulets. *Rijksmuseum Kröller-Müller, Otterlo.*
Writhing like a nest of serpents encircling the two tiny figures in the middle distance, the landscape and vegetation are one of the most vehement and expressive examples of the Saint-Rémy period.

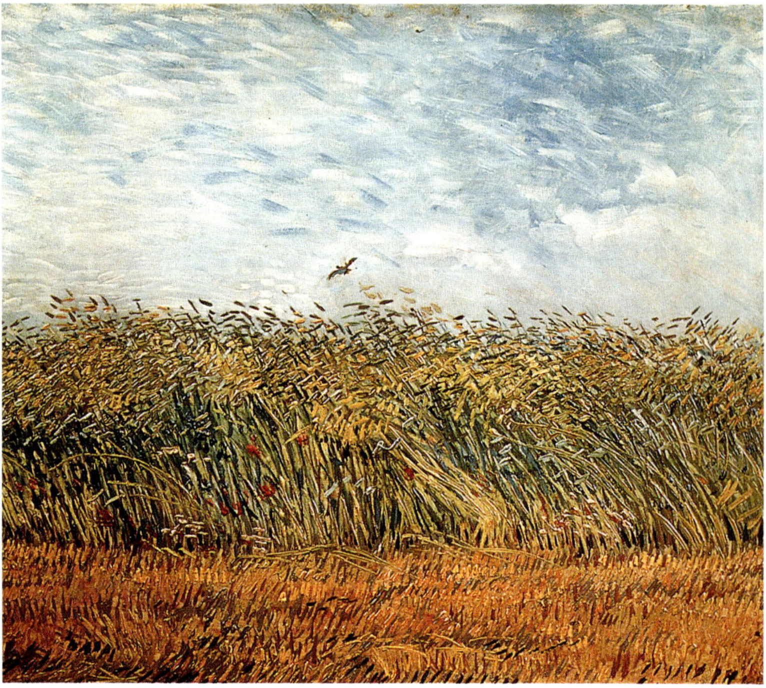

Wheat Field with Skylark. *Rijksmuseum Vincent Van Gogh, Amsterdam.*
By its serenity, one of Vincent's most atypical landscapes, prefiguring like an omen the ultimate flight of crows over the wheat fields of his suicide in Auvers.

Green Vines. *Rijksmuseum Kröller-Müller, Otterlo.*
The earth and sky are united in a counterpoint of agitated tremors, as if shaken by the same obscure and mysterious force.

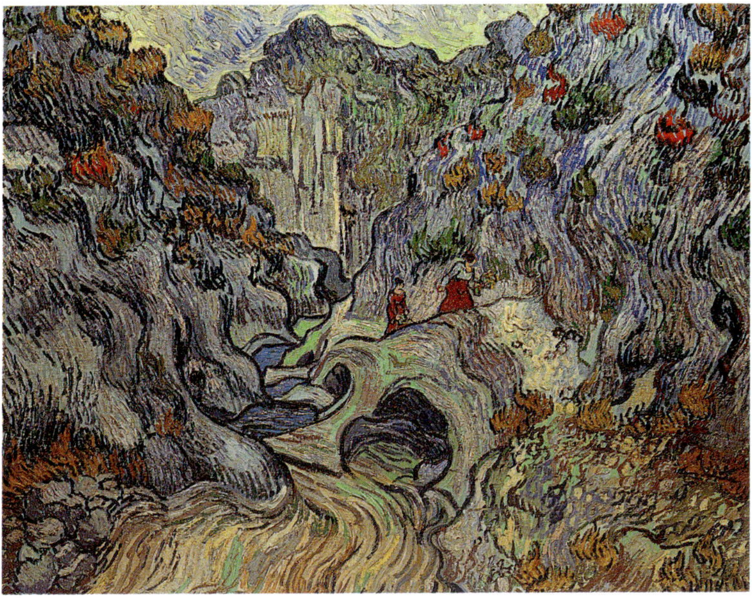

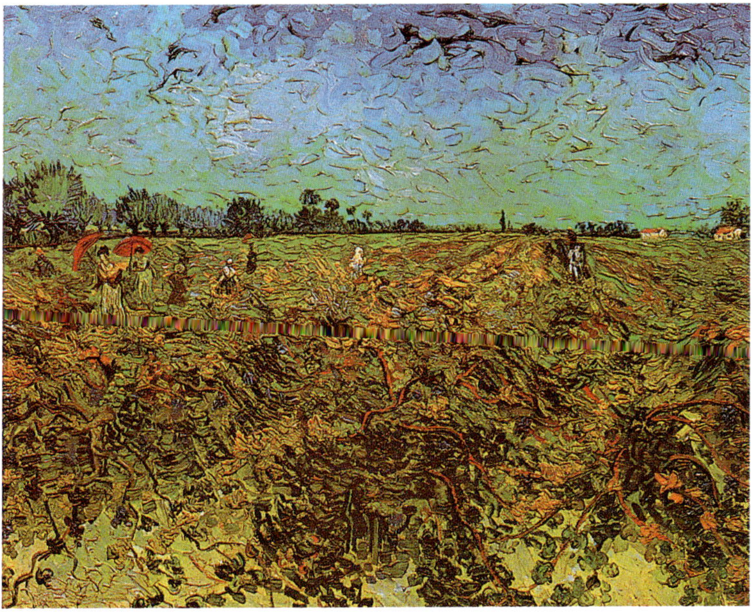

Confinement

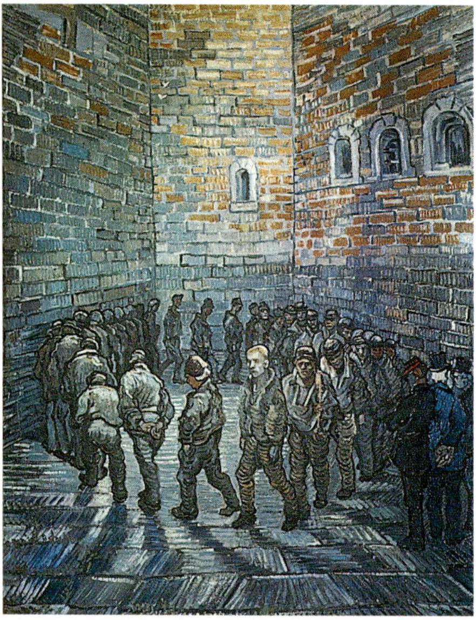

Prisoners Exercising *(after Gustave Doré). Pushkin Museum, Moscow. All forms of confinement were bitterly resented by Vincent. Here, he expresses his feelings through a brutally explicit image, unadorned by any of the more poetic mannerisms he often employed. Although Vincent's painting was inspired by an existing work by Doré, it is a clear and highly personal reference to his hospitalisation in the Saint-Rémy asylum.*

The police discovered Vincent semi-conscious in the Yellow House on December 24, 1888. Gauguin left for Paris the next day. According to police and hospital records, Vincent was taken to the municipal hospital of Arles (l'Hôtel-Dieu) where after treatment for his mutilated ear, he was placed in isolation for further observation. In the days that followed, he progressively regained his calm and on January 7, 1889, he returned to the Yellow House.

Suffering from hallucinations after a month of liberty, he was readmitted to the hospital on February 7, once again returning to the Yellow House after his release.

This time he was received with overt hostility by his neighbours, whose systematic persecution provoked a new crisis; a petition demanding his placement was signed and Vincent re-entered the hospital - this time diagnosed as insane - on February 25, 1889.

Forcefully committed and a prisoner of the establishment, Vincent - oblivious of the enormous scandal he had created - wrote to his brother Theo: "Here I am, passing my days locked by the guards in my little room, without

Self-Portrait with Severed Ear.
Courtauld Institute Galleries, London.
"I was born violent," said the poet René Char. Wounded in his soul, Vincent turned his violence against himself in a desperate act of self-mutilation.

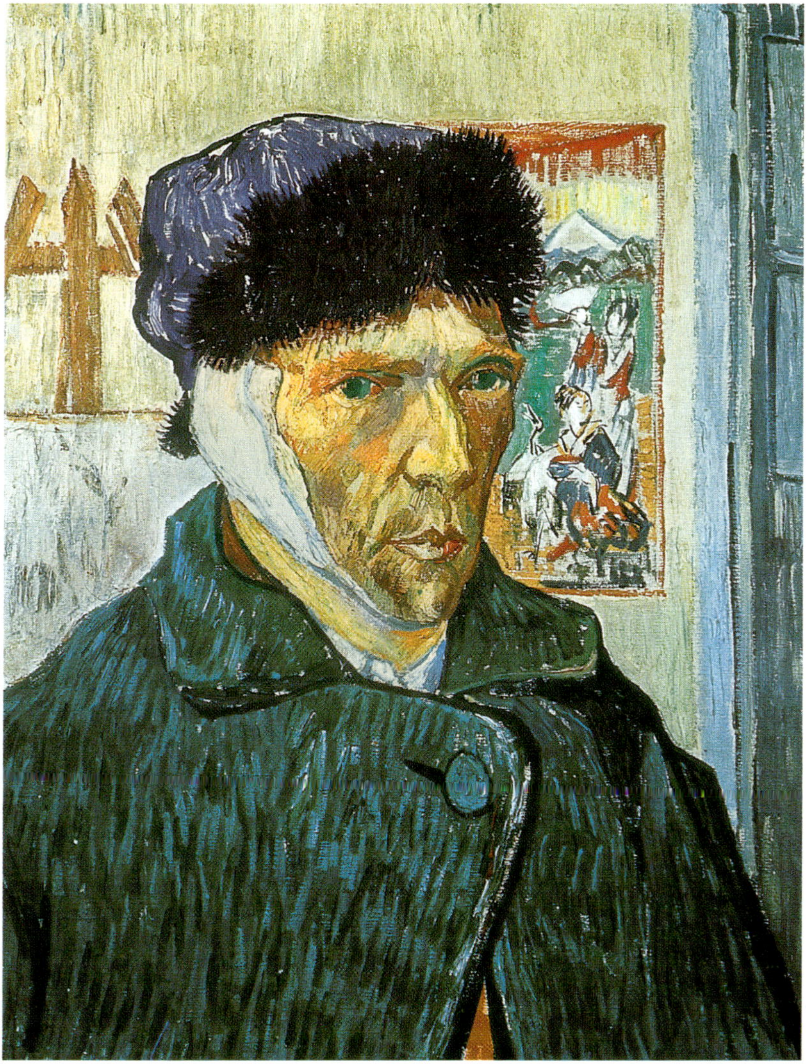

anything having being established or even demonstrable."

Dr. Rey, an intern of the hospital with whom he sympathised, allowed him a relative liberty of circulation. Much of his time was spent in reading: *Ceux de la Glebe,* by the Belgian humanist Camille Lemonnier, *Uncle Tom's Cabin,* by Harriet Beecher Stowe, *A Christmas Story,* by Charles Dickens and *Germinie Lacerteux* by the Goncourt brothers. When he turned thirty-six on March 30, Vincent looked years older: a man weakened and aged long before his time.

Suffering from general exhaustion, he remained in the hospital until May 8, when he was transferred at his own request to the asylum of Saint-Paul-de-Mausole, on the outskirts of Saint-Rémy-de-Province.

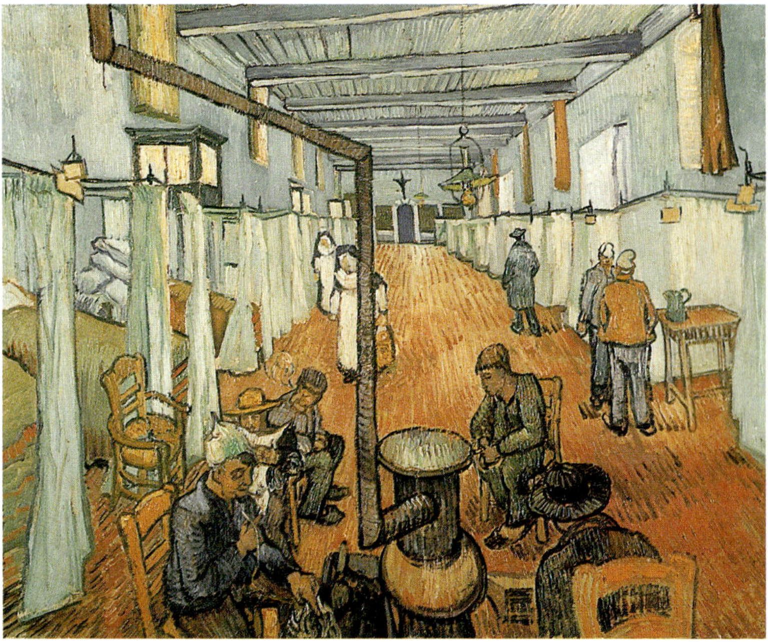

The Hospital at Arles. *Oskar Reinhart Collection, Winterthur.*
Vincent always painted from life, portraying the reality of his immediate environment. Hospitalised in Arles after severing his ear, he produced a series of works depicting his new universe inhabited by dream-like patients awaiting their destiny in the common ward of the poor.

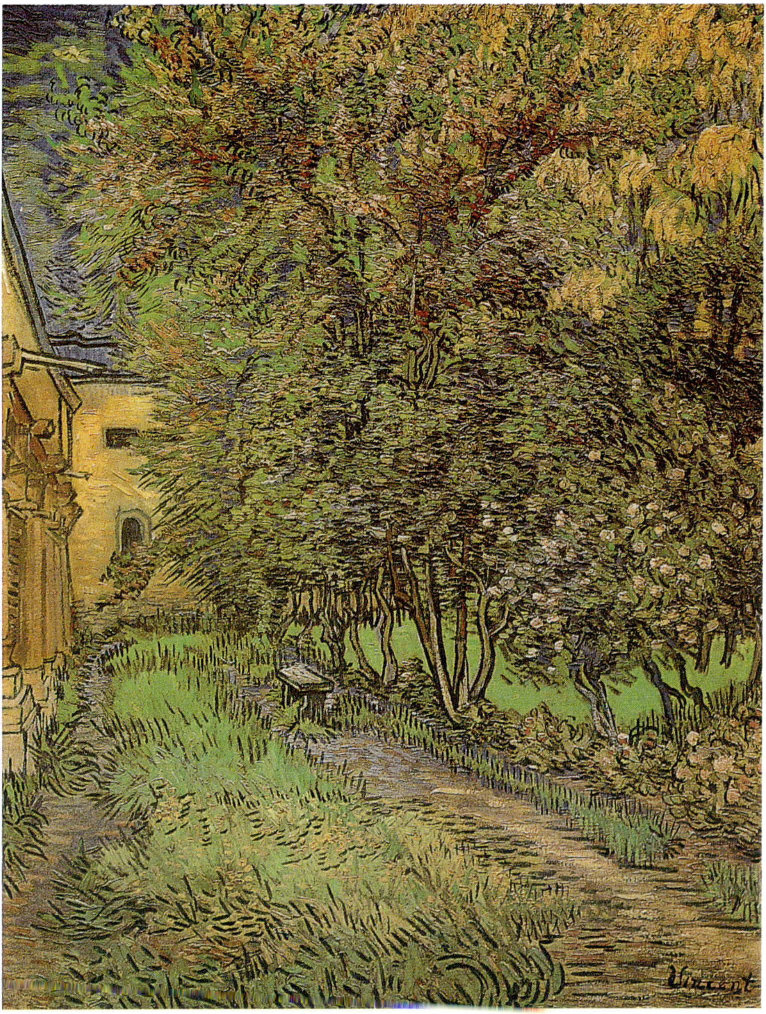

Garden of the Saint-Paul Asylum.
Rijksmuseum Kröller-Müller, Otterlo.
Following his hospitalisation in Arles, Vincent was transferred at his own request to the asylum at Saint-Rémy, where he continued to sketch and paint scenes of his daily life within its walls.

Memories of the Madhouse

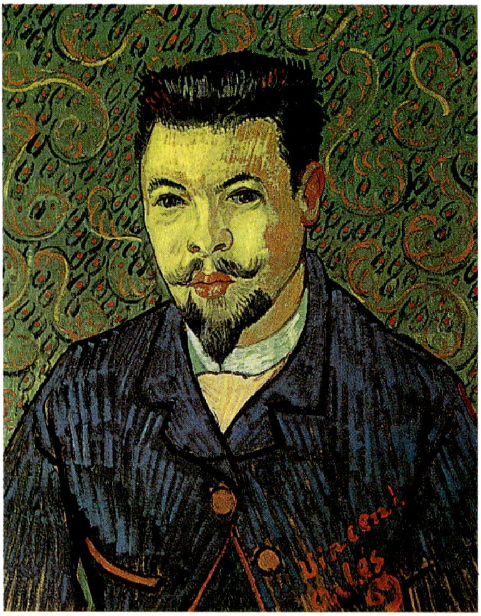

Portrait of Doctor Rey. *Pushkin Museum, Moscow.*
Painting was considered to be a therapeutic activity for Vincent during his hospitalisation. Doctor Rey, with whom he sympathised, posed for this portrait which Vincent adorned with a richly decorated background.

His internment at Saint-Paul was a voluntary and lucid act. He had refused the offer of a new studio, frightened by the idea of attracting the hatred and persecution of the local population. Because it was considered therapeutic by his doctors, Vincent was allowed to paint: "The idea of painting again occurs to me often, and I believe that all my faculties will return to me soon. When one's soul cries to express itself, it should never be stifled. I'd rather die than suffocate, for that which is inside oneself must be expressed."

Although confined within the asylum's walls, Vincent found the haven he so desperately needed: "Even though I continually hear people shouting and screaming like animals in a zoo, the patients here know each other well and aid one other constantly... When I paint in the garden, they come to see me, and I can assure you that they are much more polite and respectful of my tranquillity than the good citizens of Arles."

In describing his immediate environment, he alluded to nature, always an important element in his life and art: "My little room is papered in grey-greentones...

Corridor of the Saint-Paul Asylum. *The Museum of Modern Art, gift of Abby Aldrich D. Rockefeller, New York. The perspective plunges to infinity, as if Vincent was expressing his own plummet into madness and his search for sanity within the resounding emptiness of the asylum corridors.*

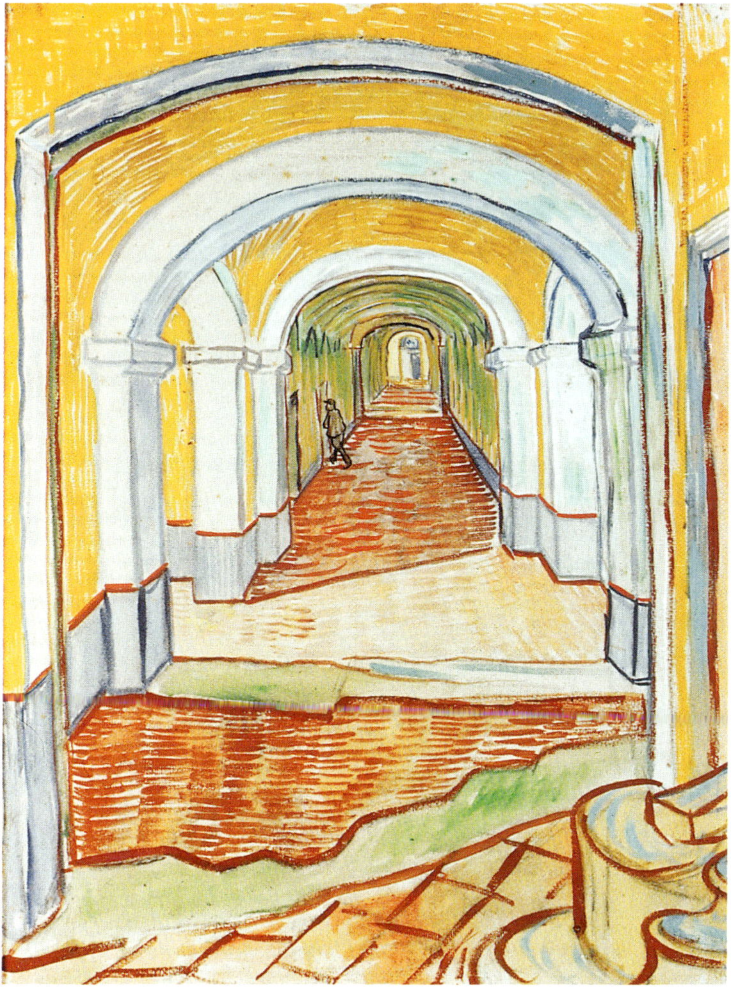

through the iron bars of the window, I can see a fenced-off field of wheat and a perspective like a Van Goyen, above which the sun rises gloriously every morning".

He began by painting close-ups of the flowers in the hospital garden and once allowed outside of its walls, fields in which the silhouettes of cypress trees soared upward like dark flames.

The scenes seemed to tremble and vibrate as if possessed by a strange inner frenzy of their own, swept up by the fury of their own energy and light before disintegrating into shadow and darkness.

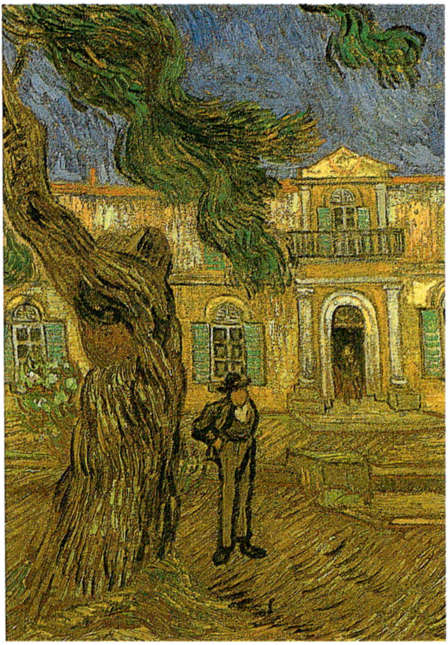

His eerily majestic *Starry Night* resumed all of the strangeness of this period. Here, Vincent had clearly ventured beyond the simple representation of reality: it was as if all of nature had attained a state of supernatural incandescence and fusion.

Along with these works marked by a vision of a universe in perpetual metamorphosis, others expressed an sense of confinement and claustrophobia. He had become obsessed with creating a detailed visual account of his confinement, of which *Prisoners Exercising* (after a work by Gustave Doré) represents the most pessimistic example: at the bottom of a dark courtyard closed in on all sides by heavy brick walls, a circle of haggard convicts march listlessly in a tight circle as their guards look on.

Vincent's *On the Threshold of Eternity* portrays a seated man, his head in his hands and hunched over in despair. The painting was like the echo of the *Sorrow* of his early years; it closed a long circle of wandering and sufferance which had terminated in his breakdown and confinement.

The situation was paradoxical: if Vincent was protected from the world and its dangers, his prolonged hospitalisation had failed to improve either his mental or physical health.

It became imperative to find a solution. In Paris, Theo discussed the situation with his friend Doctor Gachet, who treated cases similar to Vincent's. It was decided that it would be beneficial for him to move to Auvers-sur-Oise, a small village near Paris where the doctor spent his weekends and could more or less aid in his recovery. In reality, Gachet would be the impotent witness of Vincent's final breakdown during the short period preceding his suicide and death.

Hospital Garden in Arles. *Oskar Reinhart Collection, Winterthur.*
In the spirit of Vincent's "window" scenes, in reference to his confinement in the municipal hospital of Arles. An overall view, in which each detail is expressed with an almost maniacal precision.

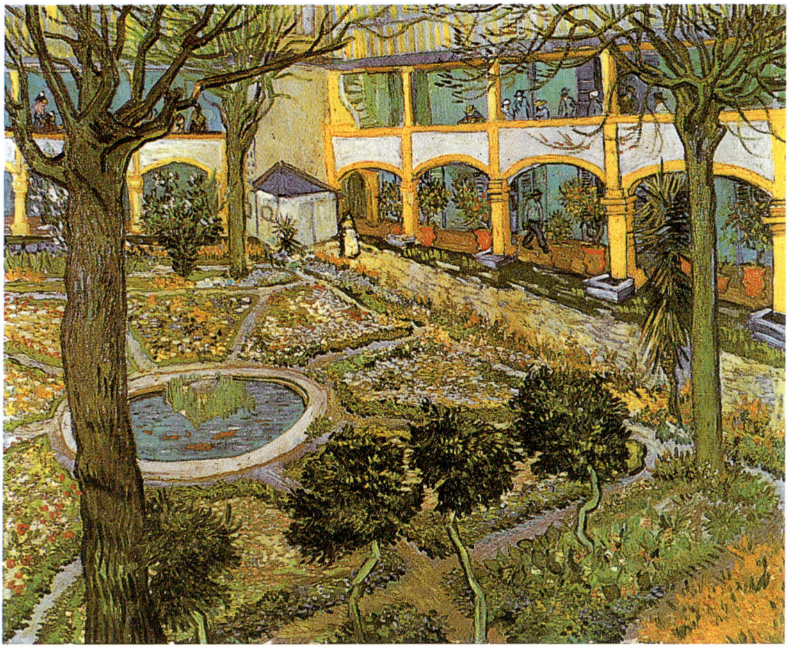

The Saint-Paul Asylum in Saint-Rémy. *Orsay Museum, Paris.*
Although it is not certain that Van Gogh was the author of this work, it portrays his universe and is strongly suggestive of his style, particularly in the representation of the monstrous vitality of the tree whose powerful trunk seems to be seared by an inner flame.

Auvers-sur-Oise

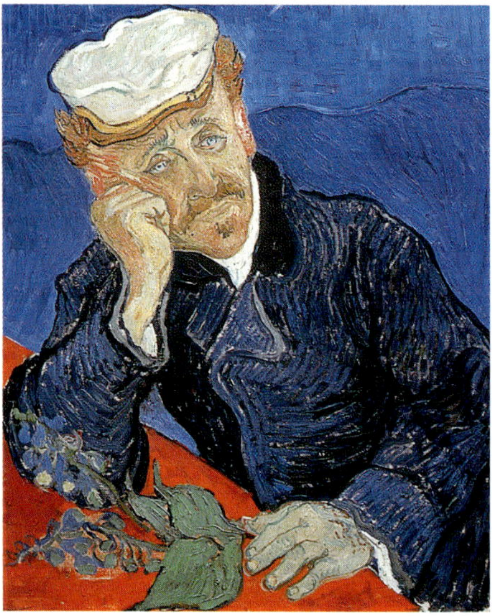

Situated on the banks of the Oise and surrounded by farmlands, Auvers counted slightly more than 1,500 inhabitants in 1887. It is thought that the poet François Villon was born there, for the village is mentioned in one of his poems:

My name is François
I'm pleased to say
My surname, Corbeul
I was born in Auvers,
near Pontoise,
And am also known as
Villon.

Vincent arrived in Auvers on May 21, 1890. After a short stay in a local hotel, he took a garret room

Portrait of Doctor Gachet. *Orsay Museum, Paris.*
Whether by choice or simple habit, Vincent's treatment of Gachet is in the manner of his landscapes, inhabited by a mute inner force and rendered in the characteristically undulating brushwork he usually reserved for inanimate objects.

The Church at Auvers. *Orsay Museum, Paris.*
Permeated with mystery, the enormous and squat bulk of the church is portrayed like a ship at sea, floating upon waves of vegetation which threaten to capsize it.

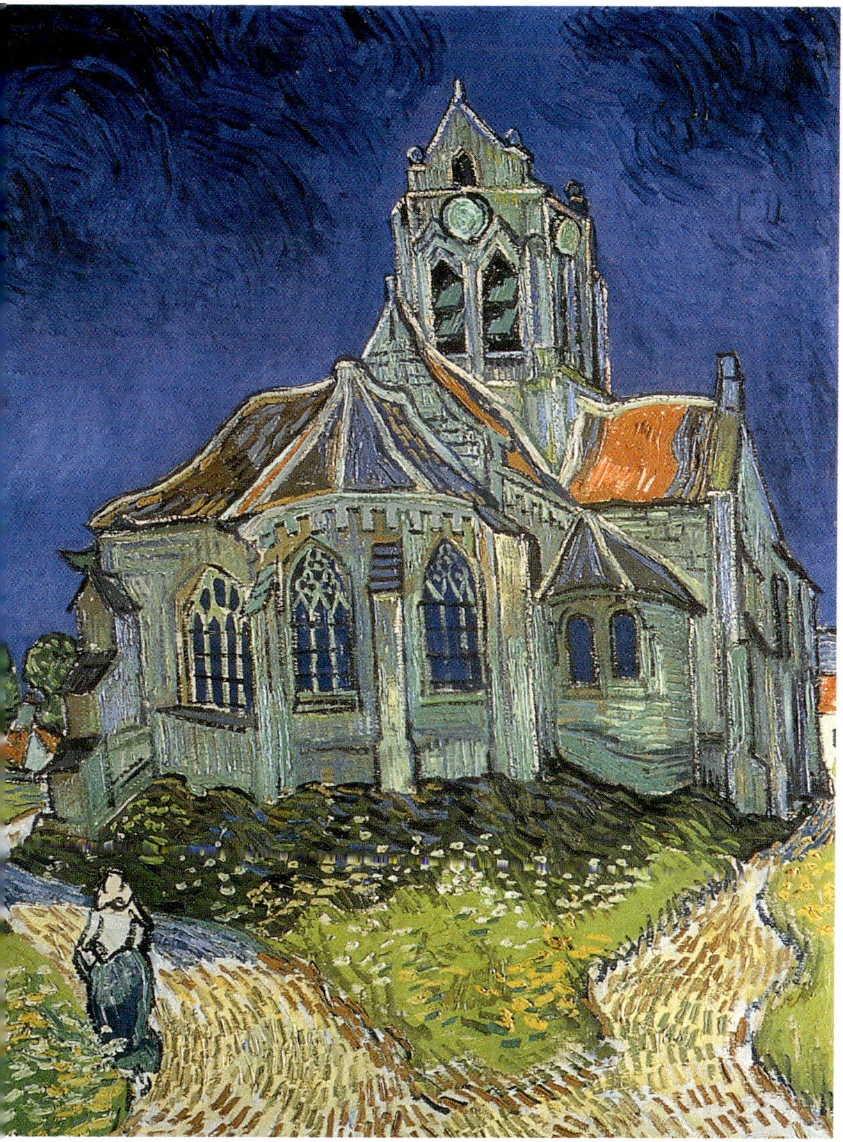

above the Café Ravoux, facing the town-hall.

Both the village and its outlying farmlands enchanted him. The rural atmosphere with its thatched cottages, gently rolling fields and generous horizons perfectly corresponded to his love for nature and panoramic landscapes.

Auvers was reputed for offering a congenial environment for artists. Daubigny had moved there in 1860, Jules Dupré lived in the region, Pissarro inhabited a few kilometres away in Pontoise, and Daumier had resided in the nearby village of Valmondois.

Gachet himself was a central figure in the history of nineteenth century art. An accomplished engraver - Cézanne had studied with him - Vincent would execute his unique *eau-forte* under his supervision.

Although Gachet's practice was in Paris, he spent his weekends in the village, where he possessed a comfortable country house. His home

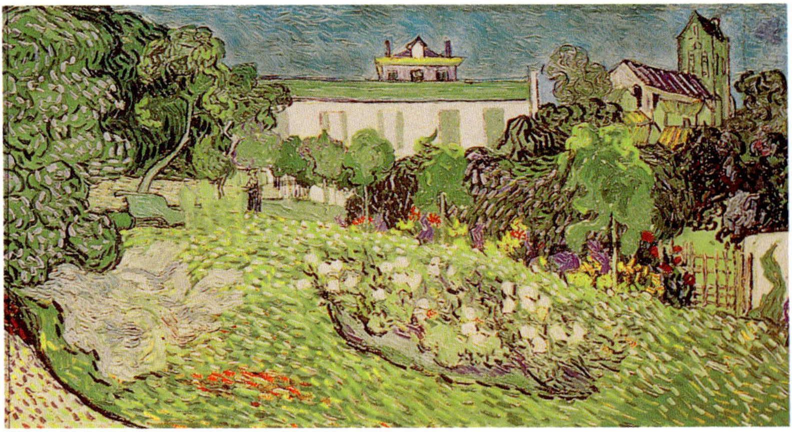

Daubigny's Garden. *Hiroshima Museum of Art, Hiroshima.*
One of Vincent's last and most accomplished works, completed four days before his suicide. As his personal crisis became acute, Vincent liberated all of his talent and energy in an ultimate transfiguration of nature.

had been frequented by many of the leading Impressionists and Cézanne, Pissarro and Guillaumin were among its familiars. Vincent rapidly became part of the family circle and on several occasions, painted the portraits of both Gachet and his daughter.

Vincent's feelings toward Gachet were curiously ambiguous: "I've met Doctor Gachet and my impression is that he's rather eccentric. His activities treating mental illnesses must help him maintain his own stability, but he appears to be as seriously affected as I am."

In a letter to Theo, Vincent also described the interior of Gachet's home: "With the exception of his Impressionist paintings, his house is full of old dark, dark, dark objects. He has a beautiful work by Pissarro - a winter scene with a red house - as well as two floral compositions and a village by Cézanne." This was in fact only a partial description of Gachet's remarkable collection, which included works by Renoir, Monet, Manet, Courbet, Sisley, Guillaumin and Daumier.

Although Vincent's mental and physical condition remained mediocre, his art, which up to then had always been either ignored or dismissed with contempt, finally began to attract the attention and praise of critics. Albert Aurier, a young writer for the influential *Mercure de France* and a standard-bearer of the Symbolist movement, had published the first critical essay on Vincent's work earlier in the year, while six of his works had appeared at the prestigious "XX" Exhibition in Brussels. It was the beginning of the recognition which had always evaded him, the confirmation that his years of effort had not been in vain.

Doctor Gachet, whose attitude as described by Vincent was somewhat off-handed and distant, nevertheless encouraged him to paint. Vincent responded by executing seventy works in the seventy days that preceded his sui-

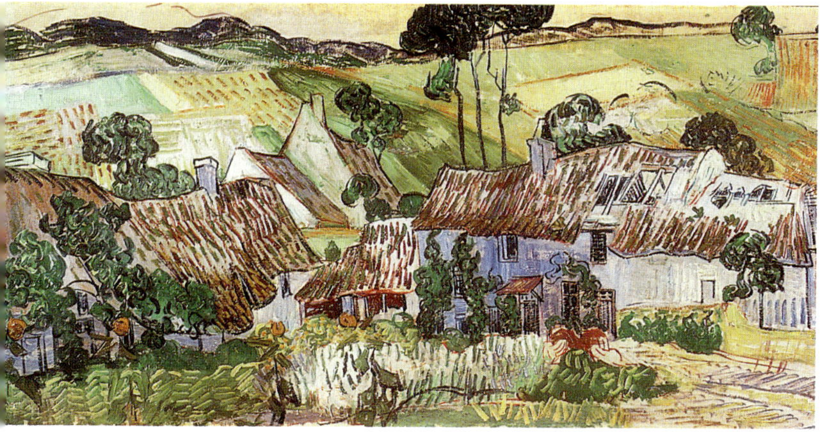

View of Auvers. *Tate Gallery, London. Vincent's long personal and artistic quest began in the Brabant region of his native Holland and ended in Auvers, on the banks of the Oise. His journey could be read in his works, among the last of which is this panorama of the village in which he died.*

cide. To sustain this unrelenting rhythm, he would arise at dawn and spend the day at his easel.

His brushwork became more dynamic than ever, translating his emotions and perceptions into a succession of flowing forms and perspectives, capturing the vital forces of nature, the green intensity of the vegetation, the blue sheen of the rooftops, the brilliant yellow of the gardens and the white fleece of the clouds massed on the vast horizon.

Mademoiselle Gachet at the Piano.
Öffentliche Kunstsammlung, Kunstmuseum, Basil.
The last woman in Vincent's art, but as distant as all the others that preceded her. By her social rank and the context in which she is presented, she could be the subject of a charming painting by Renoir were it not for Vincent's flat, dull colours and stiff treatment of her body, expressing the distance that separated their two very different lives.

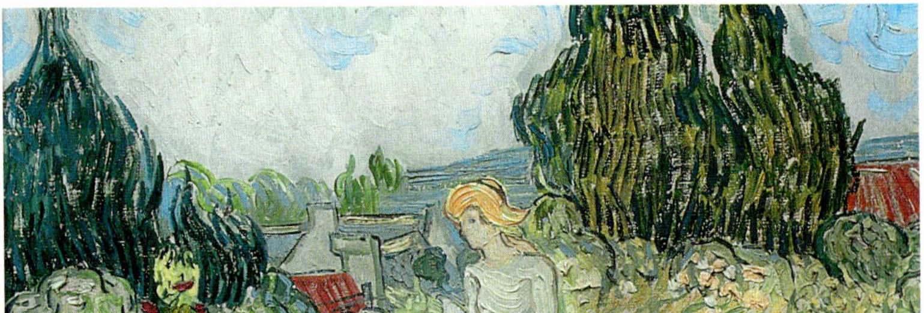

Mademoiselle Gachet in Her Garden.
Orsay Museum, Paris.
Women often appear as elements of added charm in the scenes painted by the Impressionists. But here, Vincent's treatment of Doctor Gachet's daughter is strangely spectral, as if devoured by the exuberant vegetation of her garden.

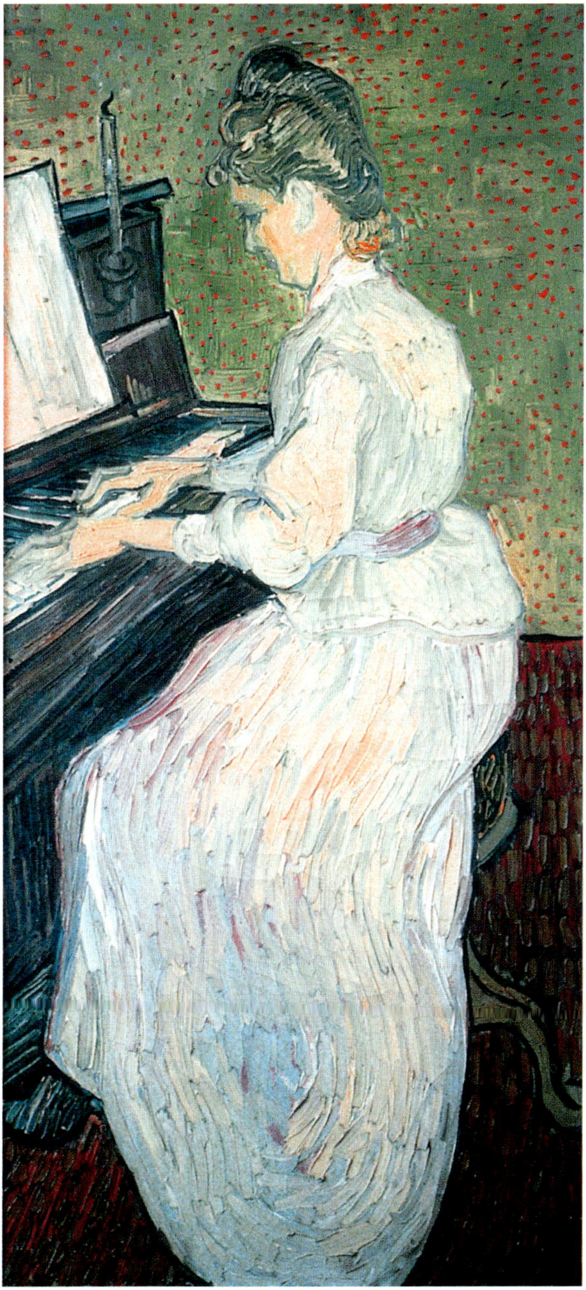

Birds of Evil Omen

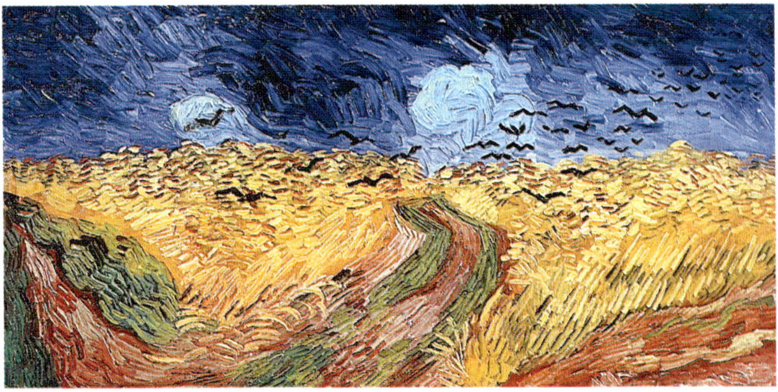

Sundays were spent at Doctor Gachet's, and on several occasions Vincent, Theo, his wife Johanna and the couple's new-born son - Vincent's namesake - were received for lunch. The atmosphere was warm and familial, and the company often included the doctor's daughter, the celebrated "Mademoiselle Gachet" of Vincent's portraits. If he was in love with her, nothing in his attitude suggested it. It is more likely that Vincent was totally beyond such hopes at this point in his life, and that he had displaced the elusive possibility of happiness within the timeless dimension of art.

Vincent often painted the countryside surrounding Auvers, setting up his easel on the edges of the fields. He also haunted the sloping streets of the village, whose church he immortalised in a darkly brooding work. Here, space has been reconfigured to his own personal measure. It was clearly no longer that of his fellow-men, who looked upon him as a half-crazy, talentless imbecile.

Seventy works in as many days: it was as if Vincent had been

Wheat Field with Crows. *Rijksmuseum Vincent Van Gogh, Amsterdam.*
By its panoramic quality, vehemence and determination, the work resumes both Vincent's artistic career and presages his ultimate crisis. The scene reveals all the hidden contradictions of existence of which Vincent was so painfully aware, and which he spent a lifetime attempting to master through his art. Here, the forces of nature and the elements sublimated by the labour of man are menaced - as was Vincent - by chaos and destruction, symbolised by the jagged bat-like forms of the crows wheeling overhead like birds of evil omen.

Fields Under a Stormy Sky. *Rijksmuseum Vincent Van Gogh, Amsterdam.*
The view extends to the far horizon, darkened by a heavy curtain of storm-clouds. Once again, a vision of the immanence of an approaching cataclysm.

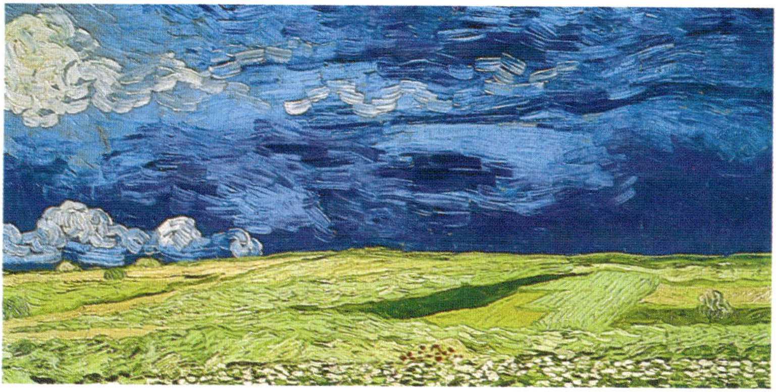

caught up in a race against time. Time indeed had nearly run out: death lay in wait on the edge of a field just beyond the village, but he would use his energies to their utmost before entering its out-stretched arms.

It was on a blazingly hot day in July - one of those Sundays in which Doctor Gachet's family and guests sought shelter from the heat under the great trees of his garden. Doctor Gachet: at once well-meaning and somewhat lost, an art-lover and the artist's friend, but incapable of saving the one artist who had painted his very soul, revealing a distress which was perhaps even greater than his own.

A Sunday in which Vincent's sense of isolation became acute, in a world where people marry, have children and attain their share of happiness, a world whose measure and reason he had forever aban-doned and which he neither wanted nor was able to return.

Even his beloved brother Theo had progressively become distant; for Vincent that Sunday, there remained only the field and its wheeling flocks of coal-black crows. He had painted them as such: dark menacing slashes circling above the golden harvest - a fitting crown for his own tragic genius.

On that Sunday in Auvers, the world was a place in which there was no place left for Vincent. The limits of Theo's love ended where Vincent's deep helplessness began, the space between them now bridged only by his brother's financial support and dutiful fraternal affection. Profoundly bourgeois, Doctor Gachet's preoccupations were situated elsewhere than in the life-and-death struggle of the artist living in his midst. Vincent was merely one of a series of such encounters; in the comfort of his country house, surrounded by his family and paintings, how could he ever have understood such a man?

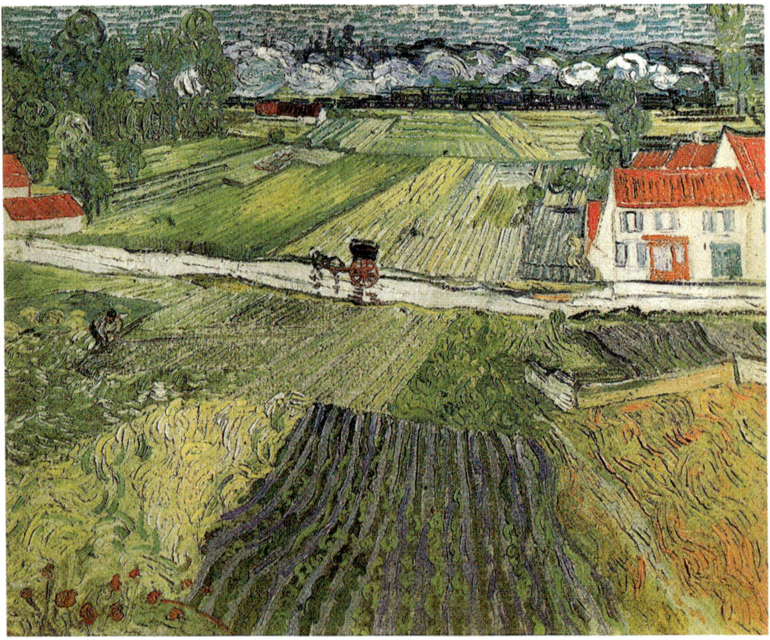

Landscape at Auvers with Cart, Train and Houses. *Pushkin Museum, Moscow.*
The toy-like image of the train on the horizon lends itself to multiple interpretations, ranging from the intrusion of "modernity" within a highly-traditional landscape to the yearning for a return to the simple innocence of childhood.

Auvers Plain Under a Cloudy Sky. *Bayerische Staatsgemäldesammlungen, Neue Pinakothek, Munich.*
Vincent's early works were filled with images of labour - an unconscious metaphor of his own efforts to affirm himself as an artist. Those executed at the end of his life are often splendid homages to the plenitude of nature, testifying to his maturity as an artist and the mastery of his craft.

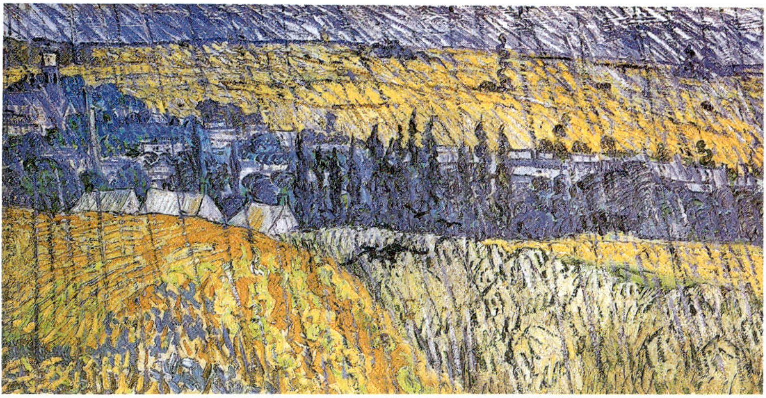

Rain. *National Museum of Wales, Cardiff. The Oriental calm of the landscape is broken by the violence of vertical lines traversing the scene like the slashes of a knife.*

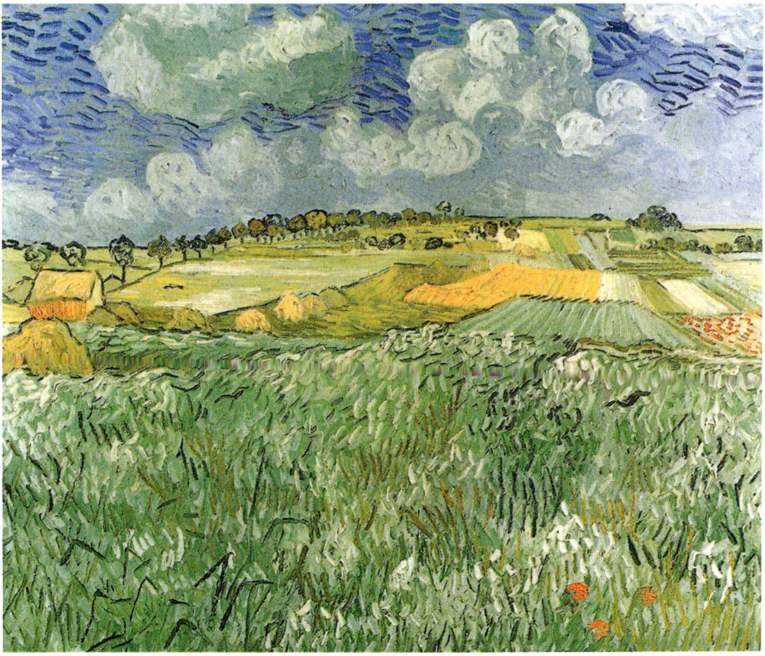

Death in a Garret

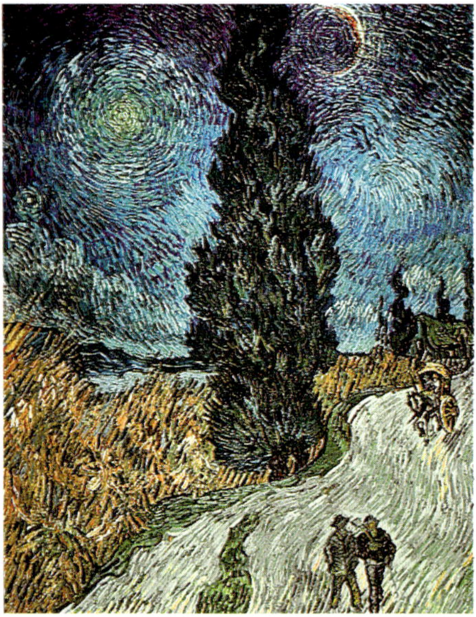

Road with Cypress Tree. *Rijksmuseum Kröller-Müller, Otterlo.*
A luminous energy from the depths of the earth rises through the plants and tree, filling the evening sky with the vibrant beauty of its swirling ascension.

The Sunday lunch of July 27, 1890 was excruciating for Vincent. Murmuring a few hasty words of excuse, he abruptly left Gachet's table. It was the last that anyone would see of him that day.

He stalked off into the wheat fields. The moments passed. A sharp detonation rang out, startling the omnipresent crows. The man with the severed ear had shot himself.

The pistol-shot echoed across the silent fields and was swallowed by the horizon. It is not known whether he cried in desperation or pain: his only witnesses were the birds and the burning sky. Although the shot was not immediately fatal, he fell under its impact and struggled to his feet, making his way back to his garret room. The Ravoux family saw him enter their café doubled over in pain, cross the room and mount the staircase leading to the garret: "Night was falling, and in the semi-darkness only my mother noticed that Monsieur Vincent was holding his stomach and seemed to be limping. His jacket was buttoned. He walked past us like a shadow, without saying hello. My mother said, 'Monsieur Vincent, we were worried about not seeing you today. What's happened?' He

Sunset at the Chateau d'Auvers.
Rijksmuseum Vincent Van Gogh, Amsterdam.
Even the most banal sites were infused with a sense of drama and underlying tension by Vincent's brush. As in his life, his art was frequently charged with intensity and passion.

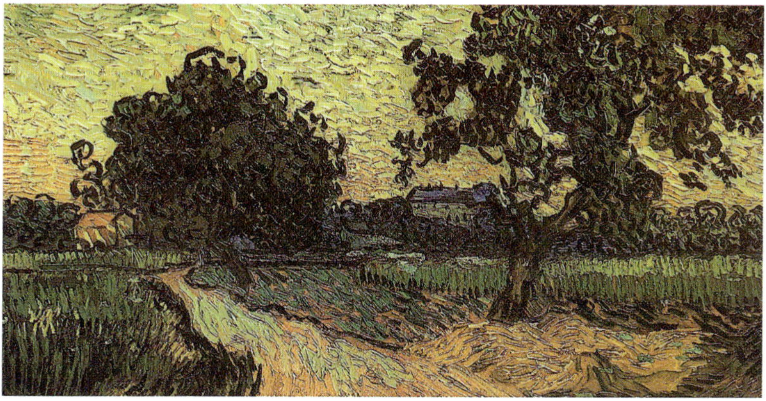

stopped for a moment, leaning against the side of the billiard table to keep his balance and answered in a low voice: 'Oh, nothing. I've hurt myself.' Then he walked up the steps to his little attic room with its white-washed walls and skylight window."

Vincent collapsed upon his bed, his head against the wall. He was discovered later that evening, soaked in blood and moaning. A doctor was summoned, and then Gachet. It was decided that it was useless to operate: Vincent would be left to die.

Theo arrived the next day. In the hours that followed, Vincent lay propped up in his bed calmly smoking his pipe, his eyes staring into space with "an expression of madness." As the end approached he murmured to Theo: "Don't cry, I did this for everyone...". And shortly thereafter, "A lifetime of sadness...".

Vincent Van Gogh died at 1:30 in the morning on July 29, 1890. As the writer Stefan Zweig aptly commented, "only that which was mortal in him disappeared."

The burial took place the next day. The funeral procession included Theo, Dr. Gachet, Charles Laval, Emile Bernard and the faithful old 'Papa' Tanguy. As word spread of Vincent's death, visitors began arriving from Paris, and among the first, Lucien Pissarro and Albert Aurier, the only art critic who had ever had a good word for his work when he was alive.

Vincent's grave still lies in the small cemetery of Auvers-sur-Oise. The headstone that bears his name, half-hidden by ivy, also bears another: that of his brother Theo, who died only six months later. United in death, did each

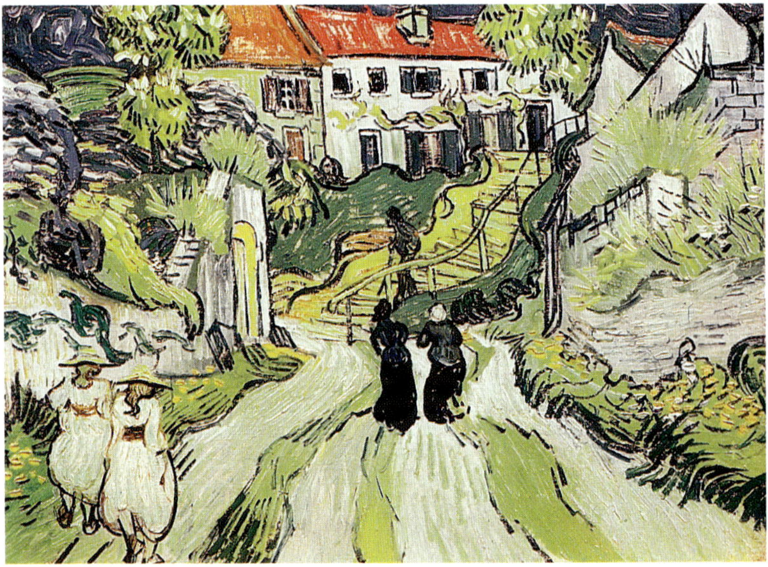

The Steps at Auvers. *The Saint Louis Art Museum, Saint Louis (Missouri).*
Nothing of the village life in Auvers escaped Vincent's regard. Setting up his easel in its streets, he captured the minute details of daily life, infusing the scenes with the haunting quality of a mysterious and parallel universe.

find the peace that was denied them in life? Inseparable protagonists in a tragic drama, each was intimately connected to the destiny of the other.

Beyond the low cemetery wall, the luminous fields still roll to the horizon; above them, the dark crows still circle, as if in homage to sorrow and genius.

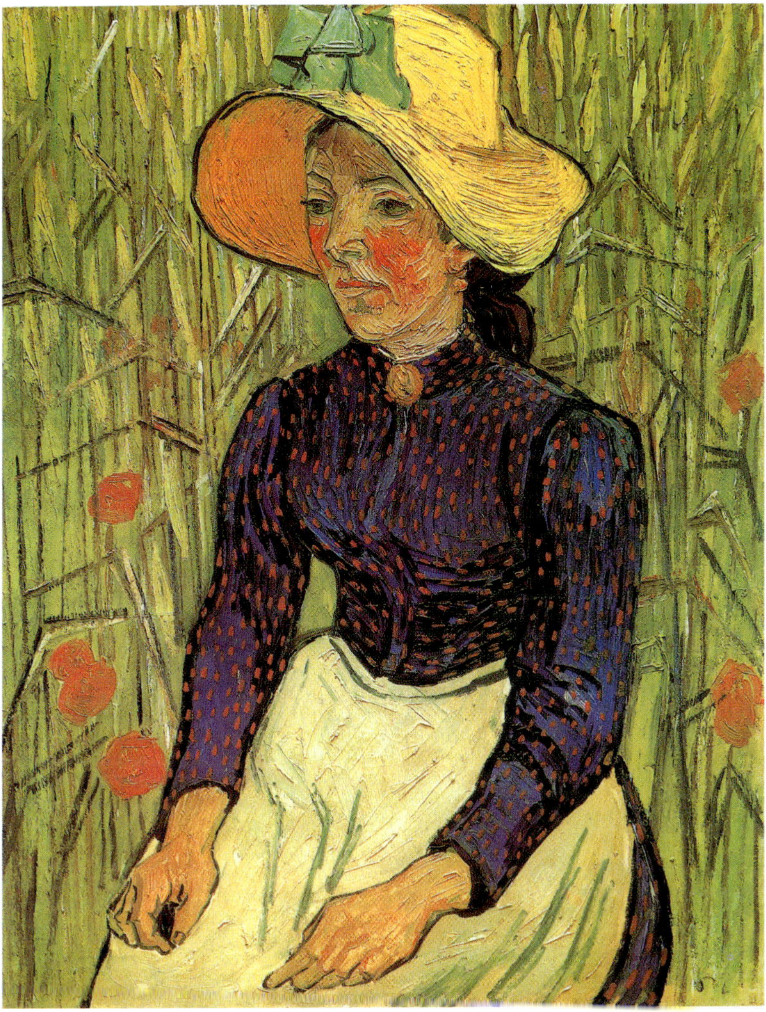

Peasant Girl with Bonnet. *H.R. Hahnloser Collection, Berne.*
Like the statue of a primitive divinity, the rough-featured study is less a representation of womanhood than a reaffirmation of Vincent's roots to the land and its people.

The Voice of the Poet

One can live for the infinite.
- Antonin Artaud

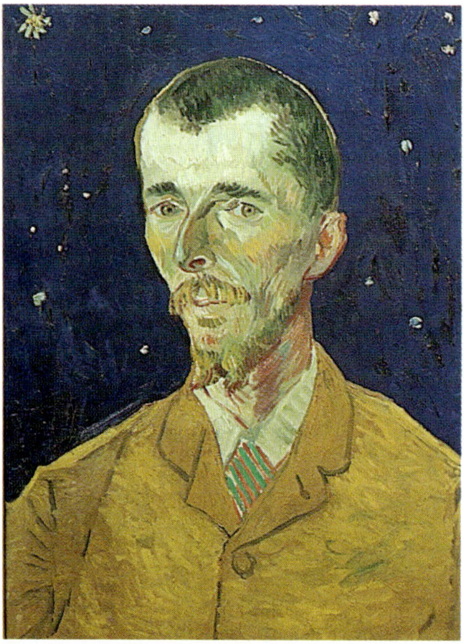

Portrait of Eugene Boch. *Orsay Museum, Paris.*
In this hallucinatory portrait of his friend the poet and painter Boch, the treatment of the visage expresses the anguish of an individual poised on the edge of the dark abysses of existence.

For Artaud, Van Gogh was not mad; it was society that broke his spirit and finally executed him: "Van Gogh's death was not the result of his madness, for he was the living incarnation of a conflict that has beset man's iniquitous mind since his very origins. The conflict is that of the flesh and the spirit, the body and the flesh, and the mind with both of them. And just where, in all this confusion, is there a place for simple human identity?

Van Gogh searched for his identity with uncommon energy and determination all his life, yet his suicide was not an act of madness provoked by the illusion of failure, for he had already succeeded in becoming exactly who and what he really was. It was society, in punishment for what he had accomplished - for having left it behind - that *suicided him.*"

This encounter in 1947 between Van Gogh's existence and the magnificent, unbroken spirit of the poet Artaud was an electrifying event that illuminated the life and work of both artists: that of Van Gogh, deported from society to a no-mans-land of his own solitude, and that of Artaud, emerging from his long confinement in a mental hospital into the morally fractured

Cypress Tree and Two Women.
Rijksmuseum Kröller-Müller, Otterlo.
The vertical thrust of the tree expresses Vincent's Promethian quest for a horizon beyond human sufferance, a journey upon a sacred path.

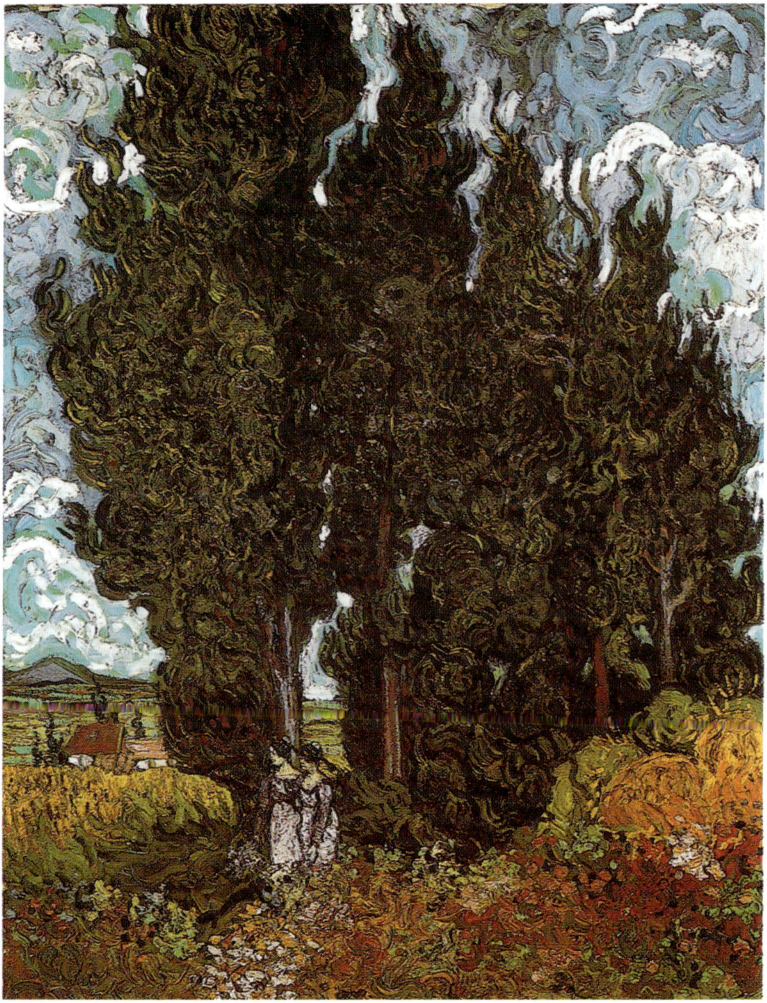

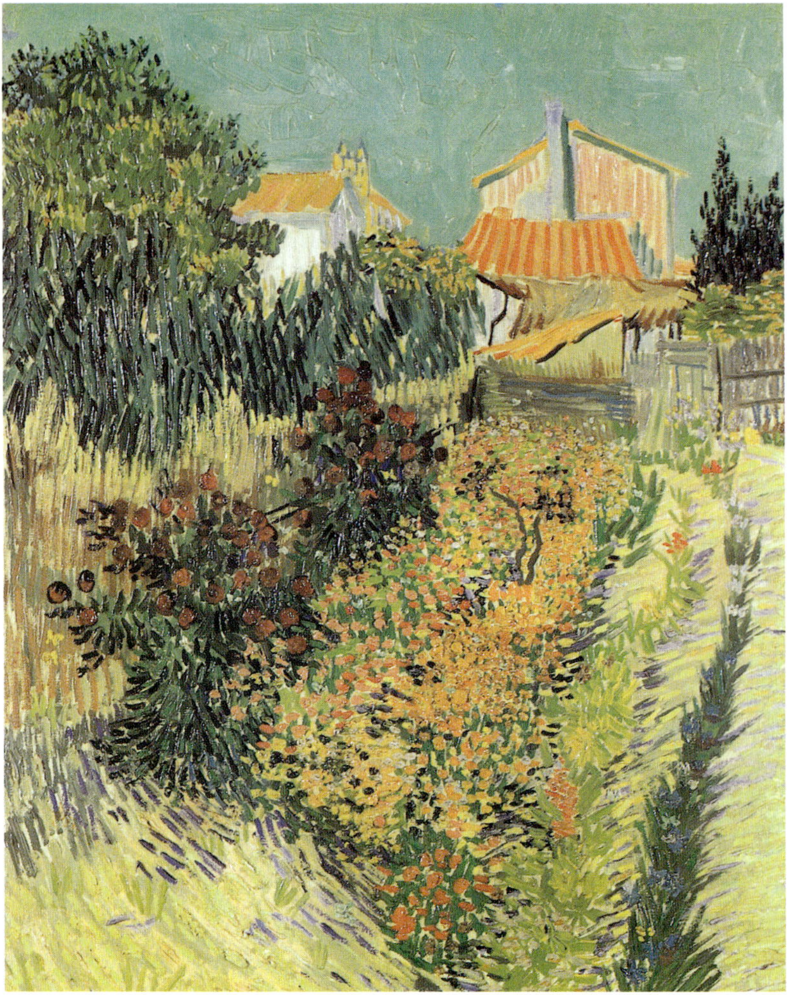

Rear Garden. *Kunstmuseum, Zurich.*
A small plot of land can transform even the most humble homes into a quiet paradise. For Vincent, it was worthy of being treated like the most noble subjects, for it was his painter's eye which saw it as such.

Four Sunflowers. *Rijksmuseum Kröller-Müller, Otterlo.*
More than representing a simple bouquet, Vincent expressed the miracle of nature's renewal and the life-giving forces of the sun, of which these flowers were the flamboyant symbol.

environment of post-war France with the redoubled force of his emotional and querulous intellect. The result could only have been a text such as this, filled with Artaud's indignation at Vincent's suicide and his outraged condemnation of the society that had provoked it.

Doctor Gachet had advised Vincent to "paint from life, to bury himself in the details of a landscape to escape from the pain of

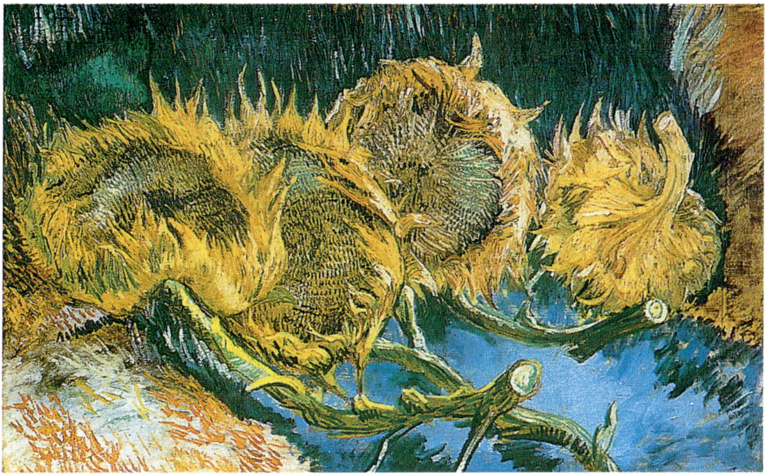

thinking." Following the good doctor's counsel to the letter, he became so absorbed in his work that it became the reflection of his own troubled mental state. Disoriented, he began to lose himself within it, his spirit inebriated by the energy of his frenetic passion. Creation was no longer a voluntary act of free-will, but that of survival itself, practised with an obsession a which contained the lethal seeds of his own destruction.

Considered to be mad by those around him, Vincent nevertheless possessed a remarkable sense of lucidity. But at the very moment his painting began to achieve the universal quality that characterises all great art, his mind began to buckle, wracked by the repeated sorrows of his tragic existence.

He had been born with the guilt of usurping the life of the stillborn brother who preceded him, had been rejected by every woman he had ever loved, and even the faithful Theo had all but abandoned him, sharing an attachment that had formerly been Vincent's alone with a wife and new-born son. In this ultimate abandon, Vincent lost the last hope for understanding and affection that still remained. Redoubling his efforts, he continued to paint, searching in his art all that life had denied him.

"One day Van Gogh's paintings,

with all of the fever and force of their creator, will scatter the dust of the imprisoned world that his heart rebelled against." Artaud's visionary words capture both the immense importance of Van Gogh's art and its future destiny. For Artaud, it was more than a simple question of aesthetics, for the significance of Vincent's art went far beyond the formal dimension of painting. It can be found in his deepest objectives, those which made him an artist beyond all schools and styles, rejected by society because he was unclassifiable, incomprehensible, and ultimately, subversive.

Rather than constituting an impassioned defence of the artist, it is clear from Artaud's words that he found in Van Gogh a kindred spirit, a brother of the soul, for his battle was so much like the poet's own: "Society is responsible for the deaths of Villon, Baudelaire, Nerval, Nietzsche, Poe, Lautréamont and Van Gogh, who no one as yet has really attempted to understand."

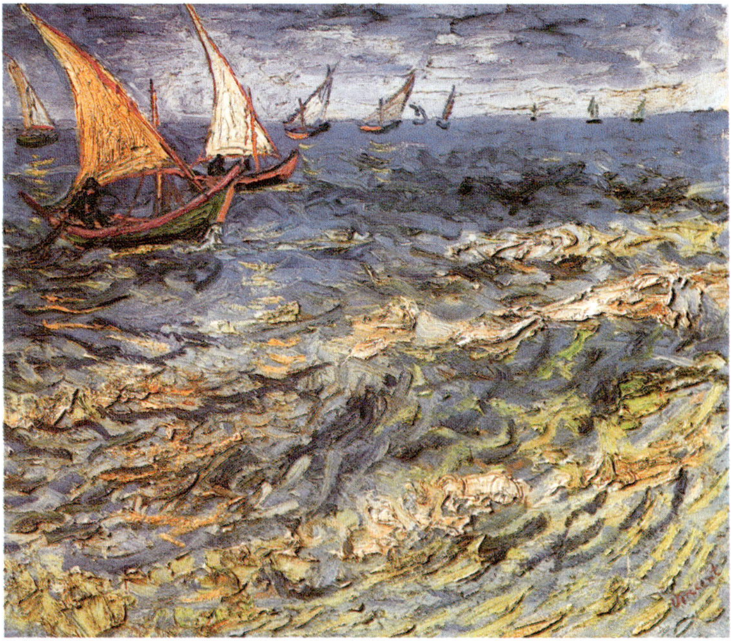

Fishing-Boats at Sea. *Pushkin Museum, Moscow.*
Rarely chosen as a subject by Vincent, the sea was portrayed with the same vehemence as his landscapes, and animated by the obscure forces of nature. A meditation on the eternal abyss.

If for Artaud, Van Gogh is always present, his physical degradation and death are described with a poet's vision and reiterated like a reproach: "...he is sinister, shocking, mournful: an old tired man with a mauve-coloured beard, who one summer's day will commit suicide by shooting himself in the stomach."

Artaud's loyalties are to the citizens of that "higher nation" of art, justice and spirituality invoked by Novalis. Within this context, one could say that Vincent's confinement in the asylum at Saint-Rémy at the same moment that Nietzsche succumbed to madness in the streets of Turin signifies a rite of passage into the citizenship of that nation whose visionary members are most often considered by society to be insane.

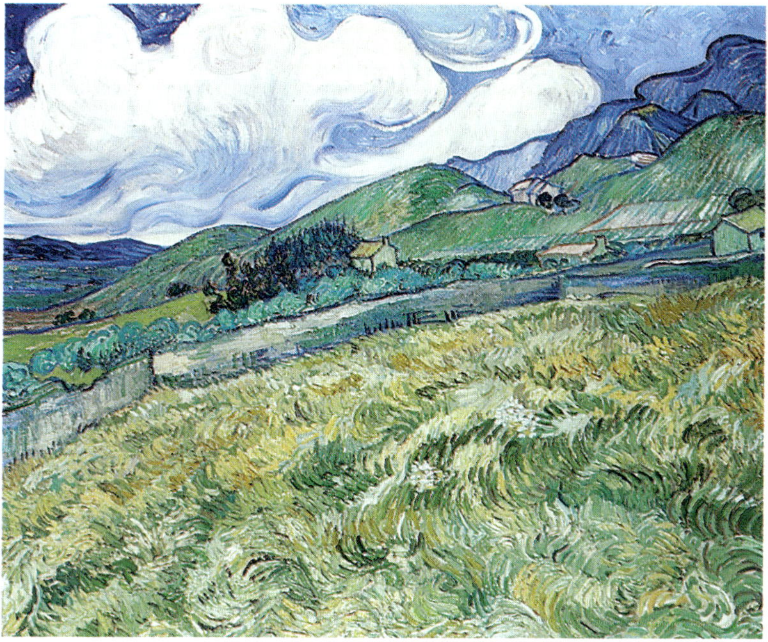

Mountainous Landscape. *Ny Carlsberg Glyptothek, Copenhagen.*
A serenely harmonious panorama of mountains, earth and sky. The presence of man, symbolised by the tiny houses scattered on the hills, is dwarfed by the immensity of nature. Above the undulating line of the horizon, a vaguely anthropomorphic cloud seems to be extending its arms over the landscape in a gesture of silent benediction.

The Autopsy of an Artist

By its innovation, creation and destructivness, refusal of accepted dogma and challenge to established order, authentic art is always visionary and ahead of its time. In its definitive break with the past and relentless exploration of new possibilities, art - like all progress - is based on the refusal of the present.

The originality of Van Gogh was that the modernity of his art - beyond the strictly representational sense of the word - was in the radical transformation of the objectives and functions of art itself.

The Impressionists had changed the manner of painting rather than its essence; Van Gogh's art introduced the radically new elements of passion and personal signification.

His advance was less a question of style or technique than his manner of communicating the reality of his own feelings, the intensity of his own experience and perceptions.

His modernity was born of an imperative need to communicate his vision of reality in a manner other than that of the empty formalism of the Academy, whose aesthetic conventions rendered the representations of such reality impossible.

He rejected the aesthetic of the Academy because he deemed it artificial and its works hollow and devoid of real meaning. His desire was to express with passion and generosity a vision of existence charged with such charity and compassion as to situate it within a dimension more religious than aesthetic: for Vincent, art was the means of expressing truths which lay beyond superficial appearance. By opening the way to a spiritual rebirth in which all hypocrisy and egoism was absent, his art was - in the true sense of the word - religious in its quest for the absolute.

His entire life was a striving toward an idealisation of the human condition. As an aspiring evangelist, he practised the charity and compassion of the Gospels with a sincerity that disconcerted his superiors. Judged as unfit for the calling he so fervently desired, he was rejected from their midst.

Van Gogh never compromised with the world, but confronted it head-on, fuelled by a higher ideal. Indeed, there was something of Saint Francis of Assisi in him; for those who had perceived this quality, he was simply "Mister Vincent." As an artist, he would sign his paintings this way, using only his first name, as if in memory of their heartfelt and respectful homage.

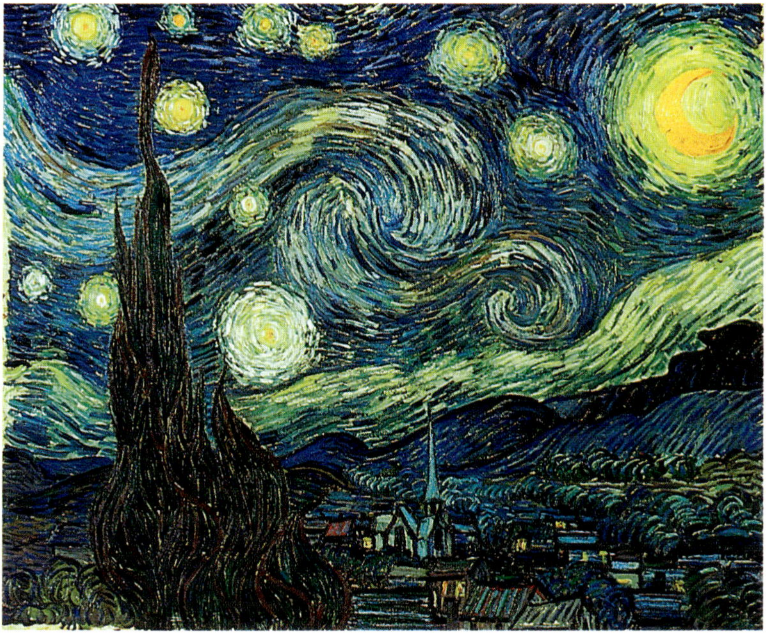

The Starry Night. *Museum of Modern Art, New York.*
One of the most spectacular works of Vincent's Arles period. An hallucinating vision of supernatural intensity.

A Voyage to the End of the Night

For a person who all of his adult life would never enjoy the stability of a permanent home, families had a great effect on Vincent, beginning with the one where he was born. Growing up in a home filled with heavy Dutch Calvinist piety imbued Vincent with a life-long quest for a luminous transcendence which he equated with deliverance.

Vincent once exclaimed, "Why should the stars in the heavens be less accessible to us than the points on a map?"

Much of his work reveals this same impossible yearning. It was more realistic than may appear at first sight, for Vincent was not referring to a physical journey but of the transcendence of all which - beginning with his ungainly body - weighed him down to earth. The quest was channelled into his manner of painting, into which he poured his desire for a space with was no longer that of our world.

Psychologically, Vincent was a child of darkness sprung from the first, primitive ages of man, issued from his mother's womb as from a cave, into an environment of empty piety, a world of pain and misery.

He was a child of the dark fields and heavy cloud-filled skies of Holland, whose horizons were as restricting as the prison of his own graceless body, a stranger to the gratuitous pleasures of childhood. Of his early years, little is known; it as if they had been covered by a veil, as if from the very beginning Vincent had been condemned to live apart, excluded from the world yet burning to understand it, observing its mysteries from the lonely outpost of his acute solitude, and all the while dreaming the outcast's dream of possessing "wings to soar above life."

To have chosen art implied the possibility of transcendence, the leaving-behind of the isolated and disoriented being that he had become. Like a monk entering the service of his order, he would progressively divest himself of his attachment to the material world, beginning with the limits of his own body, which he would strain against and ultimately demolish. The exalted dreams of the child became those of the adult; in the end, it was society that broke them, and with them, his spirit.

The grandeur of his ideals demanded that he constantly surpass himself, and in so doing, abandon the constraints of this world to attain another, more perfect world of the Divine.

Self-Portrait. *Rijksmuseum Vincent Van Gogh, Amsterdam.*
Vincent was haunted by the duality of the flesh and the spirit. In his life as in his art, he strove to transcend their limits in a quest for the clear flame of spirituality in which all contradictions are consumed, and man's original wholeness revealed.

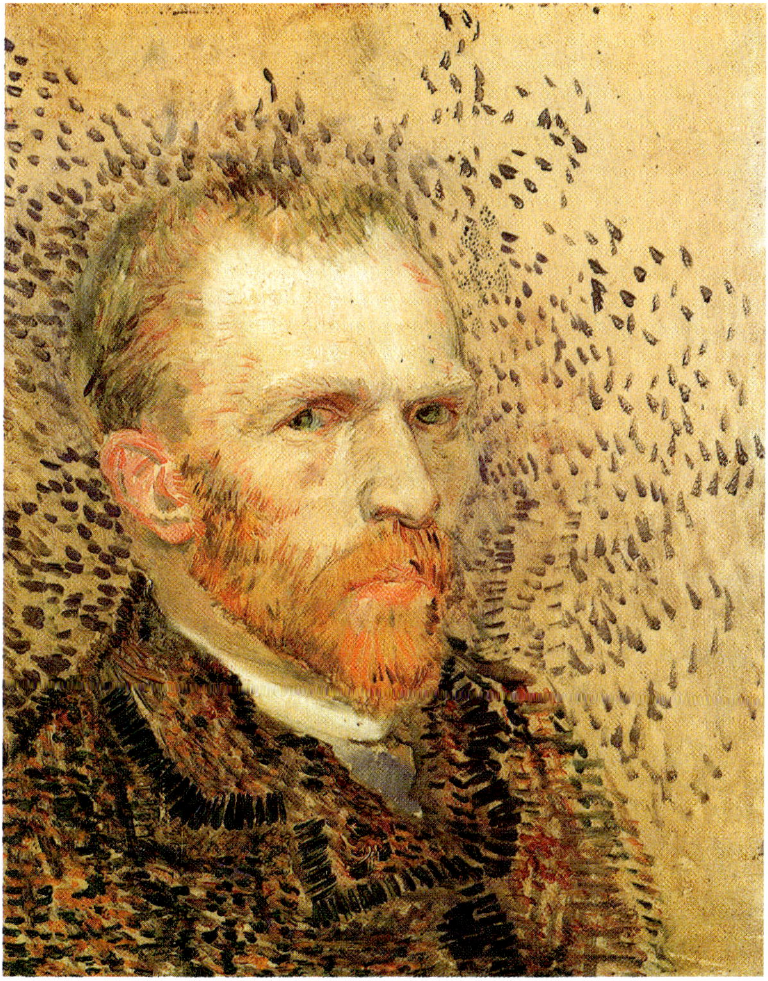

For Vincent, the world of man lacked the spirituality that had so impressed him in his studies of the Bible, for it offered no viable solutions to the misery and sufferance he saw all around him. Rather than an ethereal deity of idealised images and pious prayers, Vincent worshipped a living God of universal love and brotherhood, whose glory he first attempted to express through an absolute devotion to his fellow-man, and later, through his art. The representation of misery, so prevalent in his early paintings, would progressively give way to works charged with the dignity and simple beauty of the common people who were so often Vincent's subjects, and

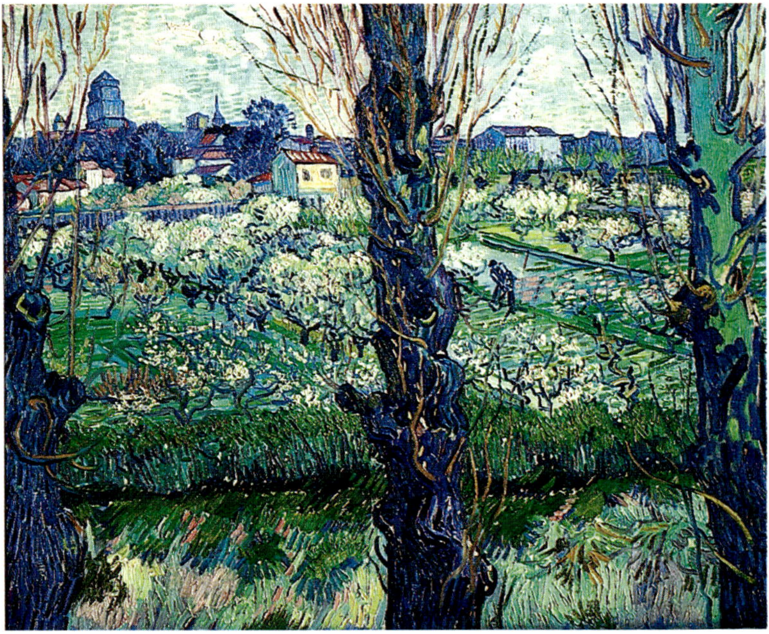

View of Arles. *Bayerische Staatsgemäldesammlungen, Neue Pinakothek, Munich.*
Vincent frequently painted Arles and its surroundings. Here, he expresses their objective reality with all the mastery of his sense of perspective and line. The palette is expressly subdued, as if to render the colours of the Provençal spring in all their delicate and elusive subtlety.

which, through the alchemy of his intense self-identification, would become his own qualities.

The failure of his last ideal of an artists' cooperative united around the Studio of the Midi was his ultimate disillusion and perhaps the most serious, for he had desired its success with all of his heart.

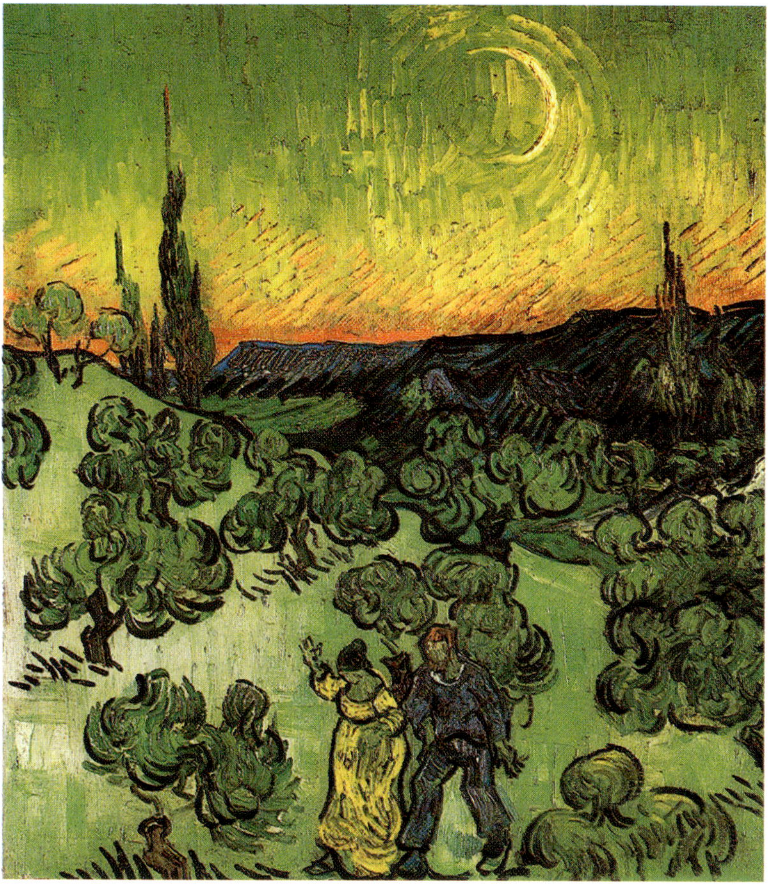

He was able to surmount his experiences of unrequited love by the substitution of prostitutes for the unattainable women in his life; his alienation from society was an incessant yet tolerable source of pain, but the failure of so many of his personal ideals was fatal.

The asylum of Saint-Rémy was the last step before his tragic appointment with destiny in Auvers-sur-Oise, where the collective weight of all these failures and an unfavourable psychological envi-

Evening Promenade. *Museu de Arte, San Paulo (Brazil).*
A work filled with the earthy nocturnal perfume of the Midi. A dream-like vision of an ephemeral moment.

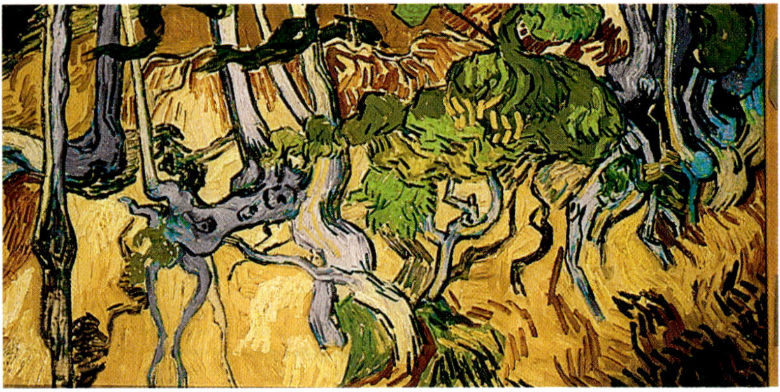

Undergrowth. *Rijksmuseum Vincent Van Gogh, Amsterdam.*
By its reduction of forms to a rhythmic pattern of volume and line, the work prefigures abstract art and reflects an Oriental vision of the complexity of nature reduced to the simplicity of its basic elements.

Pollarded Willow. *Stavros S. Niarchos Collection.*
A tangential perspective cuts across the canvas, suggestive of an escape toward an invisible horizon and the promise of a new life.

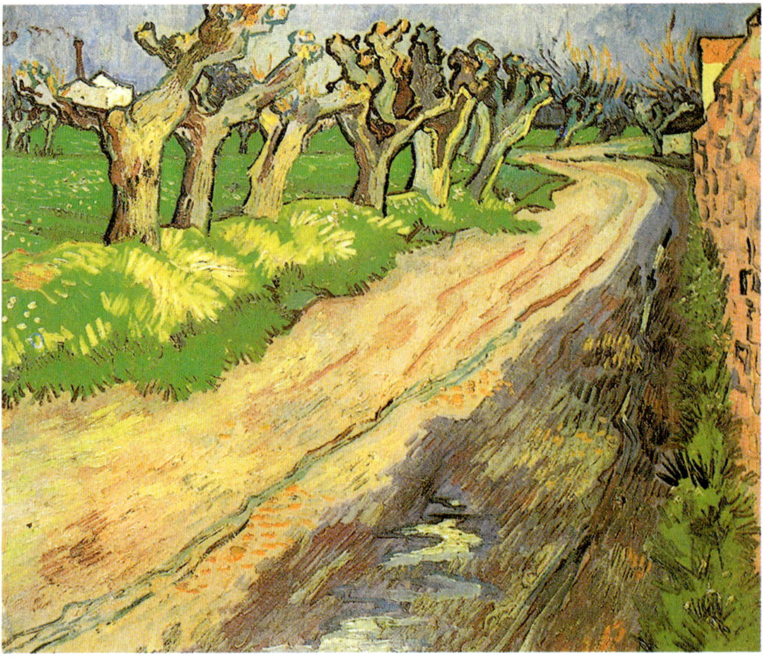

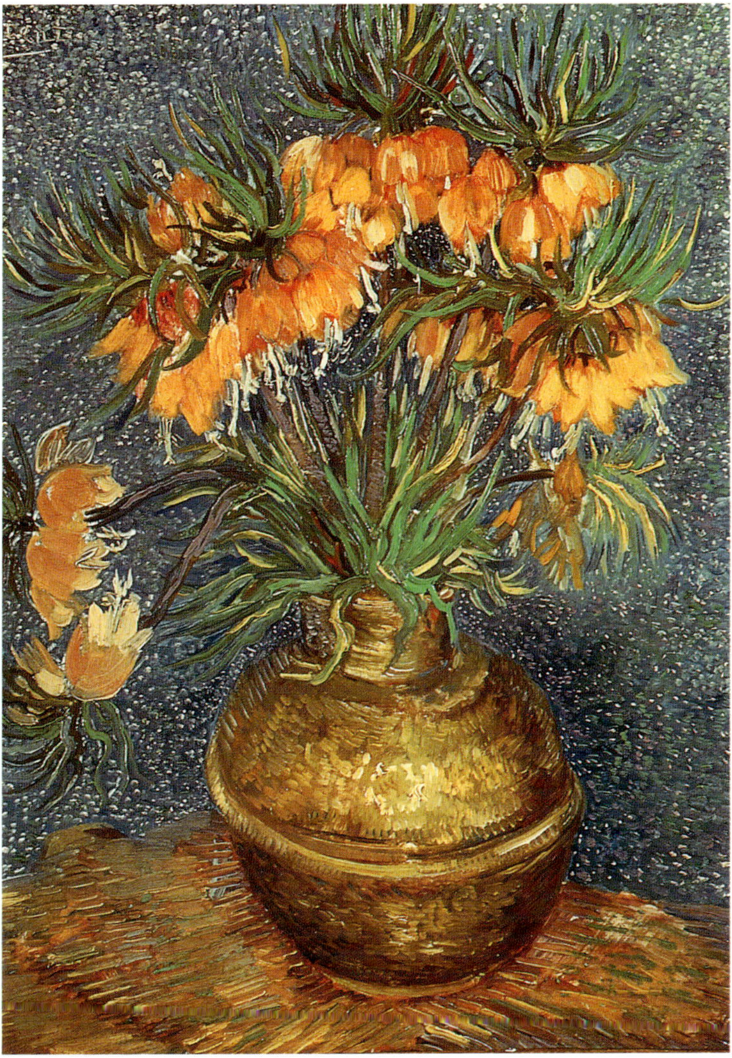

ronment would make his death ineluctable.

Abandoned to himself, he would meet it head-on, turning his face to the July sun as if performing the ritual sacrifice of an ancient religion.

Fritillary Plant in a Copper Vase. *Orsay Museum, Paris.*
One of Vincent's numerous floral studies. More than traditional figurative exercises, their exuberance is expressed within the context of conventional realism.

The Itinerary of an Artist

Zundert (Holland): Van Gogh's father Theodorus, a Calvinist Pastor, moved here on April 1, 1849. Vincent is born on March 30, 1853.
Sevenbergen: Vincent is a live-in student at the Jean Provily school from 1864-65.
Tilburg: Vincent continues his studies at the Hannick Institute, 57 Korvel Street, from 1866-68.
The Hague: In 1869, Vincent is employed by the Goupil art merchants, 14 de la Place. He takes room and board with the Roos family, 32 Marché des Bêtes.
Brussels: Vincent is employed at the Brussels branch of Goupil in 1873.
London: Vincent, sent to London by Goupil in 1873, lives in a boarding-house run by the Loyer family and then with his sister in Kensington New Road.
Paris: Temporarily posted in 1874 to Goupil's headquarters in rue Chaptal, Vincent inhabits the quarter of Montmartre.
Ramsgate: After resigning from Goupil in 1876, Vincent moves to Britain and works as a teacher's assistant at the Strokes School in Ramsgate.
Isleworth: In July 1876, Vincent obtains a post as assistant preacher in a Methodist seminary headed by T. Slade Jones.
Etten (Holland): Return to his family's home in December, 1876.
Dordrecht: From January to April 1877, Vincent is employed at the Blussé and Van Braam bookshop. He lodges with the Rijken family, rue du Pont au Péage.
Amsterdam: Vincent studies for the entry examination to the Faculty of Theology; he lives with his uncle Johannes. (1877-78).
Brussels: Vincent prepares for admission to the Evangelical School; Place Sainte-Catherine and Laeken-les-Bruxelles, 1878.
Borinage: Vincent moves to the Borinage, a coal-mining region in Belgium. He boards with the Van der Haegan family, 39 rue de l'Église in Pâturges, and successively in Warquignies, Wasmes and Cuesmes in 1878 and boards with Jean-Baptiste Denis, rue du Petit Wasmes in 1879.
Brussels: In 1880, Vincent moves to Brussels to study drawing and anatomy; lives at 72 Boulevard du Midi.
The Hague: Sojourn with the painter Anton Mauve, his paternal uncle, in 1881. Lives at 138 Schenkweg.
The Drenth: Vincent moves to the provinces of Holland in 1883, boarding with the Hartsuiker family in Hoogeven and Hendrick Scholte in Nieuw-Amsterdam.
Nuenen: Returns to his father's Presbytery in 1883.
Antwerp: Inhabits 194 Longue-rue-des-Images from 1885-86.
Paris: Vincent inhabited 25 rue de Laval (today rue Victor-Massé) in March 1886 and 54 rue Lepic in June of the same year. From 1886-88, his haunts (cafés, cabarets, theatres and artists' studios) included Le Cabaret du Chat Noir, 12 rue de Laval; Café Guerbois, 9 avenue de Clichy; Le Pére Lathuille, 7 avenue de Clichy; Le Moulin de la Galette, 79 rue Lepic; Le Café des Arts, 33 rue de Clichy; Le Tambourin, 62 boulevard de Clichy; l'Atelier Cormon, 104 boulevard de Clichy; l'Elysée-Montmartre, 80 boulevard Rochechouart; Le Mirliton, 84 boulevard Rochechouart, La Revue Indépendante, 79 rue Blanche; Le Théâtre Libre, 96 rue Blanche, Bing, articles de Chine, 19 rue Chauchat; Tanguy, 14 rue Clauzel; Toulouse-Lautrec, 19-21 rue Fontaine; Anquetin, 86 avenue de Clichy; Signac, 20 avenue de Clichy and l'Atelier Signac, 130 boulevard de Clichy.
Arles: Arriving in February 1888, Vincent first inhabited the Carrel Hotel, 30 rue Cavalerie and after May of the same year, La Maison Jaune (the Yellow House), 2 place Lamartine. Enters the municipal hospital (l'Hôtel-Dieu) in 1889.
Saint-Rémy-de-Province: Vincent interned in the asylum of Saint-Paul-de-Mausole from 1889-90.
Auvers-sur-Oise: Vincent lives at the Auberge Ravoux, in front of the Auvers town-hall. After an attempted suicide in the afternoon of July 27, he dies in his attic room on July 29, 1890.

Cité Pigalle. *Vincent lived there his last Parisian days.*

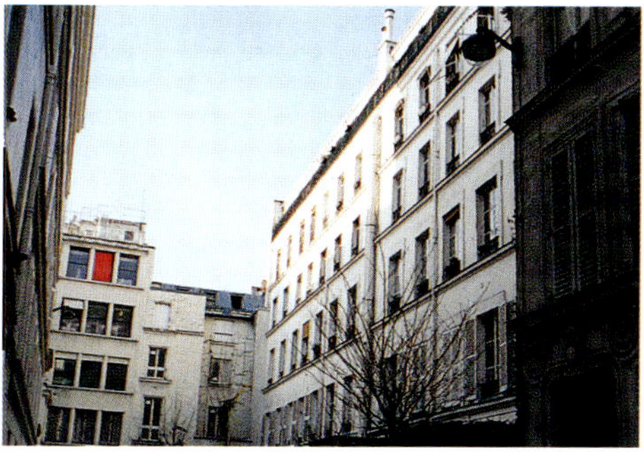

During his stay in Paris, Van Gogh lived with his brother Théo at 54 rue Lepic

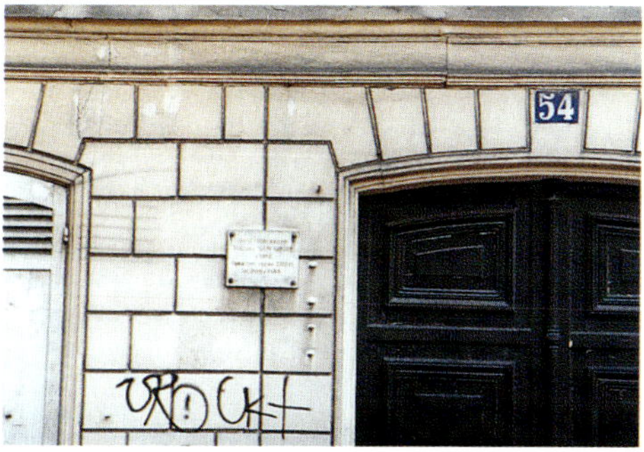

Lower right: "Papa" Tanguy's home, rue Clauzel.

43 cité Pigalle.

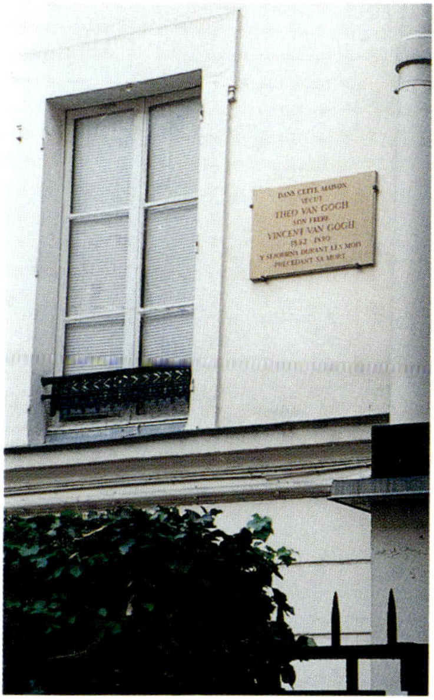

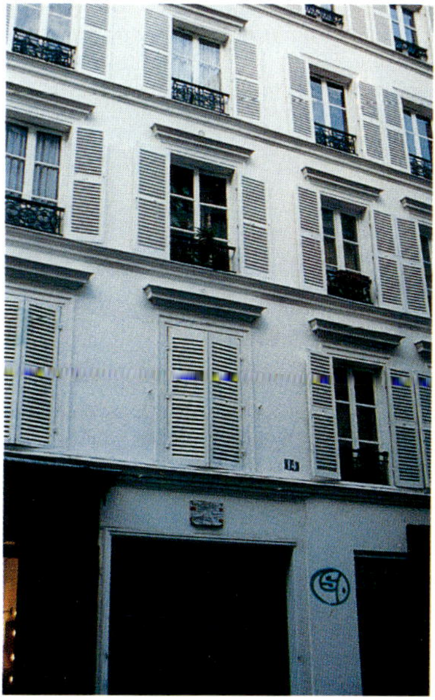

A Comparative Chronology

1853: Birth of Vincent Willem Van Gogh in Groot Zundert (in the Brabant, a northern region of Holland), the eldest child in a family that would include five other brothers and sisters. His father Theodorus, was a Calvinist pastor; three of his paternal uncles were art merchants. Anna Cornelia Carbentus, his mother, was the daughter of a book-binder at the Royal Court of The Hague.
Courbet: *Les Baigneuses*; Millet: *Le Repas des moissonneurs*; Meryon: *L'Arche du pont Notre-Dame*; Gavarni: *Masques et visages.*
Victor Hugo: *Les Châtiments*; George Sand: *Les Maîtres sonneurs*; Renan: *Vie de Jésus*; Charlotte Brontë: *Villette.*
1857: Birth of Theodorus (Theo) Van Gogh, who would provide moral and financial support for Vincent until the latter's death. Vincent's life-long correspondence with Theo remains a touching and unique literary monument.
Courbet: *Les Demoiselles de la Seine*; Millet: *Les Glaneuses*; Daubigny: *Le Printemps.*
Baudelaire: *Les Fleurs du Mal*; Banville: *Odes funambulesques*; Flaubert: *Madame Bovary*; Champfleury: *Le Réalisme.*
1864: Vincent attends the Jean Provilly School in Zevenbergen.
Fantin-Latour: *Hommage à Delacroix*; Corot: *Souvenir de Mortfontaine*; Millet: *Bergère et son troupeau.*
Zola: *Contes à Ninon*; Goncourt: *Renée Mauperin*; Michelet: *La Bible de la Humanité*; Fustel de Coulonges: *La Cité antique*; Erckmann-Chatrain: *L'Ami Fritz*; Labiche: *La Cagnotte.*
1866: Vincent attends the Hannick Institute in Tilburg, 57 rue Korvel.
Courbet: *Le Sommeil*; Manet: *Le Fifre*; Bazille: *Réunion de Famille*; Renoir: *Le Cabaret de la mère Antony.*
Verlaine: *Poème saturniens*; Hugo: *Les Travailleurs de la mer*; Goncourt: *Manette Salomon*; Henri Monnier: *Paris et la province.*
1869: Vincent begins his apprenticeship as a clerk at the Goupil gallery in The Hague. Becomes an enthusiastic reader of contemporary authors such as Daudet and Zola, whose works he frequently cites in his letters to Theo.
Carpeaux: *La Dance* (statues created for the Paris Opera House); Puvis de Chavannes: ornamentation for the municipal museum of Marseille; Monet and Renoir: *La Grenouillère*; Cézanne: *La Pendule en marbre noir*; Manet: *Le Balcon.*
Verlaine: *Fêtes galantes*; Flaubert: *L'Éducation sentimentale*; François Coppée: *Le Passant*; Lautréamont: *Les Chants de Maldoror.*
1873: Brief sojourn in Paris; posted to London by Goupil, where he boards with the Loyer family and falls in love with their daughter Ursula.
Manet: *Le Bon Bock*; Cézanne: *La Maison du pendu*; Berthe Morisot: *Le Berceau.*
Rimbaud: *Une Saison en enfer*; Zola: *Le Ventre de Paris*; Daudet: *Les Contes du Lundi*; Corbière: *Les Amours jaunes*; Jean Richepin: *La Chanson des gueux.*

1874: Clash with Ursula Loyer. Vincent moves in with his sister on Kensington New Road in Ivy Cottage. Returns to Paris in October, departs again for London.
The first Impressionist exhibition is organised by Nadar.
Carpeaux: *Les Quatre Parties du Monde*; Frémiet: *Jeanne d'Arc*; Pissarro: *Gelée blanche*; Manet: *En bateau.*
Barbey d'Aurevilly: *Les Diaboliques*; Verlaine: *Romances sans paroles*; Hugo: *Quatre-vingt-treize.*
1875: Posted to the Paris branch of the Goupil gallery, rue Chaptal. Reads the Bible assiduously.
Auction of Impressionist paintings organised by Drout yields disastrous prices.
Bartholdi: casts the *Lion de Belfort* and *The Statue of Liberty* of New York; J.P. Laurens: *L'Excommunication de Robert le Pieux*; De Nittis: *La Place de la Concorde après la pluie*; Menzel: *Paysage industriel*; Burne-Jones: *L'Histoire de Persée.*
Rimbaud: *Les Illuminations*; Zola: *La Faute de l'abbé Mouret.*
1876: Vincent resigns from Goupil and leaves for Etten. Arrives in Ramsgate in April and obtains a position in a small school headed by the Reverend William Port Strokes. The establishment relocated to the London suburb of Islesworth, where in July Vincent was appointed assistant preacher in a new school run by the Methodist minister T. Slade Jones. His health failing, he returned to Etten for Christmas.
Second Impressionist exhibition organised by Durand-Ruel.
Gustave Moreau: *Salomé*; Renoir: *Le Moulin de la Galette*; Degas: *l'Absinthe*; Clarin: *Portrait de Sarah Bernhardt.*
Mallarmé: *L'après-midi d'un faune*; Renan: *La Prière sur l'Acropole*; Duranty: *La Nouvelle Peinture.*
1877: Vincent is employed at the Blussé and Van Braam bookshop in Dordrecht. Moves to Amsterdam and lives with his uncle Johannes; prepares for entry into the Faculty of Theology.
Third Impressionist exhibition, 6 rue Le Peletier. La Nouvelle Athenès, an artist's café, becomes the meeting-place for the Parisian avant-garde.
Rodin: *L'Age d'airain*; Fantin-Latour: *La Lecture*; Degas: *Aux Ambassadeurs*; Monet: *La Gare Saint-Lazare*; Jules Breton: *La Glaneuse*; Bouguereau: *La Vierge consolatrice.*
Zola: *L'Assommoir*; Mallarmé: *Tombeau d'Edgar Allen Poe*; Flaubert: *Trois Contes*; Daudet: *Le Nabab.*
1878: Vincent leaves Amsterdam in July. Moves to Brussels and enters an Evangelist mission headed by Bokma; dismissed after three months of service in Laeken-lès-Bruxelles. Moves to the Borinage in the Hainaut mining region of Belgium and settles at Pâturages. On the basis of his earlier studies of the Bible, begins to Evangelise the poor
Paris World's Fair. Sale of the Faure and Hoschedé art collections financially disappointing results. Puvis de Chavannes paints the frescoes of the Paris Pantheon.
Gevex: *Rolla*; Bastien-Lepage: *Les Foins*; Manet: *La Serveuse de bocks*; Monet: *L'Église de Vètheuil*; L.O. Merson: *Le Loup de Gubbio*; Whistler: *La Chambre aux Paons.*
Zola moves to Médan. Rimbaud arrives in Cyprus.
Théodore Duret: *Les Peintres Impressionnistes*; Nieztszche: *Man and Superman.*
1879: Vincent is sent to Wasmes as a lay-evangelist. He is dismissed after six months because of his excess of zeal. Moves to Cuesmes in the Borinage.
Fourth Impressionist exhibition, 28 avenue de l'Opera in Paris.
Dalou begins *Le Triomphe de la République*; Bouguereau: *La Naissance de Vénus*; Cézanne: *Le Pont de Maincy*; Redon: *Dans le rêve* (a series of prints); Manet: *Chez le Père Lathuile.*

J.K. Huysmans: *Les Soeurs Vatard*; Loti: *Aziyadé*; Ibsen:*The Doll House*; Strindberg: *La Chambre rouge*; Ruskin: *The Stones of Venice.*

1880: Vincent attempts to encounter the painter Jules Breton, who he admires. Moves to Brussels and becomes friends with the painter Van Rappard.

The fifth Impressionist exhibition is held at 10 rue des Pyramides in Paris. The group begins to disintegrate. Rimbaud arrives in Africa.

Rodin works on *La Porte de l'Enfer*; Cormon: *Caïn*; Roll: *La Grève des mineurs*; Monet: *La Débâcle de la Seine.*

Verlaine: *Sagesse*; Maupassant: *Boule de Suif*; Huysmans: *Croquis Parisiens*; Léon Bloy: *Le Désespéré*; Taine: *Philosophie de l'Art*; Zola: *Nana.*

1881: Vincent returns to Etten and informs his father of his choice to become an artist. Falls in love with his cousin Kate, who spurns him. Visits his uncle, the painter Anton Mauve, in The Hague.

Sixth Impressionist exhibition is held at 35 boulevard des Capucines in Paris. Gauguin exposes his sculptures.

Puvis de Chavannes: *Le Pauvre Pêcheur*; Manet: *Le Bar des Folies Bergère*; Renoir: *Le Déjeuner des canotiers*; Pissarro: *Paysanne au repos*; Redon: *L'Araignée souriante.*

Maupassant: *La Maison Tellier*; Verlaine: *Sagesse*; Anatole France: *Le Crime de Sylvestre Bonnard*; Vallès: *Le Bachelier*; Huysmans: *En ménage.*

1882: Vincent moves to The Hague to be near Anton Mauve, who provides moral and financial support. Encounters Sien (Clasina Marla Hoornik), a pregnant and alcoholic prostitute.

Seventh Impressionist exhibition, 251 rue Saint-Honoré, Paris.

Léon Lhermitte: *La Paye des moissonneurs*; Ensor: *La Mangeuse d'huîtres*; Henri Becque: *Les Corbeaux*; Georges Ohnet: *La Maître de forges.* Zola: *Pot-Bouille*; Maupassant: *Mademoiselle Fifi.*

1883: At the urging of his family and friends, Vincent leaves Sien, with whom had been living. After moving to Hoogeven in the Drenthe, where he lives with Albertus Hartsuiker, Vincent returns to his father's new presbytery in the village of Nuenen.

Whister: *Portrait of the Artist's Mother*; Seurat: *Une Baignade à Asnières*; Rochegrosse: *Andromaque.*

Maupassant: *Une Vie*; Verlaine: *Les Poètes maudits*; Huysmans: *L'Art moderne*; Loti: *Mon frère Yves*; Paul Bourget: *Essais de psychologie contemporaine*; Stevenson: *Treasure Island.*

1884: Vincent leaves his father's presbytery and moves into the residence of the sexton of the Catholic church of Nuenen. Has an affair with Margot Begemann, who later attempts to commit suicide.

The XX Group is founded in Brussels; first Independent Artists exhibition organised.

Marie Bashkirtseff: *A Meeting*; Bastien-Lepage: *La Forge*; Gérôme: *Vente d'esclaves à Rome*; Luminais: *La Fuite de Gradlon*; Puvis de Chavannes: *Le Bois sacré cher aux Arts et aux Muses*; Degas: *Les Repasseuses.*

Huysmans: *A Rebours*; Leconte de Lisle: *Poèmes Tragiques*; J. Péladan: *Le Vice Suprême*; Daudet: *Sapho.*

1885: Death of Vincent's father on March 26 in Neunen. Vincent completes *The Potato-Eaters*, his first major work; is accused of having seduced a local peasant-girl, Gordina de Groot: the parish priest forbids villagers to pose for him. Vincent moves to Antwerp, takes a room on rue Longue des Images. Discovers Rubens and introduces a wider range of colour into his painting.

Carrière: *L'Enfant malade*; Fantin-Latour: *Autour du piano*; Seurat: *La Grande Jatte*; Gervex: *Une Séance du jury de peinture.*

Zola: *Germinal*; Jules Laforgue: *Les Complaintes*; Daudet: *Tartarin sur les Alpes*; Maupassant: *Bel Ami*; Becque: *La Parisienne*; Verlaine: *Jadis et naguère.*

1886: Vincent enrols in the Antwerp School of Fine Arts. Meets the painter Horace Mann Levens. Exhausted and in ill-health, he moves in with Theo on rue Victor-Massé and in June, 54 rue Lepic. Frequents the Atelier Cormon, where he encounters Toulouse-Lautrec, Anquetin, Emile Bernard and other artists. Encounters the Impressionist painters Degas, Pissarro, Monet, Renoir, Sisley, Seurat and Signac. Meets Gauguin in December.

Eighth and last Impressionist exhibition.

Rodin: *The Kiss*; Caillebotte: *Paris sous la neige*; Degas: *Le Tub.*

Loti: *Pêcheur d'Islande*; E. Drumont: *La France juive*; René Ghil: *Traité du verbe* (prefaced by Mallarmé); Zola: *L'Oeuvre*; Moréas: *Manifeste du Symbolisme.*

1887: Vincent has an affair with Agostina Segatori of the Café Tambourin, boulevard de Clichy. Organises an exhibition with Anquetin, Bernard, Gauguin and Toulouse-Lautrec. The group is nick-named the "Petit Boulevard" painters, in reference to the mainstream Impressionist ("Grand Boulevard") artists such as Pissarro, Monet, Sisley and Degas. Vincent was a regular visitor to 'Papa' Tanguy's art supplies shop on rue Clauzel during this period.

Emergence of the Nabis group.

Renoir: *Les Grandes Baigneuses*; Cézanne: *La Sainte-Victoire series*; Monet: *La Barque à Giverny*; Rochegrosse: *La Curée.*

Jules Laforgue: *Moralités légendaires*; Fénéon: *Le Néo-Impressionnisme*; G. Kahn: *Les Palais nomades*; Zola: *La Terre.*

1888: Vincent arrives in Arles on February 20 and takes a room at the Hotel Carrel, 30 rue Cavalerie. Rents four rooms in the Yellow House, 2 place Lamartine in May. Gauguin arrives in October; Vincent severs his ear in December.

Rodin: *Les Bourgeois de Calais*; Detaille: *Le Rêve*; Ziem: *Pêche dans le port de Venice*; Gauguin: *Jacob et l'Ange*; Toulouse-Lautrec: *Au cirque Fernando*; Sérusier: *Le Talisman*; E. Bernard: *Madeleine au Bois d'Amour*; Ensor: *Entrée du Christ à Bruxelles*; Seurat: *La Parade.*

Verlaine: *Amour*; Daudet: *L'Immortel*; Jarry: *Ubu roi*; Zola: *Le Rêve*; Barrès: *Sous l'oeil des barbares*; Strindberg: *Mademoiselle Julie.*

1889: Vincent enters the asylum of Saint-Paul-de-Mausole in Saint-Rémy-de-Province in May. His paintings are selected for the XX Group exhibition in Brussels in November.

Paris World's Fair; inauguration of the Eiffel Tower.

Friant: *La Toussaint*; Rochegrosse: *Le Bal des Ardents*; Bouguereau; *Psyché et l'Amour*; Carrière: *Intimité*; Gauguin: *Le Christ jaune.*

Verlaine: *Parallèlement*; Bourget: *Le Disciple*; Bergson: *Essai sur les données immédiates de la conscience*; Claudel: *Tête d'or*; Schuré: *Les Grands Initiés*; Maeterlinck: *Serres chaudes.*

1890: Albert Augier's article on Vincent appears in *Le Mercure de France*. Birth of Vincent Willem, Theo and Johanna Bonger's son, in January.

On Pissarro's advice, Vincent moves to Auvers-sur-Oise on May 20. His condition is followed by Dr. Gachet. Inhabits a garret room above the Ravoux café-hotel, opposite the town-hall. On July 27, Vincent shoots himself in the stomach and dies two days later, on July 29.

Monet continues his series of *Haystacks*; Cézanne: *Les Joueurs de cartes*; Toulouse-Lautrec: *La Danse au Moulin Rouge*; Redon: *Les Yeux clos*; Seurat: *Le Chahut*; Vallotton: *Le Bain.*

Zola: *La Bête humaine*; Anatole France: *Thaïs*; Oscar Wilde: *The Portrait of Dorian Gray*; Knut Hamsun: *Hunger.*

Index of Works

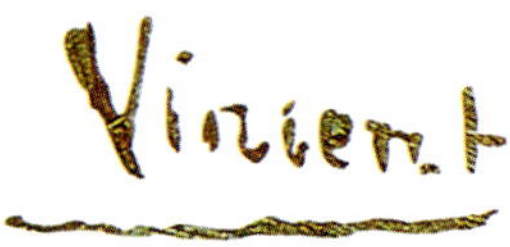

Photographic Credits

Archives ACR, DR et : Art Institute of Chicago, Chicago, p. 89. Boymans-Van Beuningen Museum, Rotterdam, p. 13. Collection Oskar Reinhart, Winterthur, p. 150. Chasserot, Annette, p. 185. Fogg Art Museum, Cambridge (Mass.), p. 86. Hiroshima Museum of Art, Tokyo, p. 158. Kröller-Müller Stichting, Otterlo, pp. 19, 34, 43, 45, 46, 52, 70, 72, 87, 99, 122, 123, 126, 127, 128, 131, 133, 147, 166. Museum of Art, Baltimore, p. 40. Museum of Fine Arts, Boston, p. 120. Museum of Modern Art, New York, pp. 153, 177. Musée du Petit Palais, Genève, p. 89. National Gallery of Art, Washington, p. 37. National Gallery, Londres, pp. 141, 142. Ny Carlsberg Glyptothek, Copenhague, p. 175. Phillips Collection, Washington, p. 135. Réunion des Musées Nationaux, Paris, pp. 59, 76, 115, 117, 133, 136, 140, 156, 157, 160, 170, 183. Rijksmuseum Vincent van Gogh, Amsterdam, pp. 6, 10, 12, 14, 15, 23, 31, 41, 44, 47, 55, 68, 69, 97, 100, 103, 108, 109, 111, 113, 118, 119, 125, 129, 138, 143, 146, 162, 163, 182. Saint Louis Art Museum, Saint Louis (Missouri), p. 168. Yale University Art Gallery, New Haven, p. 132.